HOME IS WHERE M

HOME
IS WHERE MY HAT IS

JILL WORTH

ILLUSTRATED BY PAF GRANT

PUBLICATIONS

Published in 2008 by Ad Hoc Publications
Cedars, Wattisham Road, Ringshall, Suffolk IP14 2HX
www.adhocpublications.com

ISBN 978 0 946958 64 1

Edited and designed by Roger Chesneau

Printed and bound in England by The Lavenham Press

My thanks to everyone who has encouraged and cajoled me,
especially Lisa, Mercedes and Denise and of course Jack, Paf and Roger,
without whose help my memories would still be gathering dust
at the back of a cupboard.

Contents

Introduction

IN the spring of 1984 our nomadic existence came to an end. Service wives have always been faced with the dilemma of whether they should move with their husband each time he gets a new job or put down roots and accept the separations. Whenever possible I chose the former. 'Have wife will travel,' Jack would tell his Appointer. So off we would go together—and what a fantastic and interesting life I led, even if sometimes it was exacting. I wouldn't have swapped it for the world. Now Jack was about to retire from the Navy. We had moved back into our own house and we were busy unpacking our well-travelled goods and chattels, probably for the last time.

'Where on earth am I going to put all this?' I stared in horror at the twenty place-settings of Royal Doulton that had graced the dining table during our final posting in Pretoria. When would I ever use them all again? We could barely seat eight guests round the table in our cottage. And as for all those wine glasses . . .

Eventually everything was stowed away and the crates were chopped up for firewood. My smart clothes were hung up in the closet, for the most part never to see the light of day again. These days I rarely wear a skirt: skirts are inclined to get caught in the spokes of my bicycle wheels when I pedal to the village shops. As for my collection of hats—well, I am afraid they reside in a box beneath my bed. The kind of socialising we do nowadays is mostly bare-headed, although I do have a colourful selection of fleecy caps to keep my ears warm in winter when I ride my bicycle.

We have dropped anchor for the last time and, unbelievably, twenty-five years later we still live in the same abode—which is pretty remarkable considering that for the first twenty-five years of our marriage we lived in almost that number of houses. Some of the dwellings we inhabited were terrible, others bordered on the luxurious, but none of them was ordinary.

They all have a story to tell.

— 1 —
Nightmare Lodge

THE only hat I possessed when I married Jack was a navy blue tricorn. The blue badge on the front signified that I was an officer in the WRNS. This was hardly the most glamorous headgear for a bride to wear, so I put it away in the wardrobe. On my wedding day I wore a velvet Alice band on to which I had sewn a spray of artificial lilies of the valley—the best that the shops in Elgin could offer in those more austere days in 1959.

We were married one windy Saturday in October in the little red brick church that overlooks the fishing harbour at Lossiemouth, on the Moray Firth. Although neither of us was Scottish, Lossiemouth was where we had met and spent the last two years together whilst serving at the Royal Naval Air Station—Jack as a pilot in a fighter squadron, I as the Assistant Secretary to the Station Captain. Many of our friends were based at 'Lossie', and so it seemed a more appropriate venue for our wedding than away in my hometown in Sussex where my roots were shallow.

My mother and a few of our more intrepid family and friends had flogged up on the overnight sleeper and joined the hundred or so officers with their wives and girlfriends who piled into the Wardroom after the ceremony to drink to our health in the traditional way. We were having such a good time that we didn't want to leave. Fortunately we were only driving along the road to Inverness, where we had a room booked at the Station Hotel. A week before the wedding the Powers That Be had announced that Jack's squadron would be embarking a month earlier than expected, and so our honeymoon had been reduced to just the one night. As they say in the Navy, 'If you can't take a joke, you shouldn't have joined.'

The Station Hotel, a Victorian edifice, was a building of majestic proportions. Leaving a multi-coloured trail of confetti across the acres of purple carpet, we climbed the impressive staircase to our room. The bed was as big as a boat and the bath was if anything bigger, with a huge, round, rubber plug that would have doubled nicely as a ball and chain to attach to the ankle of a convict. The Victorians did not skimp on size. We spent our one-day honeymoon on the banks of Loch Ness, not monster-hunting but cleaning the confetti out of the family jalopy. The following night we returned to the small house we were to call home for the next six months.

Finding a roof to put over our heads had been something of an achievement. In those days married quarters were at a premium, and as a childless pair of 'not-quite-weds' we were at the bottom of the housing ladder. Moreover, there was a terrible shortage of rented accommodation in the area, and most of what was on offer in our price range was pretty sub-standard. Forget modern day comforts like central heating and running hot and cold: you were lucky to find somewhere that had an indoor loo and four solid walls. Many of our friends lived in accommodation that should have been condemned, even as chicken houses. When the housing officer told me that a house on the main road between Elgin and Forres had just come on to his books I begged him to make an appointment for us to view it as soon as possible. Never mind that it was fourteen miles from the Air Station—we couldn't afford to be fussy.

It was a gloriously sunny evening in September when we first saw South Lodge. In its sylvan setting at the gateway to a large estate, the little red brick house, with its gothic windows and gabled roof, looked deceptively prestigious. The owner, Brigadier Grant-Peterkin, a tall, commanding figure in a faded kilt, was waiting to greet us.

'Worth, I presume,' he barked. Not Lieutenant, not Mister, certainly nothing as familiar as Jack; not even the offer of a handshake. My presence went un-acknowledged. I don't think he intended to be rude. It was just his natural Lord-of-the-Manor approach.

In this last bastion of feudalism, rent-paying tenants were expected to know their place, which was lowly. Fraternising with one's landlord was not something to be encouraged. From the word go it was made abundantly clear that there would be no invitations to drinks at The Big House, and no dropping by for tea with his lady wife, even though we would be helping to keep the wolf from his door. And if the threadbare rugs in the entrance hall to his manor were any indication of the state of his bank balance, he needed us as much as we needed him.

Marching ahead, he fitted a large iron key in the heavy, oak, nail-studded front door that opened straight into a living room furnished with a pair of not-so-easy armchairs with cushions upholstered in faded red velvet, three rickety wooden chairs and a small oak dining table. The only bedroom was hardly a dream bower for a pair of newly weds with its two single iron-frame beds. The electric cooker in the kitchen was a museum piece. The bathroom (a recent addition, he proudly boasted) was an add-on, corrugated-iron lean-to at the back of the house with a

'Worth, I presume,' he barked.

loo and an iron bath but no hand basin. The only source of hot water was from a boiler behind the living room fire. We were told we could collect wood from outside the house. He made it sound as if he were offering us the moon. 'Oh and by the way, as there's no weekly rubbish collection, you will need to dig a pit and bury your refuse.' Yet another bonus!

To me he turned at last. 'We've plenty of work on the estate, lifting potatoes, picking raspberries. Earn yourself a shilling or two.' I smiled sweetly and bit my tongue, refraining from telling him what he could do with his raspberries.

'Well, Worth—what shall we say? Four pounds a week, plus five bob extra for blankets and another five for pots and pans?' Cheeky considering the state of the moth-eaten blankets and rusty cooking utensils, but his tone implied that there was no room for haggling. It wasn't exactly a bargain, but South Lodge was a lot better than anywhere else we'd seen, so we sat down at the rickety dining table and signed an agreement written out in a child's exercise book. When we stood up, our laps were dusted with a fine powder. 'Just a spot of woodworm,' the Brigadier snorted. 'Soon get it treated.' Needless to say, he never did.

The night we returned from our brief honeymoon we fitted the giant iron key into the lock of our new home and were greeted with the wonderful aroma of stew that my lovely mother had popped into the antique electric oven to welcome us home.

'You had better get on and enjoy this. It might be the last decent meal you get for a while.'

I wasn't joking. My career in the Navy had including learning many new skills, from meteorology, marching and administration to looking after a division of newly recruited youngsters, but I had never cooked anything more demanding than bacon and eggs over a hot ring during the night watch.

Jack lit the fire and we drew the curtains and ate our supper whilst listening to the sound of water bubbling in the back boiler. It would have been quite snug if it hadn't been for the cold draught blowing round our ankles. We later discovered that the breeze came through a gap between the wall and the floor under the window. We stuffed the gap with sheets of newspaper and then pushed the two single beds together and attempted to continue our honeymoon without falling through the crack.

Next morning I woke early to the patter of scampering feet. There was absolutely no doubt about it: we were sharing South Lodge with Mr and Mrs Mouse and their extended family. They had eaten everything they could get their teeth into from corks in the bottles to the newspaper that we had used to fill the draughty gap. I do not find mice endearing. I do not like their dirty habits or the way they dart about. Most of all I do not like walking into my kitchen and seeing one sitting on the draining board cleaning his whiskers. From then onwards I would always stand outside crying 'Go away mices' before daring to enter.

Taking a bath was an endurance test. We would come in from work and light the fire. An hour later the water would be bubbling nicely, but unfortunately it had to travel along twelve feet of exposed copper piping before it reached the tub in the corrugated lean-to, and by the time it came out of the tap it was barely lukewarm. We would toss coins to see who would be the first to take the plunge—well, not so much a plunge as a tentative dip into three inches of tepid water, followed by a quick sprint back to the comfort of the living-room fire.

We had exactly two weeks to enjoy this domestic bliss before I had to drive Jack and his kit to the Air Station and stand with other wives watching him climb into his aircraft and take off for HMS *Victorious* somewhere in the Moray Firth. As we stood there it started snowing. Jane Giles, another Squadron wife, invitingly said, 'You don't want to go back and be all on your own, do you? Come and have supper and stay the night.' I went willingly.

It snowed all night, and then froze. It was three days before I felt safe to drive home. By the time I had skidded to a final halt, although it was only three in the afternoon it was nearly dark. Climbing out of the car, I was met by a blast of wind from the Arctic. In the porch sat a row of milk bottles with six inches of frozen milk sticking out of their necks like lollipops. Inside the house was no warmer. My teeth were chattering as I fumbled for the light switch. I looked around. Without my other half the house had lost its charm.

What I needed was a hot bath to warm me up or at least a cup of tea, but when I turned the tap on nothing happened. The pipes were frozen as solid as the milk. By now my brain was in deep freeze too, sense having flown the coop. Forgetting everything my physics teacher had taught me, I lit the fire. Soon it was roaring agreeably. Then came less comforting sounds: first a pop, then a hiss, and then a squirting noise as the thin copper piping transformed itself into an irrigation system. The passageway to the bathroom was soon awash with an unstoppable gush of steaming water.

I had no idea how to stop the deluge, and without a telephone there was no way of calling for help. Close to tears, I slithered and slid the half-mile down to the drive to the manor house and confessed to my intimidating landlord that I had flooded his property and needed help. Naturally he was far from pleased. It took him and his ghillie an hour digging in the snow before they found the stopcock so that they could turn the water off. Feeling sorry for myself, I filled the kettle with snow and, when it boiled, topped up my hot water bottle and took myself off to my bed. Next day I packed my bags and went home to Mum. If this was marriage . . .!

* * *

A month later I caught the sleeper train back to Scotland. I was accompanied by a bundle of black fur. I had this crazy idea that Simon would grow up fierce and protective, chase away the mice and generally look after me whilst Jack was away at sea. I should have bought a rottweiler, not a dumb, lovable dog that greeted everyone like a friend. The only time he barked was when the leaves fell on to the skylight.

As Christmas approached, we wives prayed for peace in this world with more than normal fervour, crossing our fingers that nothing would happen to disrupt the ship's programme. None of us felt really safe until we were told that the Squadron were airborne, on their way back to their home base.

I was so excited that I jumped into the car and reversed straight into the side of the house. Mortified, I could not believe what I had done. Crashing Jack's beloved Morris could be grounds for divorce, and we were barely married. Fortunately they built cars of sterner stuff in those days. As far as I could tell, the damage was limited to the bumper. With luck, I'd be able to save my confession at least until tomorrow.

Watching the squadrons circling and then landing one by one was thrilling. Naval life does have its compensations, I thought as I watched him climb out of his cockpit. The pain of separation was soon forgotten in the magic of reunion.

'What the hell have you got in there?' He could barely lift his baggage into the boot of the car.

'Wait and see,' I was told with a schoolboy grin.

The traders of Gibraltar must have rubbed their hands with glee when they saw my husband coming ashore to do his shopping. For the first Christmas of marriage my beloved gave me a dress watch, a gold bracelet, three bottles of an unknown perfume and a jewellery box that played 'The Wedding March' *ad infinitum*. What I really would have liked was a fur coat. The weather was something cruel.

We spent our first Christmas together cuddling up for warmth under our threadbare blankets, our breath hanging in icy balloons over our heads. But when the sun rose we stepped out into a magic kingdom of clean, white snow and sparkling ice. We walked, throwing sticks for the puppy that skittered and skidded down the tracks, appearing through drifts, his black curls highlighted with streaks of silver, and then sat down to enjoy the chicken I had roasted in the ancient oven. It wasn't until it was ready to carve that we discovered that it was a one-legged chicken. The butcher must have seen me coming.

After the New Year celebrations were over, the Squadron went back to sea. The next three months were often lonely, especially when the snow fell and the roads were to too icy to drive on, and the only time I left the house was to walk the dog. Sometimes the only person I saw all day was the postman, if I was lucky. I wasn't sorry when I heard that we had been offered one of the new married quarters that had just been built by the links golf course at Lossiemouth. A three-bedroom semi might lack character, but I was ready for a few home comforts, especially as our first-born was on the way.

— 2 —
Gamecock and Seagulls

'YOU'RE not going to believe this, but our new house is called Gamecock.' I was ringing from the chilly public telephone box at the end of the road to tell my mother that we had moved into our brand new married quarter.

'That's a funny sort of name to give a house.'

'Don't blame me—I didn't choose it. The name was already on the front door when we arrived. Our neighbours' houses are called Blackcap, Seahawk and Heron.'

'It sounds as if you're living in a bird sanctuary.'

Actually, all the houses had been named after Naval Air Stations. The Navy has an endearing way of calling all its shore-based establishments—otherwise known as 'stone frigates'—HMS something-or-other, as if they expect them to float out to sea on the next tide. Air Stations have names that come straight out of a bird anthology. HMS *Gamecock* was once the Fleet Air Arm's most inland base at Bramcote in the Midlands, so perhaps it was rather an odd choice of name for a house that stood almost on the seashore. 'Gannet' might have been more appropriate.

Gamecock was to be our home for the next nine months. By married quarters standards it was very smart, very modern; after South Lodge, it was a palace. Everything was new, from the curtains to the crates of china piled up on the kitchen floor waiting to be unpacked. In those days married quarters came fully fitted, and that meant everything from mustard spoons to bedspreads (blue and white with a nice anchor motif in the centre—very nautical). I couldn't believe how many items there were on the inventory, how many aluminium pots and pans, how many glasses from brandy goblets to liqueur, how many large white dinner plates and covered vegetable dishes, all discreetly decorated with tiny blue anchors. We had sufficient crockery and cutlery to entertain twenty guests—standing room only, for we had only six dining chairs.

When it came to electrical appliances there was almost none. Modern conveniences like refrigerators, toasters or even a steam iron were not considered essential to our way of life in those days, although it was assumed that a fish kettle large enough to poach a twenty-pound salmon was something no one could live without. It was as if we were still living in the era when servants were plentiful. There wasn't even a vacuum cleaner, just a dustpan and brush, but there was an electric clothes boiler with a wooden mangle. Okay, so in the 'sixties a washing machine was still a bit of a novelty, but I couldn't remember even my mother having anything like this museum piece.

In those far off days, before consolidation, privatisation and amalgamation, each establishment had its own department of civilian workers who were responsible for taking care of everything from the maintenance of the plumbing to the provision of knives and forks. Helpful and well-intentioned teams of builders, plumbers and providers made the houses fit for habitation, but presumably there were no interior designers or we would never have ended up with a dairy-milk purple living room carpet, a three-piece suite upholstered in marigold yellow and swirly patterned curtains that were predominantly ointment pink. Not that I was about to grumble. Anything was marvellous after the Brigadier's collection of battered furniture.

The house was on the Stotfield Road overlooking the local golf links; beyond there were sand dunes and the Moray Firth. On a perfect day in the summer the sea could look very tempting, but you've got to be hardy to swim in the Moray Firth: the only dip I took lasted precisely two minutes. But the beach was glorious, with miles of golden sand to walk the dog. It really was idyllic.

Behind the quarters stood a sizeable plot of land, divided into gardens by lines of battleship grey wire fencing. We understood that the lawn area had already been seeded, and, sure enough, within a week the garden was full of little green shoots. Unfortunately, the protective wooden fencing along the back, intended to provide a windbreak, was still waiting to be erected. The week before we moved in, a gale brought a harvest of ripening seeds of poppy, cornflower and dog daisy from the neighbouring fields. What better place to germinate than in a freshly raked piece of Ministry of Defence land? Thus, instead of a bowling green-like sward we were soon looking out on to a field of red, and blue and white. Very pretty, and very patriotic, but tough on the small, manually operated lawn mower provided.

Elizabeth Brown, my next-door neighbour and a keen gardener, couldn't wait to plant a border and grow her own veggies. The first time she tried to dig in her spade she hit something large and very hard. It transpired that the houses had been built on what had used to be tennis courts, and the tarmac foundations were still lying just inches beneath the topsoil. Grimly she ploughed on. Soon her garden looked more like a rockery than a cabbage patch. I was more than happy to use my pregnancy as an excuse just to sit and watch.

A month after we moved into our new home, it was my birthday. I was told to be sure to stay at home and wait for a delivery. Sure enough, a van drew up in the middle of the morning, not from Interflora but from Messrs Macdonald and Drew, Suppliers of Electrical Appliances. A brand new refrigerator was carried through my front door. I was thrilled. A refrigerator was such a novelty. What a treat to be able to make ice cubes and keep ice cream on tap! To celebrate the arrival of my new acquisition, I invited guests for supper and prepared a frozen fruity concoction of melons, strawberries, cream and meringue that looked absolutely delicious when pictured in the cookery book. Unfortunately, as I was a real novice, it never occurred to me to allow sufficient thaw-time before serving my guests. Triumphantly I placed my creation in the middle of the table to cries of admiration that soon turned to howls of laughter as I tried to hack off a portion of rock hard ice. Anyone for cheese and biscuits?

The refrigerator was new but my first washing machine wasn't. I had never expected to own something so high-tech, but when my neighbour left to go abroad she offered to sell me her single-tub, fully non-automatic Mark I Hoover. I couldn't resist the temptation. Fascinated, I would load small piles of clothes into the tiny tub and then waste hours watching as the washing was stirred and paddled. When I judged it clean I would then haul each item out into the sink, sloshing streams of soapy water on to the floor. Between each wash and rinse the water had to be emptied into a bucket, which very often resulted in yet more flooding. There was no spin cycle, but there was a mangle that folded out from the washing machine. Not an electrically operated mangle: I still had to turn a handle. All in all, the machine was a bit of a mixed blessing, but it was one I clung to loyally, convinced that I was saving myself time and effort. And at least we always had a clean kitchen floor.

We were very happy in our new house. Jack was based at home most of the time and was there to drive me to the hospital for the birth of our son. Knowing that our domestic bliss wouldn't last forever, we made the most of each day together. In the autumn Jack was told that he was being appointed to a frigate so that he could obtain a watch-keeping certificate now that he had a permanent commission. He would be at sea for six months, during which I time I would no longer be entitled to live in a married quarter in Scotland and would have to pack up and go home to Mum. Chances were that in six months we would return to Lossiemouth and be back at the bottom of the waiting list again. Fortunately, as it turned out we were destined to go somewhere very different.

* * *

'I've been asked how we'd feel about going to America for two years,' Jack shouted from the bottom of the stairs, having just arrived home. I was upstairs running the bath for the baby and was sure that I had misheard what he said. How could anyone impart such exciting news long-distance?

He bounded upstairs to join me.

'I've just bumped in my Appointer, Dougie Baker, who's here on a visit. He asked me if I would be happy to go to the USA to relieve Pete Newman following my frigate time. Apparently Pete is on exchange with the US Navy, serving on a test and evaluation squadron in Virginia. So what they want to know is, how do we feel about pulling up roots and serving in America for two years?'

I nearly dropped the baby in the bathwater. 'Tell them "yes" as soon as possible, before they change their minds!'

'I thought you might say that,' he grinned.

I was so excited: if they had asked us to go tomorrow I would have packed then and there.

There was only one snag, and that was that it would be almost a year before we travelled. It sounded like a lifetime. A whole year to wait with my fingers crossed, knowing that there could be a change of plan at any time. To make things worse, I wasn't allowed to tell a soul until the appointment was officially published, and that probably wouldn't happen for another nine months. Fearful that any breach of confidence might wreck our chances, I kept my lips tightly sealed.

'So, do you know where Jack is going after he finishes on the frigate?' I was asked a hundred times.

'No idea,' I would have to lie.

I tell you, it wasn't easy. I was just bursting to share my news with someone. Eventually I persuaded Jack that I had to tell my mother, promising to swear her to secrecy. Actually, I wasn't really looking forward to making the 'phone call. I was going to have to break it to her gently. We were the only family she had, and in those days America seemed a lot further away than it does today.

For a moment there was silence at the end of the line as she absorbed the shock.

'How long will you be away for?' she asked.

I took a deep breath. No good trying to hide the truth. 'Probably a couple of years,' adding quickly, 'I know it may sound a long time, but just think, Mummy, you could come and stay. How does a month in America sound?'

'So when do you go?'

'Not for another nine months. First, Jack has to get his watch-keeping certificate. I wondered if Robin and I could come and stay with you whilst he's away.' She was thrilled.

Then, just when we thought things couldn't get any better, life dealt us a blow that left us reeling with disbelief. When, late one evening, my doctor rang the bell of our front door, I was surprised. I hadn't asked him to call. He apologised for coming so late but said that he wanted to catch us together before we left

Lossiemouth and that he was very sorry but he had some bad news. Having been observing Robin for some months, he was now sure that, as he had suspected from the beginning, our baby was not normal. Nowadays it seems strange that it had taken so long for him to be certain of his diagnosis. All I know is that it came as a terrible shock to learn, after four months, that we had a Down's Syndrome baby. In retrospect, perhaps we should have suspected something ourselves: perhaps he was a little too good to be true, rarely crying, and sleeping almost all the time.

I dreaded having to break the news to my mother, but I didn't have to tell her on arrival. Not having seen Robin since he was a tiny baby, she was able to spot the problem at once. And yet it was months before I accepted that our child would never be normal.

* * *

While Jack was patrolling the freezing waters off the coast of Iceland, protecting our fishing fleet in what was known then as the Cod War, I lived in the house where I had grown up. Number Three St George's Road was part of a terrace built between the wars in a road just off the sea front in Worthing. My parents had taken on the lease during the war, when rents were rock bottom because so many houses were standing empty, begging for tenants. With its six bedrooms and three reception rooms, it was far too big for the three of us, but, knowing that my father was suffering from Parkinson's disease and that his days as the breadwinner were numbered, my mother considered it ideal for the small B&B business she planned to run once the war was over. My bedroom was the small slip room upstairs that had a door that opened on to the balcony from which I could see the sea. I loved it.

After my father died, my mother gave up the business of bed and breakfasting. She had then taken on the post of warden of a residential home for the professional elderly, and the upstairs of Number Three had been divided up and rented out as bed-sits. Knowing we were coming to stay, Mother had moved into the flat above the residential home and we took over the bottom floor of the house. The dining room was converted into a bedroom for Robin and me, and for Jack when he was home. The front room, as the lounge was known, was large and lofty and also very draughty. As the only source of heat was an open coal fire, we tended to live in the breakfast room at the back of the house, where an old-fashioned iron range gave off a comforting glow. I cooked in the scullery with its red brick floor, gas cooker and large, walk-in larder. Out the back there was a small walled garden with a coal shed and outside loo, a pocket-handkerchief lawn and a massive hydrangea bush.

It was my job to collect the rents from our lodgers and pay the bills out of the proceeds. I couldn't help feeling sorry for them, knowing that, soon, Mother would be giving them their marching orders; after we had gone, she intended to clear the house and hand the keys back to the owner.

I should have been grateful to have a refuge to run to, but time hung heavily. The children who had been my schoolfriends had long gone. The neighbours in St George's Road were total strangers. I passed a solitary winter, crossing off the days on the calendar. There wasn't much for me to do except push the pram and walk the dog along the promenade, often in a howling gale. Six months can seem like for ever, especially when you are holding your breath each time you open a letter, fearing that it might contain news of a change of plans. It could so easily have happened.

But it seemed that we were still on course for our great adventure, and, as the merry month of May approached, things positive began to happen. The same day that America launched her first man into space, the postman slotted an official brown envelope filled with instructions through our letterbox. Robin and I must be medically checked, inoculated, vaccinated and X-rayed, and we had to provide answers to a hundred questions to satisfy the US Government that we weren't a pair of subversives. How much luggage did we intend to take with us? By what means did we intend to travel to reach the RMS *Queen Mary*. Wow, the *Queen Mary*! What a way to cross the Atlantic! In those days this was the Blue Riband way across; air travel was in its infancy. My chums would have been green with envy . . . had they known!

The day of departure was fast approaching when at last the much-awaited letter from Peter Newman, the Royal Naval officer Jack was relieving, arrived. To my amazement, I saw that it had been posted in California. It seemed that VX-4 had moved to the West Coast of America a year earlier, to somewhere hitherto unheard of called Point Mugu. Unbelievably, the Appointer in London seemed quite ignorant of this rather important item of news.

Big re-think. California. That did seem like the stuff that dreams were made of. Outside a cold wind was blowing and rain was hitting the windows. In California the sun was shining. I drifted into a world of fantasy. What would the land of promise hold? Would we live in a luxury home with fitted kitchen and two bathrooms, all mod cons, everything shining and easy-care?

By the time I had finished reading Peter's letter, I realised, 'Not exactly.'

— 3 —
Blue Riband Style

A T last the day of our departure arrived. Our crates had all been packed and shipped off ahead of us. Jack's parents had been down to say their last farewells and driven away the much-loved Morris Oxford, with Simon dog-sitting in the back, a look of puzzlement on his curly black face. Now my mother and her friend, wearing hats that would have graced the *Queen Mary*'s launching ceremony, had come to Southampton to wave us off. I think they were a little disappointed when they saw the size of our cabin. I'm sure they expected something grander, but a junior officer was only entitled to travel Cabin Class and our accommodation, on 'R' deck, was more a closet than a stateroom. By the time our luggage had been delivered, there was barely sufficient room for the three of us to squeeze in, never mind swing the proverbial moggie.

Two bunk beds, a cot for Robin, a small wardrobe-cum-dresser, but nothing as luxurious as an *en suite* shower, just a cupboard containing a hand basin and a loo. If you wanted to take a bath, you had to walk to the end of the passage. The first time I did this I found the door firmly locked. According to a notice on the door, passengers must warn their cabin steward when they wanted to take a bath. He would then tell the bathroom attendant, who would run the water.

'Why cannot I be trusted to run my own?' I asked our steward, who was called Herbert.

Herbert had a well-rehearsed spiel up his sleeve.

'Well, Madam, it's like this. Ever since a passenger sued the company because she slipped and hit her head on the taps, it has been company policy only to permit supervised bathing.'

'Supervised? How supervised? Are you telling me that I must bathe with the door open?'

'Certainly not, Madam.' Herbert looked suitably embarrassed, but when challenged as to how the bath attendant would guarantee my safety from the other side of the door he shook his head, nonplussed. To add insult to injury, the bathwater tasted of salt. Only First Class passengers, it transpired, were permitted freshwater bathing.

The RMS *Queen Mary* was the Concorde of the 1930s. Her job was to carry passengers to their destinations in the shortest time possible, and luxury in all but the First Class section was sacrificed in the interests of speed. Lieutenant Jack, who was accustomed to having a steward to look after his every need when serving on board one of Her Majesty's ships, could not get over the lack of laundry facilities!

I was just thrilled to be aboard. Not until the morning we stood on the pier at Southampton gazing up at the *Queen Mary*'s three funnels did I really believe that we were truly going. I had spent the past months with my fingers crossed, quite expecting to hear that our tour to the States had been cancelled and that my husband had been re-appointed. It could so easily have happened, right up to the day before we sailed.

Dinner that first evening proved to be a bit of a bun fight. The only seats we could find were at a table occupied by three South Americans who did not understand a word we said, so we consumed all seven courses in almost total silence whilst endeavouring not to choke on the smoke from the evil-smelling cigars on which the gentlemen puffed between each forkful of food. Thankfully, for the rest of the voyage, meals were served in shifts and we were allocated our own table.

After dinner we set out to explore our floating hotel. Sadly, by the 1960s the *Queen Mary*, for all her opulence, was beginning to look her age, her 'thirties *décor* slightly tarnished. For all her gleaming brass and highly polished woodwork, plush upholstery and glittering chandeliers, she seemed more in tune with the luxury of a bygone era. There were even pots of aspidistras sitting on the staircase.

The public rooms were populated with groups of people mostly twice our age. We were beginning to think that we were the only young couple on board, until we discovered the Mermaid Bar, where it was all happening, supervised by Harry, a veteran of many crossings. On such a short voyage you had to get to know your fellow passengers very quickly, and by the end of the evening we had already formed a cosmopolitan circle—an osteopath and his wife from Chicago, a Romanian medical student, a Spanish couple who worked for UNESCO, and Alan and Mary Elgar, whom we would get to know very well as Alan was about to become Our Man in Los Angeles.

The next morning we were woken early by the sound of something being pushed under the door. It was the ship's newspaper, with world headlines and a programme of activities and entertainments for the day. There was also a list of passengers and the morning competition—ten anagrams that had to be solved—and a prize was promised for the first correct answer to be delivered to the Purser's office. I soon discovered that I had little chance of winning. A certain Mr McPherson must have been up at six o'clock with his pencil ready sharpened, for without fail his name headed the daily roll of honourable winners.

Not that there weren't plenty of other competitions to be won, the favourite being the daily sweepstake on the ship's run, when bets were laid on the distance the Q.M. had sailed during the previous twenty-four hours. When the correct answer was posted the next morning, the lucky winner picked up quite a nice little sum of money.

Most of the prizes on offer were no more than knick-knacks, but it didn't matter. We got a disproportionate amount of pleasure from winning almost anything, from souvenir key rings to tiny sailor dolls. Provided you were prepared to compete in everything from the deck quoits tournament to the fancy headdress competition, it was almost guaranteed that you would be awarded at least one prize before the end of the voyage. The booty that we laughed at then must by now be true collectors' items. I wish I still had that propelling pencil with a tiny *Queen Mary* floating in the barrel that Jack won for clay pigeon shooting!

In the morning we would leave Robin in the care of two lovely young girls from Yorkshire who ran the ship's nursery and stretch out on the sundeck. The only snag was that, although the sky was a cloudless blue, the temperature was hardly swimsuit weather: the ship was steaming at such a high speed that it was impossible to avoid the cool slipstream. The only way to keep warm was to wrap up in a rug with merely the tips of our noses showing—not exactly tanning mode. Soon, just in case we hadn't had enough for breakfast, a steward appeared with warming cups of soup.

Page one of my book had hardly been read before the tannoy summoned us to lunch. For the sake of my already expanding waistline, it would have been a good idea to miss the odd meal. Unfortunately, we couldn't resist the temptation to dine in a style to which we were not accustomed. Every meal was something special. We would have needed to cross the Atlantic Ocean a dozen times to sample all the fare.

A ballroom dancing lesson at the *thé dansant* was the highlight of the afternoon's entertainment programme. Whilst we sat sipping our Earl Grey, Rita and Paulo from Argentina entertained with a spirited demonstration of Latin American dancing, although when the music stopped we were told that it was our turn now. The next thing I knew was that I was partnering an American gentleman of bear-like proportions.

'Pleased to meet you, ma'am,' he drawled in a deep Southern accent.

'You'll have to excuse me. I'm not much of a dancer.'

He held me so tight that my nose rubbed on his blazer top button.

'One-two-three, cha-cha,' he repeated, his face a picture of concentration. But for all his trying, his outsized feet refused to move with the rhythm, his dancing more gentle jive than fiery Latin.

'I guess you drew the short straw,' he grinned, having apologised for stepping on my toes for the tenth time. Every time the ship lurched we ended up in a tangle. The audience thought we were very funny, but what my southern partner lacked in grace he made up for in charm. He really had a lovely smile.

In true cruise tradition, the last night on board was celebrated with a Gala Dinner, a final diet-busting occasion. By now we were on the best of terms with our waiter, who insisted I should try his *crêpe Suzette*—a fittingly high note on which to end our brief incursion into the world of *haute cuisine*. It was just as well that the voyage wasn't any longer: we were already having trouble doing up our buttons!

New York. There she stood, bathed in the afternoon sun—our first sight of the Statue of Liberty and the famous Manhattan skyline. The journey up the Hudson River was like sailing through an album of larger-than-life picture postcards. For four days we had been cosseted and cared for; now we had to come back to reality. It was time to disembark and start another chapter, to say goodbye to the crew who had looked after us so well, and to the Grand Old Lady who had brought us safely across the Atlantic.

* * *

Leaving the *Queen Mary* was like emerging from the safety of a chrysalis. After five days of being mollycoddled, suddenly we were confronted with a life that needed organising—a battery of immigration paperwork to be completed, twenty-one pieces of luggage that seemed to have gone walkabout, a child who thought it was time someone provided supper. By the time we were met by an understanding official from the British Consulate, we were bleary-eyed and dizzy, and more than grateful to climb into his station wagon, enormous to our Mini-accustomed eyes. The lights of New York passed in a dazzling haze as our driver sped through the canyons of skyscrapers at what seemed like an alarming speed.

Our hotel, the Governor Clinton, had been selected for its proximity to the railway station. Otherwise it was featureless. Not that the array of buttons in the elevator didn't impress me: our room was only on the twenty-first floor, Number 2100. Just coping with the lock on the super-secure, fireproof door required ingenuity. Inside, the room was surprisingly small and noisy. An air-conditioning unit—the first I'd ever seen—thudded on the wall, and even my husband switching through the dozen television channels of cops and robbers and cowboys failed to blank out the noise of screaming police sirens on the street way down below. I'd seen it on the movies, but now we were here it seemed quite surreal.

26

The following morning we boarded a splendid train with seats that revolved through three hundred and sixty degrees and settled back to enjoy our ride to Washington DC. It was Memorial Day, a public holiday. The Stars and Stripes flew from almost every porch and the pleasant tree-lined streets were very peaceful. 'You wait till tomorrow, lady,' our taxi driver told us. 'On a normal working day, it's like a madhouse out there.'

The apartment where we spent the next three nights was deliciously cool after the heat outside, which, according to the flashing overhead signs, was registering around ninety. I couldn't believe that we could be so spoilt—a bedroom, a sitting room and a kitchen complete with automatic washing machine and something in the sink made a frightening grinding noise when I accidentally flicked a switch. All we needed now was food. According to the sheaf of useful information on the table, there was a grocery store just a block away. Off we set, child in pushchair, bumping up and down the foot-deep kerbstones. In the residential district where we were living, shops seemed few and far between, and the only food shop we found was the neighbourhood 'deli'. I remember how intimidated I felt entering that shop. Even the store holder sounded foreign and was hard to understand. I couldn't think what we could eat—the food looked unexpectedly strange and un-familiar. I'd never heard of pastrami or bagels. Eggs should be safe. And ice cream. Bread. What else?

Hearing my English accent, obviously a novelty, the wife of the owner hurried over to help.

'Sausages? Sure, we've got sausages and bacon.'

She threw the contents of the freezer chest from right to left and came up with a dark brown rock and a plastic-covered flat pack that said it contained bacon though all I saw were strips of fat streaked with a few fine lines of lean meat.

'Is this all you have?' I asked timidly. 'No back bacon?'

'Back bacon?' She looked at me as if I was weird, plainly never having heard of such a thing. 'This is the only bacon we sell.' She shrugged her ample shoulders with a 'take it or leave it' gesture. Defeated, I took it, along with a plastic bag of spongy bread, some extremely expensive butter, a tub of ice cream and a carton of milk. By the time we had walked the block and a half home, the ice cream had well and truly melted.

Three days later we flew to California, but not before we had sat an exam. Whilst he was being briefed at the British Embassy, Jack had been warned—erroneously, as it turned out—that our international driving licences were invalid in California. Before either of us could drive, we would need to sit a test. On the other hand, if we had licences issued in the District of Columbia, we would be able to drive lawfully for the duration of our stay. Unlike California, the District of Colombia only required us to pass a written paper in order to obtain a precious driving licence. It wasn't that long since I'd gone through the nightmare of passing a driving test in Britain, and the thought of having to repeat the whole experience filled me with horror. I readily agreed to go for the easy option. How were we to know that this advice was load of bunkum?

We swotted up on the equivalent of the Highway Code and then took a taxi to the Department of Motor Vehicles, only to discover that the examination centre was closed for the day.

'What time do you open?'

'7.30 through 4 p.m. excepting Wednesday,' said the black lady who barred our way. 'On Wednesdays we're closed.'

Sod's law: today was Wednesday. Tomorrow we were flying to Los Angeles at 10 a.m., but by now we had the bit between our teeth and refused to be beaten.

'How long does it take to sit the test?'

She shrugged. 'Maybe thirty minutes. If you get here real early, maybe less.'

Back in the apartment, we packed everything ready for departure and the next morning were in a taxi by six. Outside it was pelting with rain and already the humidity was ninety per cent, according to the newscaster. The ride back to the examination centre was relatively trouble-free, so that we arrived before the doors were open. Unbelievably there was already a line of twenty people ahead of us.

Impatiently we waited our turn, moving up at a snail's pace, checking our watches by the minute. Eventually we were each handed a test paper, but not before the official had examined our international driving licences with a micro-scope. Clutching a bewildered-looking child in my arms, I raced down the corridor, arriving at the desk in a sweaty heap, and collected my test paper.

'Tick box 1, 2 or 3.'

I'd never seen a multiple-choice paper before. It was amazing how easy it was to get the answer wrong, even though the questions were pretty simple. Of course, my clever husband got them all right, but then he didn't have chubby fingers trying to grab the pen out of his hand.

By the time I'd had my paper marked and been told I'd passed, it was nearly 8 o'clock and we still had to have our eyes tested on a desktop monitor (more child-wrecking opportunities) and then 'wait in line' whilst we were 'checked out' to make sure that there were no black marks against our record. At last, trium-phantly waving our new driving licences, we hailed a taxi and raced for the air terminal.

As it transpired, the whole exercise had been a complete waste of time. As a nice Highway Patrolman explained politely three months later, 'If you're resident in California you need a Californian driving licence, ma'am.' In our opinion, the letter we wrote to a certain someone in Washington pointing out the error of his information was far too courteous.

It was amazing how easy it was to get the answer wrong . . .

We landed at Los Angeles airport in the middle of the day. The Newmans had promised that they would meet us, but there was no one waiting at the barrier. An hour later we were still waiting. Jack decided it was time to make a 'phone call.

'Could I speak to Lieutenant-Commander Peter Newman?'

The voice at the other end sounded puzzled. 'I don't seem to have a Reverend Newman listed.'

'Not Reverend.' He spoke very carefully.

'Oh, *lootenant*. Pardon me,' she hooted. 'It's the British accent,' and put him through to VX-4.

'Pete isn't here,' Jack was told by the duty squadron officer. 'He's gone to meet his Brit replacement.'

'I am his replacement.'

'Is that right? Well, welcome aboard!'

An hour later Peter and his wife Micky appeared, amazed to see us waiting by our luggage like a bunch of refugees.

'Was your flight early?'

We shook our heads. 'No, dead on time.'

Somewhere along the line there had been a breakdown in communications, a miscalculation caused by the three-hour time difference in time zones. We hadn't been expected to touch down till later in the afternoon.

By the time we had joined the freeway, it was the height of the rush hour—eight lanes of bumper-to-bumper madness. I was glad my view was obscured in the back, where Robin and I sat with Micky and her son Christopher.

'Tomorrow I'll take you to see the house at Rancho Lomita, where we've lived since we moved out here,' she told me. 'If you like it, you can move in as soon as you've agreed the lease with the owner, Stuart. Until then, I hope you don't mind sharing the house on the base where we are living temporarily.'

Forty miles later, we turned off at the sign for Point Mugu (pronounced *Magoo*, as in the cartoon character) and drove through the gate of the Pacific Missile Base, our six-thousand-mile journey finally over. For me the next step was into the great unknown, but for Jack it would be a Naval aviator's paradise. He had left the Fleet Air Arm's Scimitars, Venoms and Sea Hawks behind and had now joined one of the US Navy's top squadrons. As I understood things, its rôle was to test, operationally, and evaluate the latest fighter aircraft and missile weapon systems. Phantoms, Crusaders, Demons and Skyhawks would now be the order of the day for him.

— 4 —
Rancho Lomita

FOR the next four nights we would stay with the Newmans in a house reserved for families-in-transit: two bathrooms, walk-in wardrobes, a kitchen fitted with every modern convenience—the epitome of the all-American lifestyle I had pictured back home, and quite different from the house that was be our future home.

On day two, whilst Jack was making his number with his new squadron, Micky took me to see the house. After driving for about twenty minutes we turned off the Los Posas Road where the sign on the wall read 'Rancho Lomita' and parked beneath the shade of a huge palm tree, beside a metal hutch post-box with the number 610 painted on the side. Through the picket fence I caught my first glimpse of the green-shingled roof of the white-painted, wooden bungalow.

As we climbed out of the car, the air was deliciously warm and perfumed. Eucalyptus mingled with the scent of the exotic cash-crops of stocks, tulips and iris growing in the neighbouring field. Earlier the weather had been cool and foggy, but now the sun had burned through the early-morning mist and the temperature was rapidly rising. Inside the back door, the house felt blessedly cool.

The kitchen was large and roomy but nothing fancy—definitely not the designer utopia I had drooled over in glossy magazines. There was no stainless steel unit, there were no fitted cupboards, there was not even a proper work surface, just a large picnic table with two benches, a stone sink, a free-standing electric stove and an ugly though capacious refrigerator.

'This is the living-cum-dining room,' said Micky, watching for signs of approval as she led me into the light and airy room with two doors, one leading to the main bedroom and the other opening on to a wooden verandah. I wondered if it was an optical illusion: did the floor slope from left to right?

'Definitely. You have to climb uphill to go to bed,' Micky laughed. 'Termites are munching their way through the foundations, but there's nothing to worry about. The house will still be here long after you have left.' That was comforting to hear.

When Peter and Micky moved in, the gateway house—like most rented homes in America—was unfurnished. Not being over-flush with funds, they had bought most the furniture second-hand from the Salvation Army thrift shop. The rest they had begged or borrowed from friends. We had agreed to buy whatever they owned, which turned out to be two well-used armchairs, a rug and the bedroom furniture.

'The mahogany dining table, the four chairs and the red-lacquered Chinese coffee table belong to John and Brookie Wissler.'

'Don't they want them back?'

'Yes, I guess they will when they move. But in the meantime they are happy for you to use them as they haven't got room in their house—as you'll see when you go there.'

'Still, it's very kind, considering we haven't even met them yet.'

'Don't worry, you'll find everyone on the Squadron equally generous. Most Americans are.'

The one bathroom was blessed with a matching sea-green suite and a very efficient hot water system, the only snag being that because it was in the middle of the house it had two doors, one to each bedroom. This was not a problem until we had visitors, when we had to remember to lock them both before we took a bath—something we forgot to do on more than one occasion!

Our tour ended in a garden filled with brightly coloured flowering bougainvillea and hibiscus, succour to minuscule metallic-green humming birds hovering like iridescent bees over the coral-pink trumpets. A huge, handsome date palm stood in the middle of the rather bumpy lawn.

Micky explained that the devastation was the work of gophers.

'Gophers?' Not creatures I had ever heard of.

'Bit like a mole only much larger with huge buck teeth. Sometimes when you're washing up, they pop out of their burrows and grin at you through the window. They're very cute, but terribly destructive.'

Termites, humming birds, gophers! I wondered what other kinds of unusual wildlife I would be sharing my home with.

'Do you think you're going to like it here?'

I said I loved the house. It might not be the modern, all-American des-res of my dreams, but it had so much rustic charm and character that I felt at home right away. I had my reservations about the location. Gophers might be very endearing but were hardly a substitute for a friend in need.

As we had driven the ten miles inland from the base, I had seen few houses, only miles of open fields of sweet corn, tomatoes and beans, interspersed with groves of citrus trees. Had Micky not been lonely?

'Heavens, no! If I am, I just go to the top of the ranch and visit Brookie Wissler. Anyway, you'll be all right. Very soon there will be three other Squadron families living on the other side of the field, once their new homes have been delivered.' She made it sound as if they were coming mail order.

Sure enough, when I had been living there for a couple of months three new houses arrived, not in flat packs, but on the back of trucks, followed by an army of workers who connected the electricity, water and telephone and landscaped their gardens. A week later the Keenes, the Petries and the Macdonalds and their six children took up residence.

Back in the car, Micky said she would take me to see the nearby town of Camarillo. 'We can drop off a load of washing at the laundromat and then I can show you where the doctor and dentist have their offices and some of the shops you might need.'

When I first saw the town of Camarillo, it was a sleepy little place with a population of fewer than three thousand, the main street, with its shops and offices, wide enough to have been used as a set for a spaghetti western. Many buildings still had a very Spanish look, a reminder of the days when southern California was part of Mexico.

Micky humped a load of dirty washing out of the car and packed it into one of the giant machines that lined the wall of the laundromat. Here there was no authoritarian lady attendant; the machines were churning unsupervised whilst the owners of their contents went shopping. No one seemed to worry that they might return and find their underpants missing.

I confessed that I had hoped to find a washing machine in the house.

Micky shrugged. 'We weren't expecting to be out here very long, so it hardly seemed worth investing a lot of money when I could take care of our laundry at twenty-five cents a load.'

Later, when I asked Micky if she would be sorry to leave, she said 'Yes' emphatically. 'I could happily stay for ever.' If she had told me that soon I would feel the same, I wonder if I would have believed her.

That evening the Squadron had organised a barbecue, a combined 'hail and farewell' party for the Newmans and Worths.

'What should I wear?' I asked.

'Anything will do—nothing fancy,' she said and then, when it was time to depart, appeared looking absolutely stunning in a sunshine-yellow pant suit, leaving me feeling less than glamorous in my modest blue and white cotton dress. Peter wore a tartan shirt and carried a set of matching bagpipes.

The party was being held at a house on Sparrow Drive, in Camarillo. By the time we arrived, the house was already wall-to-wall with people, the noise deafening. For the next half-hour we shook hands non-stop. Everyone wanted to meet us. My fingers tingled from being squeezed.

'Jack and Jill—gee, isn't that just *darling*,' cooed a lady who introduced herself as Peaches.

'Hi, I'm Rudi and this is Chic, and the big guy is Chuck. The lady over there is Dottie—she goes with Glenn.'

Soon my head was spinning. Suddenly the introductions were all over and, like the Red Sea, we parted—the boys to the kitchen where they could talk aeroplanes, the wives and girlfriends to the sitting room for a good gossip. I was amazed, quite unused to such automatic segregation.

The 'girlie' conversation was all about the children's schools and teachers, about hairdressers and diets. Which store had the best line in Capri outfits (whatever they were)? At least I learned the going rate for a baby-sitter. The wives were all dressed in a kind of uniform—long slinky pants and contrasting tops, a cross between Chinese coolie suits and maternity wear in psychedelic colours (were these the mysterious Capri outfits, perhaps?). Frocks were out.

'Help yourself,' said our hostess, showing me to a table groaning with a dozen different salads, baked potatoes in nests of silver foil, baskets of muffins and bowls of dressing. Her husband selected a massive T-bone from the barbecue grill and plonked it on my plate.

'Haven't you got a smaller one?'

He hadn't. Thank God they had a dog with bad table manners.

After supper it was time for farewell gift presentations. Pete stood up and made a witty speech and, when pressed, Micky performed a brilliant impersonation of Julie Andrews singing 'All I Want is a Room Somewhere' to rapturous applause. Then it was time for dancing, not rock-and-roll or square but Scottish, a spot of crossover culture introduced into the Squadron's party life by the Newmans. Peter fetched his bagpipes and started to tune up.

'Do all British officers play the bagpipes?' I was asked by Dottie or was it Nadine. It would take me weeks to get their names sorted.

'Absolutely not! Sorry to disappoint you.'

'Gee, that's a shame,' she sighed nostalgically. 'We just love to hear Pete play.' What a talented pair the Newmans were. We had a lot to live up to.

Unfortunately the neighbours did not share her enthusiasm for Scottish music. Half way through a chaotic Eightsome Reel, the police arrived.

'Sorry, folks, but we had a complaint that someone's sitting on the horn of a Volkswagen.'

Peter looked hurt. He was very proud of his bagpipes. He had brought his instrument with him from Scotland. Before he left, he presented them to the Squadron as a memento. For all I know, they are still sitting in the trophy case.

Our first priority next day was to buy some wheels. Pappy Gay said that he had a car for sale. On first sight the Chevrolet Corvair looked exactly what we wanted—a six-month-old white compact with a fully automatic gearbox. The engine ran sweetly. So why was Pappy selling it so cheaply?

Half way through a chaotic Eightsome Reel, the police arrived.

Of course, there was a catch. Pappy—so called because he was the oldest pilot on the Squadron—was rarely seen without a pipe stuck in his mouth. One night after returning from an extended 'happy hour' at the Officers' Club, he fell asleep in the car, leaving his pipe smouldering on the passenger seat beside him. Fortunately a neighbour spotted the smoke-filled car before it went up in the flames and rescued Pappy, but it was too late to prevent the once blue upholstery turning charcoal brown and the interior roof blackening with soot. Pappy said that he intended to get it fixed but that, if we were to take it as seen, then we could have it—naming a ridiculous price. Unable to resist a bargain, we shook hands on the deal, which is why for the next few weeks I drove to the supermarket sitting on a towel.

That night there was another party. How much longer would my candle last?

* * *

On the Sunday morning I awoke with a feeling of trepidation. We had an appointment to meet our new landlord. What would he be like? The recollection of our first meeting with our Scottish laird was still fresh in my memory. I needn't have worried: Stewart Abercrombie could not have been less like the Brigadier if he'd tried. Cowboy hat, cowboy boots . . . He didn't exactly tie his horse to the rails, just came in a huge pick-up truck.

'Howdy folks.' Did they really talk like that out here? 'I sure am pleased to meet you.' He shook us firmly by the hand. 'Welcome to the Rancho Lomita. Sure hope you folks are going to be happy.'

He told us to help ourselves to all the oranges, lemons and avocados we could eat, use the tennis court and even their swimming pool, when they were away.

'Shouldn't we be signing a lease or whatever you call it over here?'

'Bless me, no. Micky and Pete never bothered. We just had a verbal agreement. Why make money for lawyers? By the way, gotta a little house-warming gift for you from Lillian. She's my wife. You'll have to come and meet her one night. Stay and have some supper.'

The 'little gift' was a rib of beef, a basket of oranges, and half a dozen bottles of Californian wine. It looked as if we were also going to get along just fine with our new landlord.

No sooner had he left than the telephone rang.

'Hi! This is Brookie Whistler. Why don't you come on up and have some lunch?'

The unpacking was put on hold. John and Brookie lived with their two children at the top of the ranch in a house that had been converted from a cowshed and if anything was even smaller than ours. The setting was idyllic. Graceful pepper trees shaded the patio area, their foliage speckled with tiny red berries, and rows of orange and avocado trees grew just yards away, whilst magnificent horses trotted round the nearby paddock. Peacocks strutted, displaying their finery, or perched on the roof, screeching. A prize bull relieved himself against the adjoining wall. But then nowhere is perfect.

John, also a pilot on VX-4, was six feet four and dishy with it. His wife, Brookie, was to be my guardian angel during the coming weeks, taking over as guide and mentor after Micky left. She took me shopping, sat beside me whilst I learned to cope with driving on the wrong side of the road and in general became someone I badly needed—a friend.

Monday was final moving day, but not before I had my official photograph taken and completed an application for an identity card, my passport to an untold wealth of military privileges, from cheap shopping at the station commissary to the free use of a daytime nursery. I soon found that what I thought of as remote was just round the corner to most of the automobile-orientated population. Hardly had I arrived in the house when there was a knock on the door.

'Hi. I'm your Welcome Wagon Hostess.'

I shook her hand and said pleased to meet you.

'Why, you're British!' She was thrilled. 'Now, this is something special for a Welcome Wagon lady. We sure don't have many English ladies coming to live in this part of the country. Tell me, do you have a Welcome Wagon in England?'

'Well, not that I know of,' I had to confess. I was treated to the story of how the original pioneer women had driven their covered waggons out to meet new settlers with fresh water, food and supplies and from those early seeds had grown the present organisation designed to make newcomers feel at home.

From her basket my visitor produced today's substitute for a loaf of bread. Useful little knick-knacks—a pot holder, letter openers, a telephone pad, two tin-openers (pardon me, can-openers), shoe-horns—all discreetly stamped with the logo of the store which had donated them along with an invitation to visit any time.

That night we had more visitors. On the step stood a crowd of neighbours, mostly complete strangers, crying 'Hi! I'm Betty—this is Tom' and so on. 'We're just here to chivaree you.' (What in heaven's name was that?) 'We know you're busy, but it's traditional to drop by and leave a little something for the empty store cupboard.'

So saying, they heaped the picnic table with bags of sugar, jars of coffee, ketchup bottles and six-packs of loo paper.

'No, we're not stopping. Well, maybe if you insist—just one nip of your good Scotch whisky, and then we'll be on our way.'

Some hours later . . .

Tuesday morning I awoke knowing that the holiday was over. From now on I was back on housewife duty—bacon-and-egg breakfast to be cooked for a husband wearing an unfamiliar khaki uniform. The next weeks were tough. Jack would had to familiarise himself with new types of aeroplanes, learn to write his evaluations in Americanese, and generally behave like a US Naval officer. By comparison my problems were molehill-sized, although they didn't always look that way to me.

— 5 —

Very Much the Stranger

A WEEK later I joined a group of Squadron wives at Oxnard train station to wave goodbye to the Newmans, who had chosen to travel the first part of their homeward journey by rail. It was very much a tears-and-laughter occasion. Vows of undying friendship were exchanged, with promises to meet again. As the train pulled out of the station, everyone said how much the Newmans would be missed, then dried their eyes and went about their business. Service folk are used to such comings and goings.

As we drove back to the ranch I gazed out of the car window at the sun-drenched land. It was very pretty; in London it was probably raining. Anyone in their right mind would have given their eye-teeth to be in my position, so why was I wishing it was me sitting on that homeward-bound train, and not Micky? Why did a simple reminder of home, like discovering a tin of Tate & Lyle's golden syrup lurking at the back of the cupboard, reduce me to floods of tears? Had I been a more experienced traveller I would have known that all that was the matter was that I was suffering from culture shock. Unfortunately, in those days, who had ever heard of such a condition? I just thought I was being a wimp. Silly me!

I was feeling very much the stranger in a foreign land. No one had warned me that there would be a language barrier. I cannot tell you how many times I said the wrong thing. As George Bernard Shaw so rightly observed, 'One of the greatest stumbling blocks to Anglo-American co-operation is the illusion that the British and the Americans both speak the same language.' It is, of course, perfectly true that in theory we both use a language called English, but in practice we use it in two entirely different ways. Everyday conversation was riddled with linguistic pitfalls. Instructions as to the whereabouts of the 'nappies' left my baby-sitter looking puzzled; small visitors told me, 'Naw, that's not a biscuit, that's a cookie. *That's* a biscuit,' pointing to a scone. Happily a doughnut was a doughnut—on that we all agreed. A request for a reel of white cotton left the assistant at the haberdasher counter scratching her head, baffled, until the light dawned. 'What you want is a spool of thread.'

I was completed wowed by my first sight of an American supermarket. In the early 1960s in Britain, a supermarket was little more than a glorified self-service store. No wonder the first time I walked into a giant Safeway my eyes nearly came out on stalks. The banks of fresh vegetables and pyramids of luscious fruits looked so tempting—tomatoes the size of oranges, lettuces in a dozen unfamiliar varieties, artichokes like giant fir cones, squashes and pepper, green, yellow and ruby. Faced with such an overwhelming choice, I didn't know where to start.

A whole new food language had to be learned—cornstarch for cornflour, crackers for biscuits, jelly was jello, sweets were candies. Everything came in a dozen different confusing varieties. Did I want my milk whole or 'half and half?' I would learn to load my trolley with sufficient cartons for a week for in California: there was no friendly milkman delivering my pinta. Detergents were sold in suitcase-sized boxes, and as for the choice of cereals—bewildering. At the meat counter the cuts were unfamiliar. Even that old faithful standby, mince, was labelled 'ground hamburger'. I hadn't expected shopping in America to be so, well, foreign.

After the first nervous solo to the shops I began to enjoy driving the new car. No more dodgy gear levers or pedals to double-declutch; this was what I called easy motoring. Thanks to its automatic gearbox, driving the Corvair was a cinch and I soon became confident out on the road although sadly the car was jinxed. No sooner had Jack redecorated the smoked interior than I had a confrontation with the garage wall resulting in a six-inch gash along her bodywork.

I committed this horrific crime whilst Jack was away on a course and would not be home until the end of the week, so I had several days to dream up an excuse for my incompetence. As it turned out, I need not have worried. We were invited to a party on the Friday night, and by the time Jack got home there was barely time to say 'Hello' before he rushed off to get changed, leaving no time for confessions. It was dark when he drove the car out of the garage so he never saw the damage, and I decided to keep the bad news until next day. With an evening socialising with our new American friends ahead of us—something I was still finding hard work—I wanted us to arrive harmoniously. Anyway, that was my excuse for my cowardice.

As we were rather late, Jack decided to try out his racing driver skills. The highway ahead was as straight as a Roman road until it crossed over the freeway, where there was the gentlest of bends. Whilst another car would have taken the curve with ease, the Corvair with its weighty, rear-mounted engine refused to respond and the next thing we knew was that we were somersaulting down a thirty-foot bank towards the freeway below. I still remember an unreal sensation of drifting up towards the roof (in those days few cars were fitted with seat belts) and then down again before landing the right way up on a patch of sandy ground beside the road.

For a moment there was a ghastly silence and then Jack yelled 'Get out! We're on fire!' Actually the car was not on fire at all, but because he had been puffing on a cigarette at the time we left the road he assumed that the cloud of dust that filled the car was smoke. Dust or smoke, it still cost me a pair of tights as I leapt out of the car straight on to a barbed-wire fence, ripping them to tatters. How like a man.

'Are you all right?' The occupants of a following car peered down from the bridge above, white-faced.

We nodded. It seemed that we had had a miraculous escape.

The Highway Patrolman was with us minutes later.

'Ah, a Corvair.' He didn't seem surprised. 'These here cars sure are getting themselves a bad reputation.'

In 1965 author and consumer-rights advocate Ralph Nader had targeted General Motors' Corvair in his book—'Unsafe at any speed.'

We thanked our lucky stars for a soft landing on the verge. The fast lane of the freeway was only a couple of feet away.

'Where you good folk heading for?' the officer asked.

'Well, actually we were on our way to the Officers' Club.'

'Hop in. I'll drop you off.'

We accepted his offer in amazement. The looks on the faces of our hosts as we climbed out of the car were something to behold. It isn't every day that one's guests arrive in the back of Highway Patrol car. When they learned what had happened, they were first concerned and then filled with admiration. How wonderful of us to turn up to the party. Our glasses were topped up fast. Never mind that my hair and bra were full of sand and my hosiery in holes: they couldn't be happier to see us. I am not sure I would have chosen such a dramatic way to break the ice, but there you are. From that day forth we never looked back: we were well and truly inaugurated. As for my confession, that came six months later at a dinner party. Well, it was too good a story not to tell.

The car was duly repaired but we never felt the same about it again and decided to hunt for a replacement. Obeying the instructions of the verbose salesman on the television ad, we 'hurried on down to Hollywood Boulevard', which is where we found a silver-grey Mercury Comet station wagon with only 7,000 miles on the clock—a bargain and a great vehicle that was to be our family car for another twelve years.

* * *

In the beginning, I had trouble making myself understood on the telephone.

'Who is this?'

I would give my name, spell it out phonetically and even then would over-hear the child whispering, 'Mom, it's for you. I don't know who is calling but she sure don't speak very good English!'

But it wasn't just the language: I had to learn whole new way of life. Whether we could afford it or not, we were going to have to be a two-car family. Walking to the shops along the main highway with a pushchair was something only crazy women did, and a bus was as likely to pass my door as a dinosaur. I couldn't go on depending on the kindness of others every time I needed to buy a loaf of bread. Jack said that he would ask around, maybe visit some of the local used car lots. As it turned out, it wasn't necessary. I was offered what seemed like the perfect solution the first time I attended the Squadron Wives' Club's monthly luncheon.

Attending wives' clubs had never been my forte: all-female functions were something I'd so far managed to avoid. But when Brookie rang to offer me a ride, I couldn't find a diplomatic way to wriggle out of the invitation. I tried the 'no baby-sitter' angle, but that didn't work.

'That's not a problem. You can share mine. We'll drop the kids off on the way.'

After that I ran out of excuses.

The restaurant where we were all due to meet for lunch was called The King Arthur. Brookie said it was on Main Street in Oxnard. It wasn't hard to find. The entrance was disguised as a portcullis; the doorman wore a suit of armour. I believe that the suit was made of plastic; even so, it must have been very uncomfortably hot. Inside, I stood uncertain where to go, my eyes slow to adjust to the instant darkness.

'My, are you all right?' A lady in a straw fedora rushed to the rescue. 'What you need is one of these.'

She thrust a glass of something that tasted like melted chocolate-chip ice cream into my hand.

'I'm Bella, your hostess for the month. You must be our new British wife.'

Possessively, she bent to pin a massive corsage of orchids on my bosom and, beaming, thrust me into a group of women who looked as if they were off to a royal garden party.

Once more I'd dressed incorrectly. They were wearing high-heeled shoes, stock-ings, flowery hats and long-sleeved, pastel-coloured suits. And gloves! As for me, well, I was hatless, gloveless and bare-armed, quite unsuitably dressed for the hypothermia-inducing air-conditioning in the restaurant. Already the goose bumps were forming.

The lunch that followed was very formal. The tables were laid with linen, crystal and lavish floral centrepieces. As a new girl, it was my privilege to sit on the top table.

'And how you enjoying living here? I'm sure you must be feeling homesick,' said my neighbour.

41

Already the goose bumps were forming.

'Oh no!' I denied stoutly, my British upper lip stiffening, though I did admit to feeling somewhat isolated without any means of transportation. She was very sympathetic, saying that she couldn't begin to imagine how anyone could manage without their own set of wheels.

'Now I wonder if I don't have just the car for you. How'd you like a little Morris convertible.' I nearly choked on my prime rib steak. The last car I would have expected to be offered in this land of monster vehicles was a Morris Minor. 'It's been off the road for a while, but I'm sure it wouldn't take much to get it going. Why don't you and Jack come over tomorrow night and take a look?'

The little car was languishing at the back of a barn, a pathetic sight. Blanketed in cobwebs, dusted with a film of sand, her once shining red paintwork now tinted with a bloom of blue, she sat like the heroine of a fairy story waiting for the kiss of life. The prince fell in love at first sight, and couldn't wait to take her home. Of course she wasn't roadworthy—bald tyres, brakes non-existent, a hole the size of a cricket ball in her exhaust system. Even the gearshift was broken. But when Jack turned the ignition key, amazingly the engine roared into life. A week later he drove her home, very slowly, very carefully.

For the next six weeks, our weekends were spent not at the beach but outside the house, bleeding brakes and testing electronics. The interior needed scrubbing and redecorating, the vinyl seats patching. The bodywork absorbed a dozen cans of red spray paint before she was ready. Eventually the great day came when her proud owner drove her to the Squadron, parked her in a bay wide enough for a pick-up truck and left her sitting coyly between two enormous station wagons. Affectionately known amongst the Naval personnel as The Sewing Machine, she became as good a talking point as Peter's bagpipes.

Alas, our little red car was not long for this world. Her pistons seized (or whatever it is that pistons do) while racing John Wissler's Messerschmitt Bubble Car and Glen Keene's TR 2 home after 'happy hour' at the club. Her problem proved to be terminal. She never moved again under her own propulsion and for several weeks sat forlornly outside our gate. Soon she was joined by her replacement. This time Jack chose a native model. The Dodge cost him fifty bucks, a sort of Al Capone step-up-into model, with white-walled tyres and a wicked pair of fins and as roomy and comfortable as a London taxi in the back. It was a bit like driving a large green tank, and drank about the same amount of petrol, but at ten cents a gallon who cared? Jack loved driving it, but I had to sit on a cushion before I could see over the steering wheel.

So now we had three cars. Our Squadron neighbours thought Jack was very funny. We woke one morning to find they had hung a banner along our fence advertising 'Limey Jack's Used Car Lot'.

Sadly, the Morris had to go. The price of a replacement engine, even if one could have been found, would not have been cost-effective, so she was sold for scrap. The day they towed her away we both had tears in our eyes.

By now I was adjusting, feeling a lot happier, less an outsider. I was even beginning to think in dollars instead of constantly converting prices into sterling. My disappointment at the lack of automated domesticity long forgotten, life on the ranch was turning out to be fun. Where else would I have found such a pretty place to live?

Lomita means 'small hill' or 'rising gently above the plain'. From our house a shady, eucalyptus-lined track climbed up towards the Los Posas Hills, passing fields where armies of imported Mexican labourers picked the beans and green tomatoes. Beyond were corrals stocked with cattle, sheep and magnificent purebred horses, their coats as shiny as conkers. The road veered off behind the Abercrombie hacienda, their tennis court and swimming pool and a large paddock where Robin and I could stand and watch the ranch hands working with the finest bloodstock. A mini rodeo, in fact.

Over the top of the hill, hidden from view, the road stopped at a ditch known as Rat Canyon, where once a week the Ranch residents dumped their household rubbish rather than pay large sums of money to a firm of trash collectors. On the side of the hill, as far as the eye could see, grew groves of bittersweet aromatic orange, lemon and avocado trees.

43

I counted myself truly lucky to have somewhere so interesting to walk and safely participate in that quaint old British pastime of perambulator pushing. Today people would fork out millions to live in such a rural Eden.

Our garden almost looked after itself, apart from the so-called lawn. Mexican Joe was meant to come one afternoon a week to cut the tough Bermuda grass, though his visits were rarely that regular. The first time he came, he scratched his ample belly and sighed at the sight of my lumpy lawn.

'You got gophers bad. You need a trap.'

'Oh no! I'd rather not!' Trapping sounded too drastic.

Joe shrugged. Clearly, he thought this strange lady was a few cents short of a dollar. Instead we tried flushing them out with the hose—a complete waste of time. The little furry rodents just shot off into another part of the garden and dug out a whole new burrow system.

After puffing up and down with the mower for half an hour, Joe knocked on the kitchen door.

'Maybe you gotta little beer for me?'

Well, of course. In England it's cups of tea; in California, presumably, it's cans of beer. He settled himself down at the table, pushed his baseball cap to the back of his head and lit up a cheroot. He looked as if he was settled there for the afternoon. I began to wonder how I was ever going to get him out of my kitchen.

Finally, I coaxed him back into the garden, telling him I wanted to show him a patch of ground I would like dug over. I was planning a little vegetable garden—corn, strawberries, tomatoes, perhaps even some melon.

'Si. We grow melon. Very good ground. We grow anything.' The beer had made him very expansive.

The following week when he arrived, he brought his spade and an assistant, a sad-faced fellow with spaniel eyes whom he introduced as José. Joe was now the foreman, a rôle he enjoyed enormously, leaning on his spade, handing out the orders.

'Cut back the ice plant for the lady, José.'

'Yes, Joe.'

'Dig the patch for the lady's melons.'

Then Joe disappeared to the tool shed for a little siesta.

The following week Joe was back—alone. He was sorry, but he had no time to cut the grass. That José, he was very sick. He was obviously quite put out now that he was no longer bossman.

A month later he returned, all smiles once more. He had a new assistant. José II was a gentleman of uncertain years, who could barely walk let alone push a mower. He didn't last long either. When I asked if he, too, was sick, Joe shook his head in great sorrow.

'No. He's gone,' looking heavenward. 'Miss Lillian she says, "What do you do with all your helpers, Joe? Work them to death?"'

Meanwhile my little seeds were sprouting nicely—row upon row of healthy green shoots. As Joe had promised, everything grew at the speed of science fiction. Nothing grew faster than the melons. Following my gardener's instructions, I watered them copiously and they blew up like balloons. Proudly displaying the fruit to my neighbour, I seized a knife and plunged it into the top. A fountain of juice squirted into my face. Inside the flesh resembled a waterlogged sponge and tasted like, well, a waterlogged sponge. Mexican Joe refused to take responsibility.

'I say to you, "Not too much water."'

He didn't. Or did he? We had always had a little problem communicating.

I never did taste home-grown melons, nor strawberries. Our little friends the gophers saw to that. Like an advancing underground army, they burrowed beneath the rows. My precious plants rose in waves before them, then flopped back to earth, limp and rootless and all in broad daylight. The cheek of it! After that I rather lost interest in gardening as a hobby. It hardly seemed worth all the heart-break when the fruit and vegetable roadside stands sold such wonderful fresh produce for very little money.

It wasn't just gophers we had to contend with. Roof rats moved into the bath-room one night. I saw them sitting on the taps, washing their whiskers. Jack thought I was making a fuss.

'They're only big mice,' he mumbled from the security of his blanket.

Big mice, little rats—my love of animals didn't extend to either. We called in someone called the 'rodent control agent' to deal with the problem.

The bunch of ducks that waddled into our garden late one afternoon was far more endearing. No one seemed to own them. I asked around and even 'phoned the Highway Patrol, who assured me that ducks where not within their jurisdiction and that perhaps I ought to be calling the animal pound. By now it was getting dark, so we locked them in the tool shed for the night. Next morning they break-fasted on our abundant snail population and then enjoyed a bath under the sprinkler. They seemed very happy, but our relationship was short-lived. Two days later their real owner came and bundled them into a sack and that was the last we ever saw of them.

Our garden was always full of birds of the wild variety. Jays the colour of ripe damsons, long-tailed grey mockingbirds, whistling golden orioles and king-sized, red-breasted robins. Most beautiful of all were the diminutive, iridescent humming birds that hovered in suspended animation above the nectar-rich hibiscus and fuschia blossom, their plumage shimmering jade and malachite, their wings beating too fast for the human eye to follow. At night a nightingale sweetly serenaded us. It would have been difficult to find a lovelier place to live. I would have been more than happy to spend our whole tour living there. Unfortunately it was not to be.

The price of land in the area was soaring; the developers were on the march. One by one the bean fields were sold for building plots and the hedges of scarlet and flame bougainvillea that used to grow in glorious profusion along the Los Posas Road were torn out, to be replaced by stone walls and high fences. Who could blame the Abercrombies for selling up and moving to an even more beautiful ranch near Santa Barbara? Their hacienda was converted into a boarding school for girls. The rest of the land became the Rancho Lomita Estate.

In time the citrus orchards were rooted out to make way for executive homes. Where once flowers had grown, houses sprouted. Life on the ranch was never the same again. The tennis court and swimming pool were out of bounds; our friends from the top of the ranch had long gone. The letter asking us to leave at our own convenience came as no surprise. The week after we moved, they bulldozed our little house to the ground. Where the gophers used to play they built an estate office.

Lark Drive

FINDING a new abode was not a problem. The Housing Officer at Point Mugu promised he would have a quarter available within the month. So we decided to move in style.

For some time we had been promising the neighbours that we would invite them over for supper and serve them that quintessential British dish, fish and chips. The Saturday before we moved from the ranch seemed as good a time as any. The house was due for demolition, so there would be no one to complain if we left it smelling like a chippie.

'Gee, what a great idea! We'll be there!' promised the Petries, the Macdonalds and the Wisslers. Dottie said that she and Glenn would love to come but her sister and brother-in law-were staying.

'Bring them too—the more the merrier!' Was I mad? How can anyone cook chips for twenty in one small chip pan?

At the early-morning market in Ventura there were all kinds of fancy seafood on sale. Had I wanted giant prawns or Alaskan crab, I could have bought them by the crateful, but there was not a single cod. Cod, it would seem was off—that day at least. Judging by the blank looks my enquiries received, it was probably never on. However, on Otani Izzy's stall there was a nice line in red snapper on offer. The Oriental stallholder assured me that red snapper would be a delicious substitute and that he was happy to fillet the fish for me, which was a relief because fish filleting was not one of my culinary skills. Back home I made a huge basin of batter. The chips were easy. They came in bumper bags, frozen.

We greeted our guests wearing shiny plastic Union Jack pinnies (a Christmas present from Mother) and then left them to make merry on their own whilst we locked ourselves away in the kitchen and turned up the heat under the pan of oil. Whilst the chips and fish frizzled side by side, enveloping the kitchen in a haze of blue smoke, sweat poured down our faces as the temperature in the kitchen climbed with the addition of each fresh batch. It was a miracle that the fat didn't catch fire.

Scarlet-faced, I bundled the crispy fillets into sheets of the Airmail Edition of the *Daily Telegraph* that I had been hoarding for weeks and rushed the paper bundles through the swing door, begging folks to go ahead and eat. By the time the last fillet had been fried and the last chip crisped, we were exhausted. Compliments flew; the meal was pronounced delicious. 'You'll have to do it again.' No chance. It was days before I got the smell of fish out of my hair.

The house into which we were moving came fully furnished with a three-piece suite, coffee tables, beds and giant-size side lamps—practically everything we needed. The only items we had to buy from the previous tenants were their curtains (or, rather, drapes)—floor-to-ceiling, pinch-pleated, lined beige linen, beige being the colour favoured throughout the house. They were very good quality, and also very expensive.

Before we moved, we advertised all our furniture that we no longer needed in the local paper, but sold nothing. On the Saturday morning, in desperation, Jack hung a banner along the fence: 'Furniture for Sale'. Incredibly, in less than half an hour the house was overflowing with passers-by, keen to relieve us of what an hour before we had been ready to consign to Rat Canyon. Everything was sold

Scarlet-faced, I bundled the crispy fillets into sheets of . . . the Daily Telegraph . . .

48

except our double bed, which we loaded on to the top of the car, not knowing what else to do.

Half way along the Los Posas Road, a pick-up truck came screaming up alongside, hooting, the driver waving his arm through the window.

'Hi! That bed for sale?'

'As a matter of fact it is.'

'I'll give you twenty dollars.'

Just as we dragged it off the roof, something very unusual happened. It started raining.

'So how much did we make?' Jack asked his treasurer when she had finished counting up the dollars and cents.

'Enough to pay for the living-room drapes. Just.'

There are few things sadder than an empty house, especially when you know that in a few days' time it is due for demolition. We said very little as we drove. I may even have shed a tear. I'd learned to love that little house with its white picket fence.

Nevertheless, thanks to a quirk of fate, my earlier wish had been granted and we were moving into a model house complete with two bathrooms (or rather one and a half; the second had just a shower), both with power showers, acres of parquet flooring that never needed polishing, sliding glass patio doors and lots of closet space. The kitchen had a double stainless-steel sink fitted with a garbage disposal unit, and there was a double oven and a built-in automatic washing and drying machine. What more could a girl ask for? This was going to be easy living.

Our new address was on Lark Drive. All the residential roads on the base were named after missiles. So romantic! The base had all the facilities of a small town— a commissary, shops, schools, a gas station, a cinema and all kinds of sports and leisure facilities, even a space-age chapel, a very modern example of ecclesiastical architecture with a built-in 'crying room' for babies. It would have been quite possible to live one's life without ever going outside the gates.

The streets had sidewalks along which I could safely push Robin in his buggy (by now, 'American-speak' was coming naturally), much to the amazement of passing automobile drivers who couldn't understand why I turned down their offers of a ride. The truth was I needed the exercise. My waistline was spreading from too many hamburgers, too many sour-cream-stuffed potatoes, too much chocolate-chip-and-pistachio ice cream, too much good living.

Almost every weekend there seemed to be a reason to party—someone's birthday, hail and farewells, a monthly theme evening at the club or an impromptu barbecue with the neighbours. Thanksgiving and Christmas guaranteed non-stop feasting, and then there was the entertaining we did ourselves. On the Fourth of July, defiantly, we flew the Union Jack and invited the neighbours over to play a drunken

49

game of croquet with a set of mallets left by the Newmans. No one knew the rules and both teams were quite sure they had won. But then, there was a lot of national pride at stake.

Leave was at a premium, but when we were given the opportunity to hitch a ride with the Military Air Transport Service to Hawaii, we jumped at the chance. There were few places more romantic for an overdue honeymoon, especially the unspoilt Hawaii of the 1960s, when there was still space on Waikiki Beach to walk between the sun-tanned bodies.

We touched down in Honolulu, on the main island of Oahu, at five in the morning and the aircraft taxied up to a long wooden building with a single word illuminated above the door—'Aloha', that all-embracing Hawaiian greeting. At the bottom of the steps a lovely barefoot maiden in a grass skirt waited to greet us with garlands of flowers and kisses on both cheeks. The warm air was heavy with the scent of waxy pink and cream blossom on the plumeiria trees. Coconut palms stood silhouetted against a sky that slowly turned from indigo to butter as the sun came up. Already the jungle dawn chorus was tuning up. I thought I'd gone to heaven.

We checked into the rest-and-recreation accommodation, an ex-army, single-storey barrack block used by US service families at Fort de Russy, right on Waikiki beach. Our room was basic—two beds, a communal bathroom down the passage—but who needed luxury when right outside our door a palm-shaded lawn sloped down to one of the most famous beaches in the world? Where any time we liked we could stroll down to a cobalt-blue sea or walk along coral sands to where the imposing Diamond Head jutted out into the ocean, and all for two dollars a night?

That evening there was a knock on the door and there stood old friends Glenn and Kathy Tierney, waiting to greet us in the traditional fashion with kisses on both cheeks and leis of orchids and plumeiria which, custom dictated, we had to wear round our necks for the rest of the evening. Glenn, ex-executive officer of VX-4, had been transferred with his family to Hawaii for a three-year posting—a tough assignment! We caught up on the news whilst sipping *mai tais*, a delicious Polynesian rum concoction topped with fresh pineapple. During dinner they insisted we borrow their second car so that we could explore the island at our leisure.

And what an island! The windward coastline, bare and rocky where the sea crashes on to the shore in giant 'Hawaii Five-O' waves beloved of the surf-kings; the gentler leeward side, protected by a spine of purple-green volcanic mountains, lush and verdant; the sea, an emerald green and turquoise coral garden. Dense, steaming rainforest and rushing mountain streams, agricultural plains heady with the sticky scent of pineapple and sugar cane, and everywhere happy people, a

50

hotch-potch of white, yellow and brown faces, every major race represented, harmoniously integrated under one huge smile.

For ten glorious days we submerged ourselves in the Polynesian way of life, waking to piped-steel and string-guitar music playing 'Aloha Oe,' the unofficial anthem of the island. We ate our breakfast of fresh pineapple, papaya and hot rolls outside in the flower-filled garden, with cheeky sparrows and doves clearing up our crumbs around our feet and a mynah bird who kept saying 'What a smasher!' Then we were off to the beach with our grass mats.

In the local market, I bought a gaudy cotton *muumuu* or 'Mother Hubbard', a tent-like dress introduced to the island by early missionary ladies who insisted that the local girls 'cover- up'—about as sexy as a sack but wonderfully cool. Not to be outdone, Sir, normally the most conservative of dressers, selected an acid-green aloha shirt patterned with grinning hula girls.

We fell off surfboards more times than I care to remember and visited the touching memorial to those who died at Pearl Harbor and the Ulu Mau Village to learn about the island culture. In the Botanical Gardens, we admired never-before-seen species of trees and plants, like the gingerbread palm, the kapok and the sausage tree hung with weighty seed pods as long as salamis. We were model tourists.

Our friends invited us to a *luau*, where we squatted on the ground round a low table decorated with vibrant, scented blossoms and feasted on pig wrapped in banana leaves (and baked in a pit full of hot volcanic lava rock), sweet yams, breadfruit, salad and *poi* (the local staple diet, a gooey purée of ground-up taro root served in a coconut shell and eaten by dipping in the fingers). Then we made fools of ourselves dancing the hula-hula.

If only we had had longer, but duty beckoned; our 'honeymoon' was nearly over. Two days before our deadline to be back at Point Mugu, Jack went to put our names down on the list for the first available seats home, expecting that we would have at least one more day in Paradise, but, as luck would have it, there were two seats free on the very next flight, so it was *aloha* and back to the real world (which actually wasn't that bad either).

It would be easy to recall our life in the States as just one big 'jolly', but the truth was that Jack spent long hours working at an extremely demanding job, sometimes all week-end. This was especially so towards the end of 1962. With the onset of the Cuban Missile Crisis I saw very little of him, the Squadron being tasked to provide an airborne solution to the night threat of missile-armed Cuban fast patrol boats. When President Kennedy issued an ultimatum to Nikita Khrushchev stipulating that, if the Soviets refused to remove all the missiles from their base on Cuba, he would blockade the island and blow their ships out of the water, the nation held its breath. For the first time in living memory, the Americans were looking at war on their doorstep—or even world war. No one could guess how the Russians would react.

The military were put on red alert. The Civil Defense department warned the civilian population to prepare for any contingency, from bombing raids to nuclear attack. It all got very scary. Families were advised to stock up their houses with at least two weeks' rations—which of course led to mass panic. The supermarkets were besieged by legions of women charging up and down the aisles, emptying the shelves of cans and packets. The suppliers couldn't keep up with the demand. The queues at the check-out tills were horrific. It would have been funny had it not been so serious.

Of course, as history tells, the crisis was peacefully resolved when Khrushchev agreed to dismantle all his missile installations, but at the time it was easy to believe that this could have been the beginning of World War III. We sat glued to our radio, listening to every news bulletin, just as we had done at home during the Suez Crisis, and as our parents must have done in 1939. There was an enormous feeling of patriotism. Few people failed to back the President, and when it was all over he was proclaimed a hero and his popularity rocketed. The whole episode had occupied less than three weeks, and yet, whilst it was going on, it seemed to last for ever. We all felt as if we had been living on a knife-edge—and one from which we climbed down with immense relief.

Time was running out and the two-year appointment was due to end. We should have gone home early in 1963, but the Commanding Officer of the Squadron requested that Jack stay on until the end of the summer to finish the project he was working on. I leapt for joy when permission was granted. It was like a reprieve: every day in California was precious. We had to be home by November because Jack was due to take up his new appointment as Commanding Officer of 736 Squadron, the Scimitar training unit at Lossiemouth. Of course, I was thrilled for him, but, after two and half years of almost perpetual sunshine, even the thought of Scotland's bracing climate made me shiver.

Not that the Californian weather was perfect all the time. As the song goes, 'It never rains in California, but, man, when it does it pours.' In February it rained for five days solid. All the drains were blocked and the downtown streets were turned into rivers. A drunk drowned in a hole in the road and, in Hollywood, million-dollar homes were washed away in mudslides. But when the sun came out again the desert blossomed and for a few brilliant days the hills were like a Monet painting before everything dried up again. I was in love with California: I thought the landscape equally beautiful—brown, green or yellow.

Jack's successor was due in September and, like it or not, plans had to be made for our journey home. A firm of carriers had to be contracted to pack and ship our heavy baggage. The rules were strict: three quotations were obligatory, so three different gentlemen came armed with clipboards. The problem was deciding what to take and what to leave behind. We only had a limited capacity allowance. So it was 'no' to the picnic table and the fancy garden furniture, but should we take a washing machine with us? Back home the appliance industry had not advanced beyond the twin-tub, and the memories of all that water sloshing about the kitchen filled me with horror. In the world of full automation, I'd been spoilt.

'No reason why not.' Jack could not see a problem.

'You're joking. What about the electrics? Aren't they all wrong for the UK?' American machines ran on 110 volts; anything more would cause instant burn-out. Not one to be defeated once he had the bit between his teeth, Jack had a word with a squadron petty officer who, he knew, ran a successful moonlighting business repairing home appliances.

'Not a problem, Lootenant-Commander, Sir. I can fix you up a good second-hand machine and build you a transformer.'

And he did. A shiny good-as-new appliance arrived complete with transformer. We christened the machine 'Big Bertha'. You needed good biceps to lift her transformer, but it meant that now I could go ahead and book her passage.

We were also taking home the silver Mercury Comet compact station wagon— not too much of petrol guzzler and spacious enough to use as a family transporter of kit and caboodle. It would be sailing with us on the *Queen Mary*, but first it had to carry us over three thousand miles across the States to New York on our journey home—an experience bound to challenge our pioneering spirit.

Jack's successor and his wife arrived and I knew that our stay in California was almost over. The house in Lark Drive, once stripped of our personal belongings, no longer looked like home, so we moved out, left it to our successors and went to live with friends until the final handover was complete and it was time to pack up and say goodbye. This took a little longer than planned but, finally, on one pretty afternoon in September 1963, we packed the car with our suitcases and a heap of last-minute farewell gifts, including a cartwheel-size Mexican hat presented to me by the Wives' Club. Each wife had contributed a little token to be sewn on to the hat—miniature cowboys, squadron badges, flags, silver charms. The sombrero still hangs on the wall upstairs, a touching if now rather dusty memento of those very happy times.

— 7 —
Homeward Bound

I COULDN'T see for tears as we drove through the gate of Point Mugu for the last time. My consolation was that for the next three weeks we had the opportunity to take an amazing cross-continental drive before we embarked on the *Queen Mary* for the last leg of our journey—a rare opportunity in those days, when travelling to faraway places was an experience enjoyed only by the more affluent.

The first scheduled stop on our three-thousand-mile trek was to be Salt Lake City. From Point Mugu this meant crossing seven hundred miles of mostly desert that would be blisteringly hot in the daytime—not much fun in a car without air-conditioning. So we chose to travel by night, taking it in turns to drive and sleep. At 1.00 a.m. we were cruising down The Strip in Las Vegas. Today's Vegas is a huge, sprawling metropolis that the traveller to Salt Lake City bypasses on a busy three-lane freeway with barely a glimpse of a neon light, but in the early 1960s almost all there was to the town was one long street with casinos and motels on either side. Somewhere in the midst of the battery of flashing lights I read that the temperature was still ninety degrees.

By 4.00 a.m. we had crossed into Utah State, and at noon we stopped in Salt Lake City. One day we'll go back to Salt Lake City and see it through eyes a little less bleary.

Next day we headed for the remote corner of Wyoming where the Grand Teton Mountains rise like sharks' teeth from the valley floor with no foothills to reduce their visual impact, and from there to Yellowstone National Park, just in time to take in the primæval landscape of steaming fissures, bubbling basins of sulphur, stinking mire, hot springs and geysers before they closed the gates for the winter. There was hardly a car or visitor to be seen—a far cry from today's scene.

The next stop was in Buffalo Bill country. In the café where we ate, men uniformly dressed in stetsons, jeans and fancy leather boots fed quarters into a jukebox that played only country and western. 'Howdy partner. How ya doin'?'

Robin was doin' fine. He always loved being in the car. Some two-year-olds would have gone crazy driving hour after hour, but Robin was perfectly content. Back on the road once more, we were still climbing, snaking up and up until, at 9,000 feet, the road levelled out and we were driving across a flat, wooded plateau with pasture and cattle grazing for more than twenty miles before we began the long descent on to the prairies.

In Buffalo I paid a visit to the local 'social centre', otherwise known as a launderette. This was a very busy place with lots of long, lean, tartan-shirted, spurred and booted individuals sitting watching their Y-fronts flying round in circles. In the corner the proprietor was doing a brisk trade cutting hair. The inevitable Western Soul music was turned up to full volume so that it could be heard over all the spinning and rinsing.

Next day we drove in non-stop rain into South Dakota and from there to Mount Rushmore when, wonder of wonders, the sun came out in time for us to admire this impressive masterpiece of rock sculpture known as the 'Shrine of Democracy'— the sixty-foot-high faces of Presidents Washington, Jefferson, Lincoln and Theodore Roosevelt. We detoured into Deadwood, a time-warp frontier town, to pay homage to the memory of Wild Bill Hickock and Calamity Jane, the notorious crack-shot and horsewoman, before moving rapidly on across the Cheyenne River, where a cattle drive was taking place. Unfortunately we missed it, though its course was reported hourly on the radio as the top news story of the day. This and the birth of the Dakota quins were all we heard about, in between an endless and unvaried diet of mournful Western ballads. Was there another world out there?

After two days of flogging across the flat agricultural plains of eastern Dakota, we crossed into Minnesota and then Wisconsin, into dairy-farm country, white-washed Dutch barns with roofs all different colours, cheeses and bright red shiny apples for sale on roadside stands. And trees that were turning red and yellow with autumn hues—the first autumn colours we had seen for two years. Like kids, we scuffed through the heaps of leaves. Finally, we joined the Northwest Tollway, and our journey was coming to an end.

After weeks of empty roads, suddenly we hit major traffic in Maryland, feeling as if we had driven in from Hillbilly Land. In all, we had stayed in eleven hotels or motels. The most expensive was The Old Faithful Hotel at Yellowstone, where we paid the princely sum of $13.50 per night; the cheapest was a motel in Wisconsin where we paid just $7.00. The most we paid for dinner for the three of us was $4.50. The entire experience had cost us under $500. Happy days!

Our final days in the USA were like our arrival in reverse. We stayed with friends for two nights in Washington whilst Jack debriefed at the British Mission, and then there was the final lap to New York, where we dropped the car off at the Cunard Pier and boarded the *Queen Mary* for our return transatlantic journey.

There was, however, an important difference. Although still officially Cabin Class passengers, somehow we had been allocated First Class cabins on 'B' Deck, organised by 'Mr Fixit' from the British Consulate. We had a proper bathroom *en suite*, complete with fresh water to bathe in. We had a wonderful trip home, with a really interesting group of fellow passengers with whom we laughed non-stop.

Sadly, the voyage was too soon over: five days later we disembarked in Southampton on a grey, October day. I knew that we were home when the coffee at the dockside café was made with bottled essence. Given half a chance, I would have leapt back on board and sailed back to America.

* * *

For the next two weeks Jack was officially on leave, and we used the time to visit relatives before driving north to Lossiemouth in the hope of finding somewhere to live. By now it was November, and winter had well and truly set in. We planned to break the journey in Newcastle-upon-Tyne but did not arrive there until after dark. We needed somewhere to stay and stopped at the local AA office for help. The girl behind the desk offered us a choice of two hotels, one a five-star and the other a one-star. Frugally we chose the latter: after all, it was only for one night. What a mistake that was. If asked 'What was the worst hotel you ever stayed in?' I can say without hesitation that it was that one in Newcastle—which, in fairness to the present owner, shall remain nameless. It was freezing cold and badly lit, and it stank of boiled cabbage. The mattress on our so-called double bed was lumpy and only four feet wide and the blankets were gossamer thin; outside our door there was a long, lino-covered passage that led to the only bathroom, where the tub was rusty and scum-rimmed and the hot water barely lukewarm. Fellow guests clip-clopped up and down the passage and banged their doors all night. I can't remember what they served for breakfast. I was probably too tired to eat.

We should have reported the hotel to the AA next morning but were anxious to be on our way as the snow had arrived early in Scotland. The blizzards were so bad that the Drumochter Pass was blocked and we had to take the coastal route, via Aberdeen. Our first port of call was Mr McBride, the Married Quarters Officer.

'Well, isn't it grand to see you both, and looking so well. You must be missing all that Californian sunshine.'

And a lot else, for Mr McBride had no good news to offer.

'I'm sorry to say that the married quarter waiting list has grown no shorter in your absence, nor has the choice of private hirings improved. I'll put your name down and let you know if anything new comes in. That is the best I can do.'

Our only option now was to take a room at the Laverock Bank Hotel, a red-brick hostelry known somewhat unflatteringly amongst service families forced to seek refuge in its modestly priced accommodation as 'The Lavatory Tank.'

Shivering, we piled on the sweaters before appearing in the chilly dining room for an unappetising bowl of Scotch broth followed by boiled mutton and neeps. By now I was suffering from a very bad case of re-cultural shock. Optimistically, the next day we bought the local newspaper. There was only one flat advertised. We telephoned and the lady said that we were welcome to come and look although she didn't think it would do. Desperate, we said that we'd go anyway.

We approached the house down a long drive, crossed a gungy-green moat and parked outside an ivy-covered building that had all the charm of Dracula's castle. No doubt the house had once been someone's grand residence, but now it was divided into accommodation for at least a dozen families who had littered the courtyard with an assortment of broken bicycles and prams and other even less attractive detritus.

As we climbed out of the car the lady appeared with the key. Tentatively we followed her up a slippery flight of stone steps that corkscrewed round the outside of the building. Already I knew that there was no way we could live there—a feeling confirmed by the aroma of mouse droppings as she ushered us inside. Opposite the door there was a cupboard-size space with a sink and two gas rings.

'Is that the kitchen?'

She nodded, embarrassed. Poor lady, she was just the caretaker.

There was just one bedroom, furnished with a four-poster with a mattress so old that Bonnie Prince Charlie could well have slept on it. Next door was a cabin with a basin and loo.

'Bath?'

Looking even more embarrassed, she showed us into the only reception room and lifted the top of the dining table to reveal a tin tub beneath. I caught sight of my woeful expression in a spotty, full-length mirror and began to laugh—hysterically. We beat a hasty retreat.

A few days later, still homeless, we'd had enough of hotel life and packed up and drove south to stay with Jack's sister. Hardly had we arrived when the Married Quarters Officer rang from Lossiemouth to say that he had found us the ideal place. Judging from the way he described the house, it was perfect—in a charming fishing village, within thirty minutes' drive of the Air Station with several other Naval families living in the vicinity. We took him at his word and told him we would take it unseen.

Three days later we climbed into the car for what we hoped was the last journey. By the time we arrived in the tiny fishing village of Garmouth, although it was only three in the afternoon it was already getting dark. The streets of grey houses were deserted. There was not a soul around to ask the whereabouts of a house called Braeside.

We cruised up and down the narrow winding street, searching.

'There it is.'

'Oh no!' My heart plummeted. Surely there must be some mistake.

We were looking at a grim, ugly house that had a serious case of the leans. The gutters were sagging and the windows salt-encrusted. Who in their right mind could have described Braeside as homely? My husband said it reminded him of the nursery rhyme about the old woman who lived in a shoe.

'Come on—perhaps it is better inside.' There wasn't much optimism in Jack's voice.

The front door opened directly on to the street. We knocked and waited. Nothing happened.

'Let's run away,' I whispered.

Too late, the door creaked open and an elderly crone wrapped in a shawl and rubber boots beckoned.

Too late, the door creaked open . . .

58

'Come away in.'

When I looked closer I saw that she wasn't really old, just weatherbeaten.

Even though the fire was burning in the grate, the living room felt glacial. I've been in some cold holes in my life, but this one took the *prix de freeze*. The white-washed walls in the living room were so bowed that they looked as though they might collapse at any minute. There were two tiny windows dressed with bedraggled grey netting. The only furnishings were two lumpy chairs and a wobbly wooden table, and on the uneven stone floor a threadbare rug, so faded that it was impossible to guess its original colour. We stumbled along a dimly lit, richly fungal-smelling passage and up a twisting, rickety staircase leading to three tiny bedrooms and a bathroom with a tub ringed with the scum of ages. Perhaps if we hadn't recently returned from the land of milk and honey, perhaps if it had been July and not November, perhaps if I hadn't been two months pregnant, the house might not have seemed such a horror. As it was, Braeside was my worst nightmare come true.

The very fabric of the house seemed to ooze chill. Everything we touched felt damp and clammy. I pointed to a trickle running down the kitchen wall.

'Just a wee bit of condensation. It will soon go once the house has been aired. It hasn't been occupied for a while. Maybe you should you leave the back door open.'

Leave the back door open! She had to be kidding. The house was cold enough even without inviting in the easterly wind that was whining round the walls. That night I slept with all my clothes on. Next morning we were banging on the door of the Married Quarters Officer at Lossiemouth.

'I'm sorry to hear that you are not happy.' Mr McBride looked perplexed. He shook his head and declared, 'I'm afraid there is nothing better just now.'

Then, just as we were leaving his office, the telephone rang. He signalled us to wait.

'Now you might be in luck. There's a Mr Smith on the line. He says he has a house to hire. Mind you, it's all the way out at Spey Bay, but if you're desperate . . .'

We were.

I have no idea why the funny, slate-roofed house at Spey Bay appealed to us. It just did. It was solid and windproof; it needed to be, sitting there on the shoreline. The back door opened straight on to great shingle banks of smooth cream and grey, doorstop-sized stones. From the window in the tiny kitchen there was just one big seascape of the Moray Firth. Mr Smith met us at the house and, as he walked us round, apologised.

'The house belonged to Aunty, who died only last week. We haven't had time to clear out all her things,' he confessed, peering into a drawer stacked with corsets and directoire knickers.

I said that it didn't matter: we would take the house whatever, provided we could move in by the weekend. He seemed a little staggered but agreed to do his best.

Back in Garmouth, I had great pleasure in explaining to our landlady exactly why we would not be staying. It was worth every penny of our lost deposit to watch the expression on her face. On the Saturday morning we handed back the keys and thus ended what was the shortest tenure of our married lives.

We settled in comfortably with Aunty's bow-fronted chests, high-back, plush-seated chairs and mahogany dining table. While we waited for our heavy baggage to arrive from storage in Southampton, we lightened up the walls with a tin or two of buttermilk and the woodwork with creamy gloss. Our crates and trunks were delivered on 22 November, a day I won't forget in a hurry for it was the day John F. Kennedy was shot in Dallas. Ankle-deep in packing materials, I watched with horror the newsflash on the television screen. Only a few weeks ago this man had been 'our' President. He had come to the base in California and we had joined the crowds who applauded him, and now we shared in the grief felt by the American people. It was the end of era.

Life went on, as it always must. Places had to be found for the contents of the boxes. How much simpler life would have been without possessions! Why, I wondered, had we brought our enormous American washing machine all the way across the ocean? How could we have forgotten the size of the average British kitchen? This one was really small! There was barely room for an oven, let alone Big Bertha and her transformer. Eventually she was installed ignominiously in a lean-to outside the back door, where there was neither a supply of electricity nor a water tap. On washdays the floor of my tiny kitchen looked like the snake house at the zoo with miles of hose and extension leads to trip over. At least there was no problem about what to do with the waste water: there was one enormous drain right outside the back door—the sea. We were, of course, living in pre-environmentally conscious days.

Two weeks before Christmas, Jack was due to take over command of 736 Squadron, which would mean driving twenty miles to the Air Station. It also meant that I would be left car-less, but then Jack spotted a second-hand Austin Healey lurking in the window of a showroom in Elgin. Racing green, it was all his heart desired. He just had to have it. Once more we were a two-car family—and we could not have managed any other way. It was five miles to change a library book, twenty more to Lossiemouth. In our small outpost of the British Empire there were only a handful of cottages, a tiny post office-cum-shop and a hotel attached to golf course that didn't seem to do a lot of trade.

To the east of the hotel, along the coastline, straggled the eighteen-hole links golf course, which had seen better days. Jack had never played before but he was keen to learn, so he treated himself to a set of second-hand clubs and an annual subscription to join the club, for which he paid princely sum of five pounds. As there was no professional coaching available, he taught himself to play from a paperback tutorial by master golfer Arnie Palmer. More gorse and heather than fairway, and with greens like pincushions, Spey Bay was a challenging course, especially for a complete novice. Balls that were not hit straight were lost for ever unless dog Simon, now reinstated in the family, found it.

When we walked the opposite way to the golf course along the shore, we came to the estuary where the outflowing of the River Spey met the inrushing waves of the Moray Firth in a welter of foamy explosions. Under the splash and thump of colliding water rolled the low note of the shingle, endlessly grinding on its in-and-out journey. Here, at the point aptly named Tugnet, stood the icehouse where salmon belonging to the Queen were netted from the lower reaches of the river and were sorted and boxed for market. If I spoke nicely to the boss, he might sell me a grilse, a delicately flavoured young salmon and the sweetest freshwater fish I've ever tasted. I understand that the old icehouse has now been turned into a museum, where there is an exhibition mounted to commemorate the great days when the net fishermen of this river-mouth community would haul dozens of salmon from the Spey.

The house next door to ours was empty all the time we lived there, but across the green there were two bungalows. In one lived Mr and Mrs Smith, a dear couple who very quickly adopted Robin as their surrogate grandson and spoilt him rotten. I always knew where to find him when he had disappeared, which he did often. The other bungalow was used by Jim and Kathleen Davidson and their three red-headed children as a weekend retreat from Elgin. Jim, who became Jack's first steady golfing partner, was head accountant at Baxters, where they canned high-class soups and Scottish specialities in the factory up the road at Fochabers.

The freezing weather gave way to a mild December. Christmas was just around the corner—a very different Christmas from the one we had enjoyed in California. Christmas in Scotland was not that important, but New Year . . .! Now that was something different! It went on for days and days, or so it seemed. Total strangers dropped in for a dram, frequently bringing their own bottles: ladies in hats that looked like knitted tea cosies; men with faces weatherbeaten by the salty wind; and rosy-faced children. Who knows who they were or where they came from, but we were pleased to offer them hospitality.

Slowly but surely the California days became little more than a precious memory to be momentarily relived and then returned to the family photo album. It had been such a wonderful time but life was now less pressured. There was time to stand and chew a blade of grass, and to have another baby. Russell James was born in June.

Five months later we moved again, this time into a home of our own.

61

— 8 —
Speyside

THE house we bought stood on the banks of the Spey, where the ice-cold water of this staggeringly beautiful river rushes under the road from Aberdeen at Fochabers. The Spey, an awe-inspiring spectacle beloved of salmon fishermen and malt-whisky distillers, was a magical location for a starter home.

It was early in August and I was shopping in the village store in Fochabers when I overheard the village librarian talking to the rector's wife.

'Poor Mary Dunbar,' she was saying. 'She cannae sell her house. She's getting really bothered.'

'Such a pity,' Mrs Douglas tutted. 'It must be three months or more since Donald went to work in England. She'll be wanting to move before the winter sets in.'

By now my ears were flapping. We had talked of buying many times, but so far hadn't found a house we liked or could afford. If this Mrs Dunbar wanted to move quickly, her house might be a bargain. Plucking up courage, I butted in.

'Excuse me asking, ladies, but this house—is it far from here?'

'Bless my soul, no—just away across on the other side of the river on Inchberry Road, Speyside, just next door to the old station house.'

No harm in just taking a look at the outside, I thought. The house, when I found it, was not the ancient ruin I had feared but a modern three-bedroom semi with climbing roses on the wall and an uninterrupted view of the River Spey. I couldn't understand why it hadn't been snapped up long ago.

'Come away in, do.' Mrs Dunbar brushed aside my apology for calling without an appointment. Clearly, she was excited that someone actually wanted to view. The omens were good, especially as I felt right about the house from the first moment I crossed the threshold.

'Will you be taking tea?'

I perched in the living room whilst the kettle boiled.

'What a wonderful view you have.'

'Aye, we shall be sorry to leave. But Donald is away to work in England and we have to move.'

The tour of the house didn't take long. It was small though deceptively spacious, with an open-plan living area downstairs and three bedrooms upstairs. There was a good-sized kitchen-cum-breakfast room and a wonderful walk-in larder, huge enough to accommodate Big Bertha. I liked the house because it was light and airy, yet cosy. I liked it even more for its location on the tree-lined bank of the river and for the garden that was like a miniature fruit farm with rows of strawberries ripening, raspberry canes bending under the weight of their crop and apple and pear trees heavy with embryonic fruit. I'd had my fill of gloomy, draughty, Victorian edifices. I couldn't wait to live there. Now all I had to do was convince my other half that we had to have this house, even though at three thousand eight hundred it was way above our budget. Amazingly, I did this with ease—which was an enormous relief since I was pregnant again.

Buying a house takes for ever. By the time the last legal document had been signed, the roses were no longer in bloom and there was a feel of winter in the air. We had spent all our savings on furniture—including beds, a teak dining set, a three-piece suite and a very up-market cooker that not only baked and grilled but also spun a chicken on a spit roast—and our bank balance was at an all-time low. So we gave the local coal merchant five pounds to shift our bits and pieces in his open truck. Of course, that was the day it began to snow—not just a flake or two, but a proper blizzard. Our pile of goods and chattels, when it arrived, looked like a gigantic wedding cake. Then we lost the dog.

As soon as we had returned from abroad, my in-laws had handed Simon back to us with undisguised relief, glad to be rid of the responsibility of looking after one of the randiest escape artists in the business. At Spey Bay he had been in his element, free to wander where he liked. Sometimes he would be away on his private business for hours, especially when there was a nearby bitch on heat, but he always came home at feeding time. We hadn't been in Fochabers ten minutes before he was off in search of pastures new.

This time we were really worried. He could hardly be expected to know that he had changed his address. Perhaps he was back at Spey Bay, but when I 'phoned my ex-neighbours none had seen him. The snow was getting worse. Every hour we called from the front step, but no grinning black face appeared. I was convinced that we had really lost him.

As soon as it was light, wrapped up for an Arctic expedition, we were out searching. I walked to the top of the road. There were many footprints in the newly fallen snow but none of them was canine. Depressed, I trudged home. There, standing on our doorstep, stood a tall gentleman of retirement age attired

Of course, that was the day it began to snow . . .

in matching tartan kilt and tammy shanty. In his hand he held a leash, to which was attached one unrepentant Simon.

'Is this your wee dog?'

'It most certainly is,' I agreed, overflowing with gratitude. 'But where did you find him?'

Simon certainly didn't look like a dog that had spent the night out in the snow. In fact he was looking decidedly pleased with himself.

'We live just across the river,' explained Colonel Murray, having introduced himself to me. 'We heard him at our gate last evening, calling.' His voice took on a confidential tone. 'We have five bitches; two are—you know—in an interesting condition. Shona, my wife, said she couldn't bear to think of him out in the cold all night so we took him in.'

So all the time I had lain awake, worrying, Simon had been sleeping, snug and warm, curled up on Colonel Murray's favourite armchair. He must have thought he'd gone to doggy paradise. We saw even less of him after that, but at least we knew where to find him.

Having a home of our own felt sort of special. Only about three bricks actually belonged to us—the rest belonged to the building society—but it was still ours on paper. The first thing we, or rather I, did was to re-christen it in memory of that wonderful holiday in Hawaii. A big mistake!

'Aloha? Och, Mrs Worth. That's a strange name to be calling a hoose. I wonder could you just spell it for me whilst I write it down.' How often did I wish I'd left well alone! After all, Speyside was a far better name for a house which overlooked the River Spey.

There were only six houses on Inchberry Road. The local doctor lived at the top of the row and the ex-stationmaster lived with his family in the Old Station House on the corner next to us. The other houses were occupied by various members of the staff of Baxters, purveyors of high-class food, whose canning factory was situated just across the other side of the road to Elgin. (The smell of beetroot boiling was quite strong when the wind blew in the wrong direction.) My neighbours kept my pantry well stocked with dented cans of everything from porridge to wild duck soup. I was more than happy to do a little market research on Baxters' behalf. On one occasion we were presented with a case of Victoria plums, a fruit that did not normally appear on Baxters' list of high-class groceries (but apparently the Queen had expressed an interest), so a special batch had been canned to send to Balmoral. I hope that Her Majesty enjoyed them as much as we did.

There seemed to be a special place in the affections of the folk of Fochabers for the small group of Naval families who lived in the vicinity. We were quickly accepted into their community; there was none of the 'you've got to live here for a hundred years first' attitude. Jack's Saturday morning golfing partners included the minister, Jim Davidson, and the doctor who, with Edna, the district midwife, delivered our much longed-for daughter in May.

Deborah was just six days old when Jack came home with news I really didn't want to hear. The Commanding Officer of 803 Squadron, Peter Newman (the same Peter Newman who had donated his bagpipes to VX-4) had slipped a disc and was now flat on his back, unable to embark in *Ark Royal*, which was due to leave for the Far East, and Jack had been 'pier-head jumped' to take over the Squadron. I couldn't believe it when he told me that they were to embark in forty-eight hours. Deep down inside he must have been thrilled to be given command of a front-line squadron—it was every pilot's ambition—and of course I was very proud of him, but the timing was a little cruel!

The next two days and nights we will pass over rapidly. In many ways it was almost a relief when he was gone. It had been a terrible forty-eight hours for both of us. No more bawling, though: I just had to get on with life, although the thought of looking after three small children (and of course the dog) for a whole year on my own was enough to make me want to run home to Mother. If we hadn't had our own house, I might just have done that!

At least I wasn't the only grass widow; there were other squadron wives with whom I could commiserate. The only way to escape the loneliness was to meet as often as possible, even if only for a cup of coffee. On Sundays it was especially important not to be alone, so we took it in turns to cook lunch for a small army of women and children who would arrive in their family troop-carriers with everything from baby bottles to waterproof boots, with push-chairs and with at least one change of clothes per child.

Sensible conversation was impossible; it was Bedlam, the walks along the river, or through the woods, accompanied with a frenzied chorus of 'Don't do that darling,' or 'Where the hell has that bloody dog gone now?' It was still worthwhile, however, even though, by the time the whole lot were packed back into their cars for the return journey home, the mums were shattered. On Sundays I was usually in bed by nine.

I tried to write to Jack every night, although sometimes I was so exhausted that I fell asleep with my pen still in my hand, but it was very important to keep the letters flowing, and even more important to keep them sounding cheerful. Jack had quite enough problems of his own, with a squadron of ageing Scimitars to keep airborne. I sent photos of his three offspring smiling at the camera like angels, resisting the urge to let him know that at times they were running me ragged, especially his first-born.

Robin had grown from a sweet baby into an extremely difficult child who was so jealous of his younger siblings that he would do anything to draw attention to himself—from pushing his brother down the stairs to locking us all out of the house so that I had to break a window to get in. There were days when home was a madhouse and I screamed like a harridan with frustration. I was near the end of my tether. My mother visited and decided that it was time to come to the rescue.

After much deliberation she persuaded me that, for the sake of the rest of the family, Robin would be better off with children of his own kind. It was she who found him a place at a boarding school for children with extreme learning difficulties that had just opened in Worthing, where he would be cared for by a staff of dedicated teachers and house mothers and be close enough for her to have him to stay. At the time it was hard for us to make the decision that Robin should leave, but in my heart I knew that we were doing the right thing, not only for myself but for Robin and the rest of the family.

Christmas came and went, and then Jack wrote to say that *Ark Royal* was going into Singapore Dockyard for maintenance period and the squadron aircraft would be disembarking to RAF Changi for a month. Why didn't I join him for a well-earned break?

It was a fantastic idea, and now that Robin was happily settled in his new boarding school there seemed no reason why I shouldn't try and 'bum a ride' out to Singapore with the RAF. The seed of an idea had been planted, and, given that helpful friends had offered to take care of the children and the dog, it germinated.

I filled in the appropriate form, applying for a seat on one the regular flights that went from RAF Lyneham to Singapore. The letter acknowledging my request informed me that if I was lucky enough to be offered an indulgence flight I would have to make myself available immediately. They had to be joking. At the very least it would take me twenty-four hours to organise the children and get myself from the north of Scotland to Wiltshire. Above all, I was told that I should *not* turn up at the airfield on the off-chance—which, I am unashamed to say, is precisely what I did. The nice Flight Lieutenant at the desk admonished me for breaking the rules but sympathetically hinted that he might be able to squeeze me on to a flight leaving the next day. At ten o'clock that evening, after an agonising wait, I was told that I was on the early morning VC-10 leaving for Singapore via Cyprus and Bahrain. I was so excited I hardly slept a wink. I had no idea at the time that those thrilling two weeks we spent in Singapore together were a precursor of what was to come.

* * *

Deborah took her first steps two weeks before her first birthday in May, the same day Jack and his squadron flew back to Lossiemouth. We all went to the Air Station to watch Daddy's aircraft land. It was a race involving us and the Captain and Commander (Air) as to who reached him first. For the next few months Jack commuted to Lossiemouth from home and we enjoyed an almost normal family life. We feasted on the strawberries and raspberries from the garden, took walks beside the Spey and socialised up at the Air Station—something that had been missing from my life for a year (apart from the chaotic Sunday lunch parties). This was 1966, the year England won the football World Cup. I can still recall the look of amazement on the face of two-year-old Russell when his jubilant father tossed him ceiling-high after Geoff Hurst scored the winning goal for England. It was only whilst watching replays during the celebration of the glorious win by the England Rugby Team in 2003 that I recalled how we watched the transmission in fuzzy black and white, but then in those days we knew nothing better.

At the end of September, 803 Squadron disbanded, and thus ended another chapter in Jack's service career: the command of a front-line squadron is not a job that comes along twice. Though his career would always be aviation-oriented, his days as an operational pilot were over, which for someone who loved flying as much as he did was hard. We waited to hear where the Navy was going to send him next, fearing a desk in Whitehall, but when the news came that he was to be attached to the Royal Marines as BAVO (Brigade Aviation Officer) to 3 Commando

Brigade we were delighted. Not only was 3 Commando based in Singapore, but the posting was classified as 'married accompanied.'

Before taking up his new appointment, Jack had courses to complete. The first of these was at RNAS Culdrose, where for six weeks he would learn to fly helicopters (which he had insisted he needed to do as a BAVO), and this was followed by two gruelling months of training with the Royal Marines before he would be entitled to wear the famous Green Beret.

Our days in Scotland were numbered. Once more it was time to pack up and follow. We found a tenant to rent the house and prepared to move south. By now Robin was fully settled in Worthing at his boarding school, receiving lots of love and affection from a dedicated staff as well as from my mother, who lived close by. Now we said farewell to Simon for good. Mrs Pusey, my daily treasure, said that she would give him a home, but Simon had other ideas. No sooner had we crossed the border than he decamped to the Murray's doorstep, where he stayed for the rest of his very productive life. At Christmas we received cards covered in the paw prints of his latest offspring.

The journey south was long and weary. In those days it took an age to drive from the north of Scotland to the tip of Cornwall. Even stopping off to visit family *en route* didn't make the ride any less boring for the children. Then, just as the end was in sight, we got a puncture, right on the top of Dartmoor. Naturally, the spare tyre was buried under a mountain of luggage. Soon the side of the road was littered with suitcases, uniforms and half-used packets of cereals and detergents I had refused to bin. Six rolls of toilet tissue cascaded down the hill never to be seen again. Who could blame my husband for wistfully recalling the carefree days of bachelorhood?

We rented a holiday chalet on a farm just outside the village of Breage. The accommodation was somewhat cramped. Our bedroom adjoined the cowshed, and at night we could hear the bovines peeing against the adjoining wall. The farm was real 'Old Macdonald' country, with cows, chickens, dogs and cats, run by a well-padded, rosy-cheeked couple who looked as if they had stepped straight out of a nursery rhyme. The farmer's wife made the best pasties west of the Tamar; our milk came warm and fresh, straight from the udder. Not surprisingly, it was a great place for the children, though I missed my washing machine. I'd never seen so much mud.

Those few short weeks we spent in Cornwall as a family were very happy. Jack was home by teatime every day, and at the weekends we were free to explore deserted beaches and coves and walk along windswept cliff-tops. Even though it was winter, it was never really cold. The little ones were growing fast and leading each other into all kinds of mischief. Visits to the village shop were chaotic. No sooner had I turned my back than pyramids of tins of baked beans went flying or sacks of potatoes were upset over the floor. The prospect of having an *amah* for the next two years in Singapore was beginning to look increasingly appealing.

Christmas 1965 was spent in Sussex. My mother's warden flat at the Priory Residential Home was too small to accommodate all of us, so while Jack disappeared to earn his green beret with the Royal Marine Commandos, the children and I played the waiting game in yet another rented holiday home, this time on the beach at Lancing.

The bungalow was a typical whitewashed, 1930s seaside chalet with wooden steps leading from a verandah to the road. There was no garden, just a washing line on the pebble beach. I don't remember the name of the house; Sea Spray would have been appropriate. All through January and February gales lashed the coastline, caking the windows with salt, whilst each angry wave that crashed on to the shore deposited yet another load of seaweed. By the time the storm died down the beach was covered with a gigantic gleaming eiderdown of slimy kelp. After a day or so it stank like rotting kippers.

January and February passed slowly. At the beginning of 1966 there seemed to be nothing but bad news. An outbreak of foot-and-mouth disease swept the country, and daily there were heartbreaking reports of yet more herds of cattle being slaughtered. As if that were not depressing enough, economically the country was going through one of its periodic downturns and morale was low, especially in the Fleet Air Arm, whose future was threatened when the Wilson Government announced a package of defence cuts that included the abandonment of all aircraft carriers. Our future did not look too rosy.

In March we exchanged our winter woolly caps for sun hats and flew to Singapore *en famille*, happy to escape the gloom.

Singapore

ONE a.m., Paya Lebar Airport, Singapore. 'Announcing the arrival of British Eagle flight EG 130 from London, Kuwait and Colombo,' an Oriental female voice purred. The baggy-eyed families on the trooping flight flexed their cramped muscles and gathered up their bits and pieces, ready for disembarkation.

It had been a long journey—twenty-eight hours, including two stops for refuelling. A long time to expect a two- and a three-year-old to behave like little angels. The novelty of flying had worn off somewhere over the Channel.

We had left London on a bitter day in February, wrapped up against the cold. Now, as we stepped down from the aircraft, a wave of heat rose from the sun-scorched tarmac. The humidity was so high, you felt that you were breathing in a shower cubicle. An air hostess came running after us.

'You left this behind.' She thrust Deborah's heavy winter coat into my arms— the last thing my daughter needed. I had purposely left it behind, hoping it would end up in the charity box.

'Thanks a lot,' I smiled weakly.

When Jack returned from mustering our luggage, he was looking annoyed. One of our suitcases was missing—mine. It came to me that almost every item of summer clothing I possessed was in that case. I was stunned. Promises and assurances that my luggage would soon be located were of little consolation when all I had to wear was the travel-stained woollen skirt I stood up in.

On the other side of the glass barrier Robert Creasy waved. Robert had been the BAVO for the last two years. In a week he would hand over his job to Jack and, we hoped, the keys to the house he and his family had been renting. In the meantime we were booked to stay in a guest house. We climbed into Robert's old black banger and set off for our first glimpse of Singapore.

In 2003 we went back to Singapore. What we saw was a pristine city, with not a scrap of litter in sight. In the late 1960s it made quite a different picture, with stray dogs and pigs rummaging in rubbish-filled ditches and beggars sleeping on the streets, the air heavy with that special Oriental pot-pourri of incense, spices, charcoal fires and drains. At two in the morning the streets were relatively empty; by dawn it would be mayhem.

The Magnolia Guest House was in total darkness. Eventually, after persistent knocking, a wrinkled Chinese face appeared at the grill and, grunting, unlocked the door and let us in. We followed his scuttling, baggy-panted figure down the corridor to Room 6—four single beds in a row and, thankfully, our own bathroom. Our home for the coming week.

'Missie want anything?'

'No thanks. Nothing. Just my bed.'

A bath was cool and refreshing—and a big mistake. Immediately the children came to life, screaming with excitement as if they were at the local lido. The rest of the guests at the Magnolia Guest House must have been delighted. The bed was a real shock. The only thing between my shattered body and the floor was two inches of unyielding flock mattress resting on a frame of hard planks of wood. Eventually, overcome by exhaustion, I lost consciousness . . .

Hours later I woke to find a figure, all in white, loitering at the foot of my bed. Help! My end was nigh! But this was no ghostly apparition, just the elderly 'room boy' trying to tell us something. Rubbing his hands, he grinned, revealing a princely fortune in gold caps.

'Lunchee, Missie.'

I groaned. All I wanted to do was go back to sleep, but our time clocks had to be adjusted so I shook my corpse-like family back to life.

I checked and found that my suitcase was still missing. My problem was what to wear. My choice was limited. Would it be the full-length, green lace ball gown or a faded towelling bathrobe? I chose the latter. Fortunately, the dining room was empty, the rest of the guests having already eaten.

The Magnolia Guest House was patronised almost exclusively by service families 'in transit' so, naturally, the management assumed we would want to eat good, solid, British food. In the heat of a Singapore afternoon we sat down to soup, roast meat, apple pie and custard. The aged waiters clucked with disappointment at the piles of rejected food.

With still no news of my suitcase, my top priority was to buy something cool to wear—but where from? Most people went to one of the many cheap and cheerful tailors who could knock up a designer model copied from the picture in a magazine in less than twenty-four hours. But I couldn't wait that long. The manager of the guest house suggested we try Robinson's department store in downtown Singapore.

'Where you wan' go?' asked the hollow-cheeked driver of the yellow-top taxi, squinting at us over the smoke from his burning butt.

'Robinson's.'

'Okay.' With a lurch he let in the clutch and we shot away in a cloud of fumes. I closed my eyes and crossed my fingers. Inside his cab all his gods were catered for. On the dashboard sat the Virgin Mary next to a rose-entwined Buddha. In the back, two pearl-encrusted satin cushions ensured a comfy journey for the good spirits. We certainly needed a lucky charm to get us safely through the awful traffic.

The following day we went to see our future home in Braddell Heights, a residential area in the middle of the island. Robert came to collect us in his old Vauxhall that he was hoping Jack was going to buy. As we drove he extolled its many virtues—how cheap it was to run, how reliable. What it didn't have was air-conditioning. I could feel the sweat trickling down the back of my neck. Many moons ago, the Vauxhall had been an official car proudly driven by the chauffeur of the top military man on the island; it still had a pennant holder on the bonnet to prove its pedigree. Then it was sold off by auction and since then had been through many hands. I think we would have been about the seventh owners.

As we neared the end of our journey I began to have misgivings. How could there be a respectable residential area hiding behind this incredible hotch-potch of dwellings and businesses that lined the Braddell Road? On one side of the street we passed wooden shacks with women washing laundry at the roadside standing tap, then a smallholding where a bent figure in a straw coolie hat moved up and down immaculate rows of vegetables with two massive watering cans slung from a shoulder pole; then a junk car lot; a chicken farm with thousands of sad birds crammed together on wire-covered shelves; some open-fronted shops, their goods spilling out on the roadside; a Chinese cemetery with pink and green tombstones and horseshoe-shaped graves; and a cinema, its rusty, corrugated-iron walls covered with lurid pictures of the Oriental epic currently showing. Across the road were massive blocks of flats festooned with bamboo poles fluttering with brightly coloured laundry, crouched behind banana plantations.

The wonderful thing about the Singapore of old was that you just never knew what was round the next corner. One minute you were in jumble country; turn the corner and everything was orderly, almost European—though not quite. Shady streets of colour-washed bungalows and tropical gardens had English names like Melrose Drive and Muswell Hill. We turned into Cotswold Close and stopped at Number Eight.

As we climbed out of the car, Robert's wife, Ann, came to meet us, followed by a large brown dog of uncertain breed that greeted us with a low-key growl and then slunk away into the bushes.

'Never mind,' Ann told the disappointed children, 'Pepe will soon get used to you.'

We followed Ann and Robert through the moon-gate front entrance that opened straight into the main living area—relatively cool, thanks to the constant gyrations of two overhead electric fans. A large dining table and sideboard stood at one end; the remainder of the room was simply furnished, with rattan chairs and sofa and two vast brass trays precariously resting on spindly tripod trestles.

'The house could do with some redecoration.'

She wasn't kidding. I didn't think I wanted to spend the next two years living with walls painted battleship grey. In the kitchen I met Ting Ah Ling. (I promise you that really was the *amah*'s name.)

'Ah Ling, this is Missee Worth who come to live here.' Ann automatically fell into the pidgin English that she seemed to have acquired the habit of using, even to her husband.

'Missie.' A set of gold teeth flashed at me but the small onyx eyes were unsmiling. Ah Ling wore an immaculate white tunic over wide black cotton trousers, tiny gold earrings and a tortoiseshell comb in thinning, boot-black hair worn screwed into a minute bun. Not yet familiar with Oriental faces, I couldn't tell if she was really old or whether she had just wrinkled early.

'Ah Ling is a black and white *amah*,' Ann explained.

'Black and white?'

'Ah Ling, this is Missee Worth who come to live here.'

73

'Yes, they are the *crème de la crème*—the true professionals. Most wives would give their eye teeth to have a servant like Ah Ling.'

Really? She looked a right old battle-axe to me. Nothing like dear Mrs Pusey.

Mrs Pusey had been my help in Fochabers. Once a week she had donned her apron and given me a hand, mostly looking after the children whilst I shopped. She was my friend as well as my employee. Ah Ling was definitely no Mrs Pusey. Cosy chats over cups of coffee were clearly things of the past.

Throughout tea I was bombarded with a miscellany of information from the cost of electricity to what time of day the grocer called for my daily order, whilst Jack was being told when to wear his black boots and how much to pay the gardener. Our landlord, we learned, was a wealthy Indian businessman called Mr Chidambaram.

'What's he like?'

Ann looked at Robert, who shrugged.

'To tell you the truth we've hardly seen him. So long as he gets his monthly cheque he doesn't bother us. I'm sure he'll be round to see you once you've moved in.'

Even whilst we sat drinking our tea, the weather changed. One minute there was blistering sunshine, the next the four o'clock downpour had started. Immediately, the open concrete monsoon drains surrounding the house were transformed into rushing brown rivers and the lawn into a lake. There is nothing like a drop of water for cooling down, especially when you are very young. Led on by Martin, the Creasys' son, the children threw off their clothes and raced round the garden, splashing through the pools and screaming with delight. It was the first time they had come alive since we arrived.

The following few days were pleasantly free of responsibility as we made the most of our enforced holiday at the Magnolia. On the Monday morning Jack prepared for the first day of his secondment to the Royal Marines. Fascinated, the children watched him don his unfamiliar olive-green shirt and shorts, green and blue lanyards, long khaki woollen socks, garters with 'Boy Scout' tabs, black boots and green beret. Only the observant would have recognised him as a Naval officer by the two and half gold stripes he wore on his shoulder epaulettes.

By five he was back, looking rather dazed, now officially the BAVO on the staff of HQ 3 Commando at Sembawang. Most of his colleagues were known by acronyms such as BOO (Brigade Ops Officer) and LOG (logistics). The HQ team all worked within the confines of a large, wire-enclosed building known as The Bird Cage, except the HQ pilots who flew Sioux helicopters, affectionately known as Teeny Weenie Airways.

A week later we said goodbye to the kindly staff and friends we had made at the guest house and moved into our new residence. Our boxes had arrived from

England and were waiting to be unpacked. Hopefully before long, Number Eight would begin to look like home.

Ah Ling seemed quite chirpy as she served our first meal of fish fingers and chips and ice cream, leading me to hope that my initial feeling of hostility was imaginary. She was sweet with the children.

That evening, our landlord was expected and there were a few things we needed to talk about—especially the dreary grey walls! I wandered round the house making notes. At the far end of the hacienda-style bungalow there were three bedrooms with beds very similar to those we had slept on at the guest house. By now we were beginning to appreciate how much better it was to sleep on a hard mattress—so much cooler than spongy, foam rubber, not to mention good for the back. The children loved the bathroom with its drain in the middle of the tiled floor: they could splash to their hearts' content, making waves that washed over the side of the bath without fear of chastisement. I wasn't so enamoured when I crunched on a cockroach.

None of the windows had glass in the frames, just security grills and wooden shutters. The few curtains looked as if one good pull would split them asunder; in strong, tropical sunlight, material fades and rots in no time at all. The kitchen was a real horror story—airless, dingy and far from clean. The cooker did not bear close inspection and the refrigerator was a huge, rusting monster with a motor that pounded night and day, fighting a losing battle against the incessant heat. Inside, the shelves were actually tied together with string. The *amah*'s room beyond was a no-go area.

The garden was a tropical delight—a tulip tree brilliant with firecracker-red blossom, hedges of red, yellow and orange bougainvillea and hibiscus. The short drive was lined with frangipani trees that flowered all year round with fragrant, white, waxy blossoms. The grass was broad-leafed, tough enough to withstand the climate. Behind the house there was a coconut palm, rambutan and mangosteen trees, sugar cane and a clump of banana trees with hands of tiny green fruit.

'Missie, Missie. House man come.' Ah Ling was in a state of agitation. She shuffled down the drive and opened the gate to allow a large white saloon to drive in. Our landlord had arrived. Why couldn't he have come later, when Jack was here? Heaven knows why the word 'landlord' makes me nervous.

'Good afternoon Mr Chidambaram.' I'd been rehearsing his name all day but it still came out as a pitiful jumble.

'Good afternoon, good afternoon, dear lady.' He grasped my hand. Mr Chidambaram was a short, stocky Indian who wore a perfectly cut European suit and spoke equally perfect English but suffered from a deterioration in his hearing when the occasion demanded.

'This is a very nice house, yes?'

'Yes. I like it very much. However, there are things that need doing.'

'I'm glad you like it. I'm sure you will be very happy living here.'

'I'm sure we will be too, but now—about the decorations . . .'

'You'll want to stay of course,' he beamed. 'Where else would you find such a nice house for so little rent?'

I wasn't so sure about the little rent. Five hundred Singapore dollars seemed more than enough to pay.

'Maybe, but we were hoping that something would be done about the paintwork.'

'The what? He cupped his hand behind his ear.

'*Paintwork.*'

'Ah. Now paint—it costs a lot of money. Yes,' he sighed, 'a lot of money.'

'And the refrigerator?'

Mr Chidambaram, looking perplexed, started tapping the teaspoon on the cup. Thoughtfully he said, 'I will redecorate, give you all new furniture. Lovely teak chairs and tables, new fridge.' I hardly dared breathe. 'And you pay me fifty dollars a month more rent.'

I shook my head.

'That's way above what we agreed to pay.' I was experiencing my first serious bout of Oriental bargaining.

Mr C smiled and spread his hands. 'You must choose. You take the house as it is, and the rent is five hundred or I charge you more. I am not a rich man.' Not half he wasn't.

We eyed each other across the coffee table. He knew I was fighting a losing battle: as he so rightly said, to find another house as good would not be easy. But I wasn't finished yet. I played my trump card.

'We could ask a representative of the Joint Service Housing Board to come and do an inspection. What do you think they would say about the refrigerator, or, come to that, the kitchen?'

Of course, he'd never heard of the Joint Service Housing Board, or so he said, but I sensed that I had scored a point. Half an hour later we shook hands on a compromise. He would clean up the kitchen and we would do the rest. Exhausted, I waved him off.

'Tea, Missie?'

'To hell with tea. What I need is a gin and tonic.'

* * *

Barely a week after we moved into the house, 3 Commando Brigade departed up-country on exercise. The night before they left we had a dress rehearsal, with Jack laying out all the kit he had to carry on his first expedition into the jungle. The children thought it was a splendid game, as first a small tent and then a camp bed and a sleeping bag were laid on the floor. Next came a canvas water bucket, numerous belts and little pouches, water bottles and canteens, a bush hat, boots, a mosquito net and a Sten gun. The largest haversack was packed with shirts, long trousers, socks, pots of anti-malarial tablets and tubes of ointment to discourage bugs.

Friday morning dawned yet another hot and humid day. Sweating copiously, Jack dressed in shirt and long pants, heavy woollen socks and black Army boots. One thing he had not learned during his initiation course with the Royal Marines was how to tie his puttees, the long bandages worn to protect the ankles from leeches and other nasties likely to be encountered in the jungle. No sooner was one securely tucked around his ankle than its opposite number came unfurled. The air in the bedroom grew bluer by the minute.

After breakfast the car was loaded with all the kit and the family, and we drove out to the Naval Base. The Brigade was embarking on the assault ship HMS *Fearless* prior to sailing up the east coast of Malaysia, from where they would launch their beach assaults and war manœuvres. The children had been promised that they would be taken to see Daddy's ship.

We arrived at the jetty and parked the car, and Jack kissed us all goodbye.

'See you all in ten days.'

My tears turned to laughter as one of the hated puttees began to unwind, trailing behind him like a paying-off pennant as he humped his half a ton of equipment up the gangplank.

I soon stopped laughing as I faced up to what was to be my first solo drive home. By now a thick heavy blanket of tropical heat had replaced the cool of the morning. Soaking with sweat, I wrestled with the gears of the old car, praying that one of the many ramshackle trucks would not choose that moment to spill its cargo of chairs, boxes or sheets of rubber. The road ahead was seething with decrepit vehicles, bicycle kitchens, pirate taxis that stopped without warning to cram in yet another passenger, pedestrians marching or shuffling on to the crossing without looking right or left and motorcycles driven by maniacs—the normal morning traffic on the Thompson Road. By the time Jack returned from fighting the 'enemy' I was driving round the streets of Singapore as if we had lived there all our lives. (What a liar I am!)

Before Jack departed for the 'battle front' we attended a party at Sembawang, where I met many new faces. One couple to whom I was introduced were to become life-long friends. John Leonard, a Captain in the Royal Irish Fusiliers, had, like Jack, been seconded to the staff of HQ 3 Commando Brigade. To my delight, I discovered that John and his wife Mercedes lived on Muswell Hill, another road in the Braddell Heights complex.

'So we'll be grass widows together.'

Mercedes seemed equally pleased. Like us, the Leonards had only just arrived in Singapore.

'Have you children?'

'A two- and a three-year-old.'

'Fantastic. You must come and bring them round to play with Philip. He's my only one for the moment.' She was very obviously expecting.

Mercedes, my very special wild Irish friend, would be my frequent companion during the coming two years. I had to laugh when she explained that she was the last of seven children and her parents had run out of names so they christened her after her father's beloved 1929 Mercedes Benz. In fact, we had plenty of laughs together when we mounted assaults on the shops and markets of Singapore or retreated to the cool of one of the many swimming pools. Our children became water babies together. Best of all, she was the one who spirited me away for three days to a then unheard-of magical island called Bali.

But that's another story.

— 10 —
Cotswold Close

LEFT on my own, it seemed a good idea to keep myself busy giving the house its promised face-lift. I telephoned our landlord to remind him that it was time to keep his part of the bargain. Mr Chidambaram was not an easy man to get hold of: whenever I called he was either on the golf course or in the bath, but eventually it was arranged that work on the kitchen would start the following week. In the meantime, I asked Peter of Lee Food Supplies, who delivered our daily order of everything from custard powder to cornflakes, if he knew of an inexpensive painter and decorator. Peter—really Lee Soon Seng—was a veritable walking Yellow Pages and was bound to know the right people for the job. An hour later Lim Bak Chaun and his two brothers arrived on three small motorcycles festooned with paint pots and brushes and very soon the house reverberated with sing-song chatter as one whitewashed the ceilings, another painted the cupboards and the third used long, bamboo-handled brushes to apply coats of creamy white rubber paint to the walls with graceful sweeping strokes.

For two days they worked like Trojans. The only time they laid down their tools was when they heard the honking that heralded the arrival of a mobile restaurant. At the gate stood a tricycle protected from the sun and rain by a red-striped canopy. On a counter constructed over the frame of the machine, the pedalling cook prepared meals, selecting the ingredients from the string of dried fish, vegetables and chicken hung on a pole under the awning, and from baskets of eggs, noodles, rice and bean sprouts hanging beneath the counter, cooking them in a red hot wok over a charcoal burner. It all smelt delicious but it would have been more than my life was worth to suggest to Ah Ling a change of menu. Whilst the Lim Brothers dipped their fingers into paper cones of fragrant Oriental rice dishes we sat down to boring cottage pie.

The mobile restaurant was not our only visitor. About six a.m. our slumbers were disturbed by a furious chorus of dogs barking as an elderly woman raided the bins looking for pig food, old tins and anything else worth scavenging from the plastic bags of rubbish put out the night before for collection.

From breakfast time onwards, the day was punctuated with the cry of street vendors. Every morning, Sundays included, the *pop-pop* of his motorcycle heralded the arrival of the breadman, who, immaculately dressed in a grey siren suit and large white sola toupée, dispensed loaves and cakes from a little cupboard strapped on the rear carrier. From another compartment under the handlebars came sweets and dried fruits, while crispy rolls and French bread were packed in pannier baskets. He even carried a pot of jam to make five-cent sandwiches for hungry schoolboys.

At 9.30 Peter Lee would come to collect my daily order, driving a large white van garishly decorated with brightly coloured advertisements for locally produced orange squash. My list would have been compiled already with Ah Ling's help—or hindrance, depending on the mood she was in. She would get cross when I failed to comprehend what she was trying to tell me, pointing with agitated fingers, her gold teeth sparkling unlike her eyes. How was I to know that 'dog lice' was nothing more alarming than the unpolished rice she put in Pepe's feeding bowl? By the middle of the afternoon Peter Lee was back with a box of groceries. In the tropical heat the service was a blessing.

Once a week Mr Kleen-Eeze came past the gate on his bicycle, loaded up with feather dusters and grass brooms. The Orchid Man called from the gate, begging me to inspect his range of exotic blooms, and you could smell the Satay Man with his delicious titbits on sticks half a mile away. After lunch it was a toss-up as to who arrived first—the Pineapple Man, who, for just five cents, would peel and chop a pineapple and pop it in a plastic bag, or the Magnolia Man with his ice cream. The Magnolia Man was everywhere: go out to one of the islands or into the deepest jungle, and sooner or later you would hear the familiar ring of his bell.

By the time Jack emerged from the jungle, the house was looking a lot brighter. The rickety folding brass tables had been removed and replaced with more stable models of bamboo and glass. I had even made new curtains from yards of cheap-and-cheerful material bought at the local market, using the new sewing machine we had purchased before Jack went on exercise. That had been an adventure in itself. We had driven to Changi Village, one of the many shopping villages that made a living keeping the thousands of service personnel and their families in Singapore supplied with everything from hi-fi equipment to Tiger beer. In the days before the RAF built an airfield and moved their squadrons and their families to live in the area, Changi had been little more than a handful of attap-roofed huts. Now it was a highly recommended bargain-hunter's paradise, selling everything from tools to toys, cooking pots to crocodile skin handbags—and, of course, sewing machines.

The owners of The House of Teak and Camphorwood and Lee Sin Tailor Company, famous for running up men's suits and ladies' dresses in twenty-four hours, were Chinese, as was the family that ran the grocery store where a service wife could buy anything that was available back home, including her favourite English marmalade (at a price), but the proprietors of Aladdin's Cave, a treasure house overflowing with electrical goods, watches, cameras and a host of luxury items, were Indian. Turbanned figures sat on stools or squatted on the pavement, outside the open-fronted shop.

'Good evening, Sir. Good evening, Madam. Something I can show you? Come in and look. I give you very special price.'

Jack led me firmly away, by knowing that, once inside, he'd never get me out. He knew exactly where he wanted to shop.

Deluxe Radio seemed a funny name for a shop that sold everything from a packet of needles to waterproof coats, but Jack assured me that the Singh Brothers gave the best prices in town. Who was I to argue? Jack spoke with the voice of experience. Changi Village had been the nearest port of call for the Squadron when they were ashore.

A stout, middle-aged Indian, his snow-white, collarless shirt hanging outside his floor-length, red and yellow *veti*, greeted us as if we were old friends.

'How are you Sir, Madam? Good to see you again.' His beam grew even wider when Jack explained we were looking for a sewing machine.

He snapped his fingers and sent his number three son to fetch cold drinks. Soon the counter was groaning under the weight of various models that did everything from simple seaming to fancy embroidery. The choice was baffling. How much did we want to pay? Jack wasn't saying. Singh suggested a price. Jack said he had to be joking.

'For you I knock off twenty per cent. Now I can't say fairer than that.' But apparently we had only just started.

The bargaining process, long and tortuous, was a well-worn ritual that had to be followed and had to include, on our part, threats to take our custom elsewhere and, from Mr Singh, much wringing of hands and declarations that we were reducing his family to a state of penury.

'My friend, you'll ruin me. I cannot live if you force me to sell at a loss. All right—you offer me a fair price.'

In the end, a figure was agreed.

'You're a hard man to do business with,' Ravi Singh sighed, throwing up his hands in capitulation.

The charade was over, the price was paid and the machine was loaded into the car. Did I see Mr Singh rubbing his hands with glee when he thought I wasn't looking?

'My friend, you'll ruin me . . .'

Apart from the sewing machine, we needed a lot of other things for the house. Happily, shopping in Singapore was as good an entertainment as going to the cinema. According to the booklet issued to new arrivals to the island, the place to buy things like cutlery, china and other household items cheaply was at the Pasar Malam or, as it was more commonly known, the Amah's Market.

Tuesday was the night the touring market came to Serangoon Gardens. From a mile away we could hear the blare of the latest pop music, see the avenue of stalls lit with the harsh white flares from hundreds of acetylene lamps and hear the thump of a dozen generators. A cosmopolitan crowd shuffled past stalls loaded with a conglomeration of goods, some useful, most tawdry: British 'Mems' from the nearby housing estate, Malay *amah*s at liberty now that the last supper dish had been washed, Indian and Chinese housewives, their pyjama-clad children in tow, all out just for the fun of the occasion. Some haggled, some bought without argument and others had just come to look and drink in the atmosphere. Somehow, above all the mayhem, could be heard the sing-song patter as the stallholders begged passers-by to purchase sequin-encrusted dresses, crystal wine glasses, battery-operated toy cars, a stick of firecrackers or a cheery-faced china Buddha. There wasn't much you couldn't buy, except perhaps a grand piano.

The daytime market in our local village of Serangoon Gardens was equally magical. The hawkers spent much time and effort arranging their displays. Nothing was too much trouble. Even a pile of potatoes would look like a work of art by the time they had finished.

Fruit stalls offered pyramids of apples and citrus fruits. From bamboo poles swung clusters of bananas, some tiny and yellow, others long and green, some even pink; bunches of green and purple grapes; plastic bags of tomatoes grown in the coolness of the Cameron Highlands. Piles of fat yellow papayas sat next to pineapples; coconuts and watermelons surrounded baskets overflowing with local fruits like mangosteens, starfruit and scarlet-whiskered rambutans. The stinking durians I passed on, finding it hard to believe that anything that smelt so disgusting could really taste of strawberries and cream. The 'weg-ia-tibul' man, as Ah Ling called him, artistically displayed panniers of freshly cut ingredients for the salad bowl, young carrots, cabbages, Chinese greens, spinach, artichokes, yams, peas and bean sprouts, all ingredients necessary for the essential Oriental cuisine.

The stall-holders tried to catch my attention: 'Yes, Missie. What you want?' Even in the food market haggling was expected—very exhausting in the tropical heat. Local housewives would spend hours arguing over a bundle of greens. Me, I was happy to pay ten cents for a pineapple, provided the vendor peeled and sliced it for me.

The local fish were often renamed for the benefit of the European customers. 'What is that fish?'

'Cod, Missie.'

Hmm—maybe. Heaps of prawns varying from half an inch to three inches in length looked very tempting; crabs were sold alive, nipping. A Chinese woman in a faded *samfu* sat behind a row of baskets, selling all kinds of eggs: duck and hens' eggs, tiny speckled quail eggs that the children loved to eat at breakfast, and eggs covered in black clay and sawdust—the so called 'hundred-year-old eggs.' No one seemed to have heard of salmonella.

The meat market catered for every taste. On one side lumps of beef, lamb and pork were being sawn from frozen carcasses, whilst in the corner local housewives shopped from the fly-blown choice of fatty pork and offal impaled on hooks suspended from the roof. There were cages packed with unfortunate chickens and ducks awaiting execution, either on the spot or later in the kitchen. When our Chinese neighbours held a party to celebrate the birth of a daughter, we could hear the ducks quacking right up to the minute they hit the red-hot wok.

Our neighbours were not over-friendly. It was a year before I had a conversation with the lady of the house, who made up for lost time by recounting her whole family history in half an hour before retiring back into her shell. Her husband, a skeletal figure who looked a good deal older, studiously ignored us. He went to work every morning in a chauffeur-driven car wearing what looked suspiciously like his pyjamas. I believe that he was someone quite important in the island's cinema and hotel business.

On the other hand, our *amahs* got along well, probably because they were both Cantonese. At lunchtime they would sit hunched over their rice bowls, chatting across the fence in their sing-song, monosyllabic language. To my untutored ear, their conversation frequently sounded both aggressive and angry. Paranoid, I was convinced that they were discussing the shortcomings of Missie Worth. There was little doubt that Ah Ling did not like me, but then the feeling was mutual.

Our dragon in the kitchen hated being asked to do anything that upset her routine. She made it very clear that if I thought I had a built-in baby-sitter, I could think again. She could not cope with the children *and* her housework. If I asked her to mind them even for an hour, she would mutter and grumble. Should I dare to criticise or even make a suggestion, she would throw a tantrum and rush off to her room and light a joss-stick. On a bad day the kitchen would reek of the acrid pungent fumes.

Our horticultural paradise was looked after by a gentle Tamil known only as Kabun (*Ka-boon*), Malay for 'gardener'. Around three every afternoon he would trot up the path and greet us with a military salute before stripping off his shirt, winding a towel turban-wise round his black curls and getting down to the sweeping, mowing and weeding. The tools he used to keep the jungle from the door were primitive—a hoe fashioned from a blade tied to an old broom handle with string, a wicked-looking machete which he swung in circles to cut down the long grass, a rusty parang to chop the ever-spreading bougainvillea, and his bare hands for stripping out the weed that grew so abundantly in the humid climate. For this he was paid just a dollar at day—about three shillings! I presumed he knew no English, for whatever conversation we had was conducted in grunts. He loved the children; they could do no wrong. Even when they turned the hose on him he just wagged a finger and laughed, and when they took a tumble he picked them up and comforted them. How I wished my *amah* was as easy to get on with.

For weeks I tussled with my conscience. How much longer could I go on living with an ageing Oriental crosspatch who made me feel like an intruder if I dared to cross the kitchen threshold? But if I gave her marching orders, would she ever find another job? She was hardly sprightly and, if the piles of fluff left lurking under the couch where anything to go by, her eyesight was deteriorating. Every Sunday she shuffled down the drive carrying a shabby black bag and caught the bus to Chinatown, where, she told me, her relatives lived. Perhaps she would retire and go and stay with them?

Then, after five months of shilly-shallying, Ah Ling solved my problem for me. There was nothing she hated more than the dog. 'Dirty dog! Dog out!' she would scream as she chased Pepe out of the house with her long-handled broom. No wonder the dog would cower whenever she appeared on the scene. As far as Ah Ling was concerned, we kept a dog for one reason and one reason only, and that was to guard the house against 'lobbers'. Dogs were not pets; they belonged in the yard, or even in the cooking pot! Feeding them on anything as luxurious as tinned food was a sin. Scraps were quite good enough, she told me. In our house scraps were in short supply. My children rarely left enough to feed a mouse, let alone a full-grown hound. Whenever I insisted that she open a tin, there was a lot of clucking and clicking until one day she said, 'I go.' With relief I replied, 'Yes, I think it would be best.'

While she served out her notice, Ah Ling was remarkably cheerful. The day I watched her disappear down the drive with her three-legged stool and her large leather handbag, I almost felt sad to see her go. She left no forwarding address, but I was relieved to hear that she had gone to work for a family who lived two streets away—though I never saw her again. I felt even sadder that night as I sweated over the stove. I had had absolutely no luck finding a replacement.

Good *amahs* were like gold dust. More and more the young girls wanted to go and work in the factories, not look after children. Experienced 'treasures' were handed down from family to family. Too bad my treasure had not been such a gem. I interviewed a few hopefuls, all quite unsuitable. One bright Malaysian lass said she could cook.

'What can you cook?'

'Cheeps.'

'And what else?'

She looked surprised. Did the British eat anything else? I almost swallowed my pride and asked Ah Ling to reconsider, but not quite.

For ten days I sweated in a kitchen, growing increasingly bad-tempered, and then Ah Moy walked into our lives—or, rather, arrived in the back of Peter Lee's grocer van.

'Hallo. Missie. You take Ah Moy. Her very good *amah*.'

There stood a plump, smiling woman in her early thirties, dressed in a brightly coloured, two-piece *samfu*. From the moment I saw her, I knew she was exactly what I wanted—friendly and easy-going, a joy to have around. No more sulks, no more scoldings. Nothing was too much trouble. We were now her family, and we could do no wrong.

Ah Moy was Straits Chinese. She had grown up in a village on the other side of the Strait of Jahore. Her skin was golden brown and shone like her brown eyes, and her hair was dark and curly. Although she was married and had a house near the airport at Paya Leba, she was happy to live in, provided she could bring her nine-year-old son, Peng, along with her automatic rice-cooker and her moonflower plant.

85

'Very very lucky, moonflower. When it blooms, you make a wish.'

The pale waxy white flowers opened after dark, giving off the sweetest fragrance imaginable. Next morning, the faded blooms were used to make a very special tea—excellent for clearing the head, I was told.

Sometimes Ah Moy's husband, a broad-shouldered Hokkien called Sin Kee, came to sleep, other times he stayed home to look after his many aquaria of tropical fish—according to Ah Moy, one of his many mad schemes to make money. Peng became 'big brother' to Russell and Deborah, taught them how to climb trees and led them a merry dance around the garden when it rained—if he was allowed out to play. Ah Moy was very ambitious for her son. Homework was very important. If Peng's weekly grades were poor, he was well and truly punished. Ah Moy was very strict with her own son; with my children, she was as soft as butter.

— 11 —
Pineapple Days

COTSWOLD Close was a haven for all kinds of tropical flora and fauna. In the evening, after the rain had cleared away, our garden was perfumed with fragrance from gardenia, frangipani and tiny, sweet-scented, white flowers that grew amongst the 'granny's teeth' cactus plants. By day, mynah birds strutted on the lawn, whistling provocatively at the world in general, probing the grass with bright orange beaks. Common sparrows and tawny bulbuls fought over apple cores and scraps and pecked at snails the size of whelks, and minute yellow sunbirds hovered over the hibiscus, delicately sipping the nectar through their curved beaks. After dark, a nightjar sat in the frangipani tree, *tock-tocking* till we could stand the noise no longer. A shoe flung in his general direction brought peace for a while.

In the house, bullet beetles hurled themselves against the lights and hairy spiders scuttled out of the reach of lizards that lived on our walls. Locally, these lizards were known as *chickchacks* because of the strange clicking noise they made when they went into battle if an intruder dared to invade their pitch. The Chinese said that a house without chickchacks was unlucky, the logic being that a house without a chickchack was very likely to be infested with insects.

Our little sharp-nosed friend the house shrew was meant to be lucky too. He arrived one evening when I was sitting on my own. Out of the corner of my eye I saw something small and grey with a long tail running along the wall.

'*Eek!* A rat!'

Ah Moy arrived with stout garden broom.

'Where it go?'

'There. Under the sideboard.'

Ah Moy burst out laughing.

'That no rat. That a *chi-chi*.' Presumably he was so-named because he squeaked.

'He very lucky.'

Unimpressed, I begged her to shoo it out of the house. But very soon he was back. And who could blame him. In the kitchen and bathroom we had a plentiful supply of his favourite food—nice, juicy cockroaches. Once I realised that he was harmless, I welcomed a nocturnal visit from our small pest-control agent.

Braddell Heights truly was a pretty place to stay, but all our immediate neighbours were either geriatric or had children much older than ours. Deborah and Russell needed playmates, so we went to call on Mrs Low, the headmistress of St Paul's, a highly recommended kindergarten run by Christian Chinese. Did she have room for our two next term?

Mrs Low, a dignified lady, trim and neatly dressed in a pale lilac *cheongsam*, took us on a tour of her school. In Singapore, state education did not begin until the age of seven, so the top classes were filled with local children learning reading skills but the nursery class had its fair share of blonde-haired 'tinies' having fun with paint and paper and music. It was agreed that our children would start the following week.

They loved it there. Every morning at about eight, a hoot would announce the arrival of a pink bus driven by a cheery, round-faced Malay. Wearing their new red-and-white checked uniforms, the children would run down the drive and join the Indian, Chinese, Malay and European youngsters already on the bus. By lunchtime they would be back, having had a wonderful morning. The afternoons were spent at the swimming pool, the only place to be in the heat. Both children quickly learned how to swim, mostly underwater. It never ceased to amaze me how long they could hold their breath. A combination of sun and continual immersion in chlorinated water bleached their hair greenish blonde.

It was a pretty good life for the children, once they had got used to living in the tropics. For the first few months we spent half our lives at the local clinic, mostly with minor skin complaints. It was quite normal for newly arrived children of fair complexion to walk around looking as if they were suffering from something horribly infectious.

'What on earth are these?' I asked the doctor, showing him small bodies covered with evil, red, pustulating eruptions.

'Nothing to worry about. Just monsoon blisters,' the medical officer told me soothingly. He'd seen it all before, many times. Monsoon blisters were quite a common complaint suffered by European children when they first arrived. Calamine lotion was prescribed. Measles wasn't measles, just a nasty case of prickly heat, the smallest cut could turn septic, and of course great care had to be taken to protect small stomachs. All water was boiled, and then kept in the fridge. We didn't buy bottled water, because in the 1960s it hadn't been invented.

In the guide to life on the island with which we had been issued when we first arrived, there was a host of household tips including how to get rid of foot rot, dhobie itch and round worms and how to deal with bites and stings inflicted by mosquitoes, rats, spiders, hornets, bed bugs and snakes. 'First kill your snake. Handle the body only by the tail, and take it to your nearest clinic for identification.' Really? Fortunately, the closest I ever came to having to put my courage to the test was when I took a 'phone call from my friend Mercedes' *amah*, who took great glee in telling me that there was a long green snake in the living room and, as her Missie was away, would I like to come and deal with it? I said I wouldn't.

'Ah Lee, lock the door. I'll send someone.'

I telephoned the police station, but by the time the police arrived Ah Lee had already applied the meat cleaver to its head and chopped it up for her supper.

The only immediate neighbours who were disposed to be friendly were a devout Buddhist family who lived across the road. The wife, a sweet soul, brought me a house-warming gift of bananas from her garden, but unfortunately she spoke no English and, as I was unlikely to master Cantonese, there was little chance of our becoming soulmates. Her father, who must have been well over eighty, would jog round the block every morning, an oiled paper umbrella (referred to by Naval personnel as a Wanchai Burberry) held aloft for protection from the sun. When he returned he would join his more ample son-in-law on the lawn for half an hour of callisthenics.

One afternoon I noticed a truck loaded with tables and chairs parked outside the house and a gang of workers erecting a green canvas awning over the lawn. Ah Moy told me that Grandfather had been killed by a motor car whilst out jogging.

'How awful,' I said.

She shrugged.

'It all ri'. Him an old man.' Like most Orientals, she had a philosophical attitude to death.

All afternoon and evening, relatives and friends rolled up to the house and by nightfall the garden was seething. Wreaths of flowers were hung outside the gate and red candles and joss-sticks lit along the road. As the night wore on, the decibels increased with much banging of cymbals and gongs and the click of mah-jong tiles as the mourners whiled away the hours of their vigil, which lasted until the funeral procession formed after lunch the following day.

It was rather disappointing to discover that they were using a conventional black hearse instead of one of those incredible pagoda-like, lorry-borne structures festooned with paper flowers, dragons and butterflies. The only deference to tradition was the life-sized portrait of the deceased tied to the front bumper. The coffin, draped with red silk cloth and heaped with flowers, was carried out to the accompaniment of much weeping and wailing from the mourners who formed up behind the car. A line of friends took hold of ropes tied to the front and pretended to pull the car along as it drove off at walking pace. The chief mourners were dressed in white and wore sackcloth hoods that hid their faces. At the front of the procession marched a percussion band in military uniform, and as the funeral moved off they struck up a solemn dirge, making as much noise as possible to frighten away evil spirits. A small gathering of men carrying coloured umbrellas marched behind the hearse, members of the guilds to which the deceased had belonged. Then came the inevitable line of cars carrying the rest of the guests, all draped in something red. The rear of the procession was brought up by a van loaded with bottles of soft drinks for consumption at the graveside.

The cortège moved through Braddell Heights at a dignified walking pace, but the minute it turned on to the main road, all the pedestrians, including the band, leapt on to the back of the trucks and the procession moved off at a cracking pace, the band scaring away all evil spirits with a rousing rendering of 'Is You Is Or Is You Ain't My Baby?'

Seven days later the chairs and tables and caterers were back again. A six-foot-high, two-storey, blue and silver paper house, fully furnished down to a tiny figure waiting at the door, a boat, a Cadillac, two paper doll servants, a telephone and a clock were delivered up the garden path. The clash of cymbals, gongs and woodwind music continued throughout the night. Next morning all the 'toys' had gone up in smoke, along with a wad of paper money for the spirit of grandfather to use for his comfort in the next world. There was more to come. Forty-nine days later, yet another truckload of paper goodies was delivered. This time the party was muted. Ah Moy told me they would be erecting the spirit tablet in the ancestral shrine, a narrow piece of wood about a foot in height with dates and titles of the deceased painted on in brushwork. As the evening wore on, the now all too familiar cacophony of noise was heard and robed figures were seen performing ritual dances in the middle of the drive.

After that the excitement was over and life in the Close returned to normal until Chinese New Year—but not before we celebrated our first Christmas in the Tropics. Jelly that refuses to set, icing running off the cake, kitchen temperatures over one hundred degrees, ice cream that turns to liquid as soon as it you take it from the fridge, paper chains dancing in the breeze from the overhead fans, tree lights paled by the brilliance of the sunlight, people wishing you the compliments of the season with a kiss on a hot and sticky cheek—that's Christmas in the Tropics.

Singapore is not the easiest place in the world to get that Christmas feeling, but for two years we did our best. At least there was no shortage of places to shop for gifts: the bazaars were full of temptation. Never mind their religious persuasion, Hindu, Moslem and Christian traders alike joined in the commercial extravaganza, religious prejudices set aside for the duration of the season.

'Missee, you buy lovely crocodile handbag? Very cheap.'

'How cheap?' It was necessary to feign a lack of interest.

'Fifty dollar?' He tilts his head in hope.

'Far too much.' This is said firmly.

'Missee. Have many children to feed. All ri', all ri'. I let you have it for forty-six dollar. You no buy as cheap as that anywhere.'

'Thirty. Not a cent more.'

'Solly. No good. No profit.' He goes to hang the bag back on its hook, his face crestfallen. 'Your mother, in England, she like crocodile bag very much.' It is his last line of attack. Mothers are very important in the Orient.

'Thirty-two. That's my last offer.'

He gift-wraps the bag in last week's *Straits Times*, his inscrutable features never betraying the pleasure of the undoubted profit he has made. But I am pleased too: one more present problem solved.

Down at the night street market we went through the same charade as we haggled and bargained our way from one glittering stall to another. It was all there, at rock-bottom prices—glass balls and silvery tree ornaments, yards of tinsel and twisting mobiles of colourful foil, crackers from Communist China, nativity

. . . we haggled and bargained our way from one glittering stall to another.

91

scenes from Buddhist Japan. It seemed as though the whole world had jumped on the bandwagon to help us catch the festive mood, whatever the weather.

Dripping with perspiration, we took the children by bus to downtown Singapore, disembarking outside Robinson's department store and stopping to admire the window displays. The Fairy Queen and the Ugly Sisters, Cinderella and her coach sat on a sea of artificial snow. Carols played from loudspeakers, giggling shop assistants handing out striped candy canes to the children. Inside the store, with its powerful air-conditioning, we shivered. My children had forgotten what it was like to be cold.

'Where's Santa? I want to see Santa,' small, querulous voices demanded impatiently.

Inside the store all was glisten and glitter. We could have been in Oxford Street. Perfume, pearls, silken accessories, all at fixed prices. It was such a relief not to have to bargain, even if it cost a dollar more.

'Second floor—toys and Santa.' The Chinese liftboy probably thought we were mad, paying good money to have heads patted by Uncle Yoo Fon Wong. Too young to understand my amusement at the sight of this very Oriental Santa Claus perspiring under his red cloak and white beard, the children lined up for their dollar parcels and smiled into a camera for a photograph to send home to Grandma.

The Saturday before Christmas we were invited to the children's kindergarten end-of-term concert. The programme was scheduled to start at half past three but my daughter assured me that we had to be there by two to secure seats, for they expected a full house. The show started on the dot, but at six o'clock we were still squirming on our tiny chairs. The show went on and on like a Chinese opera as yet another class of multi-racial 'tinies' performed a sketch in beautifully elocuted English. And still we hadn't reached the finale, the Nativity Play.

We had already heard much about the Nativity Play. My daughter had been unnaturally angelic for weeks. Alas, she had been rôle-playing; next day she reverted to type. And where was Russell? It wasn't until the final curtain that we discovered that he was the third bush on the right. Ten carols later, we emerged into the moist warmth of the Singaporean night.

'Santa came to school today, Mummy.'

'Really?'

'Yes, on a bicycle.' How unusual—or perhaps not. Where would the caretaker have found reindeer in Singapore?

Visitors arrived from England, including my mother on a specially chartered 'granny flight'. There were twelve of us sitting round the table on Christmas Day, including several Sea Vixen aircrew from HMS *Eagle* led by the Squadron Boss, Bob McQueen. Thank heaven for the services of dear Ah Moy, who cooked and cleared up with a grin, sweating cheerfully over the turkey and steaming Christmas pud, no doubt thinking what a mad lot we were—especially when the boys came back for second helpings. In the evening we all went down to Bugis Street, notorious for its parade of transvestites, for little boys who would challenge you to a game of noughts and crosses that you knew you would never win and for hawkers of 'genuine diamonds' that, if you haggled long enough, you could buy for just a dollar. Here many plates of Oriental cuisine were consumed. God knows where we put it all.

Soon afterwards it was Chinese New Year. 'Kong Hee Fat Choy' announced the red banners that were draped across the fronts of the Chinese stores as the world prepared to say farewell to the Year of the Goat and welcome to that of the Monkey. Houses had their doors and porches hung with red and gold paper lanterns, their verandahs swathed in red silk cloth and their lintels pasted with red paper banners bearing the Chinese characters meaning 'Good luck, peace and prosperity.'

It was very hot, and unusually dry. Ah Moy was very gloomy.

'Man got no shoes on.'

She showed me a cartoon of a bare-footed man in her Chinese newspaper.

'No rain after New Year starts. If he got two shoes on, then plenty rain; only one shoe then half dry half wet year, but no shoes—*aiyah*—very bad. Maybe we have water rationing.'

It seemed that Ah Moy's little man was right. For the next eight weeks we had no rain at all and the sun beat down unmercifully, turning normally green Singapore brown. The levels of the water in the reservoirs were dangerously low before an almighty clap of thunder eventually broke the drought.

Heat or no heat, the preparations for Chinese New Year went into full swing. First, ancestors had to be placated. Seven days before the wane of the Old Year, the Kitchen God was sent off to Heaven on a barrage of firecrackers to report on the behaviour of the inhabitants of his house. In order to ensure that he reported nothing but good, the women bribed him with gifts of food and paper money to take on his long journey. He remained away for a week, during which time the house was cleaned from top to bottom and a new portrait of his image hung over the family altar in readiness for his return on New Year's Eve.

Two days before, Ah Moy deserted my kitchen and went off on a massive shopping expedition to the local market. Money that had been saved up all year was spent on one huge splurge of feasting. She was in a hurry; there was much to do before the great day dawned. She believed that if she so much as lifted a broom on New Year's Day she would sweep all the good luck out of the house.

New Year's Eve came and a strange hush fell over the island. In the Chinese homes everyone was tucking into piles of food and the men were raising brandy glasses, saying 'Yam Seng' and downing the amber liquid in one throaty gulp. The hour of midnight approached, and we felt as if we were sitting on a time-bomb. At five minutes to twelve our Chinese neighbours threw open the windows and doors to let the good spirits enter, and at the first stroke of midnight the whole world exploded. It was like standing in the middle of a battlefield, deafening for fifteen minutes at a time as the sausage-like strings of firecrackers burst one after another. The sky filled with rockets and showers of multi-coloured stars. This was the biggest, most stupendous firework show in the world. Thousands of dollars were sent sky high in a violent expression of rejoicing. It was three in the morning before the noise died down sufficiently for us to sleep, but for the next three days the racket continued, interspersed with the sound of sirens as fire engines rushed to the scene of yet another burning wooden home.

My friend Mercedes and I were invited to take our children to visit her *amah*'s family at this time of goodwill. This was a great privilege. We dressed up in our very best: not to have done so would have been an insult. The address was in Chinatown, an area both romantic and mysterious. The narrow, airless streets of crumbling buildings bore such names as Canton, Nanking and Peking after the provinces and cities whence the residents and their ancestors originally came. Already the government was involved in a massive building programme of low-cost housing designed to integrate the citizens of the Republic, and much of Chinatown was destined for demolition. In the old days, a visit to Chinatown felt like an intrusion into an alien world; the reconstructed Chinatown we visited in 2003 is now so visitor-friendly that the sense of adventure has gone. Where there had been opium dens, funeral parlours and dark shady alleys there are now shops and stalls selling cameras, copy-levis and souvenirs. With its new, shiny, clean image, all the original character has gone.

The Chinatown of old had colonnades of frontless shops with two and three storeys of living accommodation protruding over the dark footways supported by wide pillars. The walls were flaked and dark with mildew and the shutters bare of paint, yet there was dignity with the decay. Run down it may have been, but not squalid. There were no beggars, no piles of rotting waste and not even many of the smells associated with overcrowded living. The narrow streets criss-crossed the busy downtown thoroughfare, the colour coming from the vegetable and fruit stalls, the washing slung out on bamboo poles to dry and the potted plants bravely fighting to survive in window boxes. Small boys in pyjamas played tag around Grandma's, squatting in the arcades, gaunt old men shuffled along, pausing to expectorate a globule of phlegm, and trishaw drivers in pith helmets and food vendors pushing barrows plied their trade to the passing crowd.

The Gohs family lived in one room. Opposite the door stood the family altar, a long table of gleaming, ebony-black wood adorned with a cracked porcelain vase and a brass joss-stick bowl. Two red candles burned beneath the new portrait of the household god. The remainder of the room was filled by a single massive bed in which all eight occupants slept.

First we bowed to Mother, a frail woman in a pale blue brocade *samfu* who knew no English, and then to first sister, second sister, and so on down the line. Not surprisingly, conversation was limited, with Ah Lee acting as interpreter. We smiled and nibbled sweet sticky buns and drank endless tiny cups of green tea. Our blonde-haired children were patted on the head for luck many times. As we made our departure, *hung pao* envelopes were pressed into their hands—five whole dollars each.

'Honest to God, so embarrassing,' said my Irish friend. 'They didn't look as if they had the price of a box of matches between them.'

— 12 —
Ark Royal Again

ALL good things must come to an end. Two years had passed: it was now March 1968, and it was time to pack away our sun hats and the famous green beret and return home to England. Maybe it was the right time to leave. By the second year, the sapping tropical climate had begun to take its toll, leading to varying degrees of irritability and lassitude accompanied by loss of memory and the desire to put off till tomorrow what should be done today. It wasn't until we returned to our more temperate climate that we realised that we had been firing on only three cylinders.

Politically, the climate had changed. While we were stationed in Singapore, the British Labour government had announced the accelerated withdrawal of HM Forces. At the time, the local population saw this as catastrophic, and there was much sighing and shaking of heads by those who depended upon us for a living. Seeing the Republic as it is now, it is hard to believe how reluctant they were to see us go.

We handed on the tenancy of our house and the keys of the old banger to friends Peter and Betty Williams, said our tearful goodbyes to Ah Moy and Peng and flew home to England on a trooping flight. By the time we landed at RAF Brize Norton it was past midnight. As we climbed out of the aircraft we were welcomed by an icy March wind. For weeks the children had been excited about coming home; now they could not understand what was going on. This was not at all what they had expected England to be like, but, when one is sweating in a tropical climate, how can one explain the word 'cold' to a three- and a four-year-old?

It was too late to catch a train, so we spent what was left of the night trying to sleep in a stuffy, overheated room in the transit quarters. Used to nothing heavier than a thin cotton sheets, the tightly tucked-up cocoon of heavy-duty bed clothing felt like a ton weight.

Things looked a little brighter in the thin, pale sunlight of a frosty morning. We caught the train to Worthing, where my mother met us at the station. She greeted us with, 'I've had a bit of luck. Mrs Blake died last Sunday.'

I blinked.

'Sorry?'

She hastily apologised for sound a little unfeeling.

'What I'm trying to say is that, as her bungalow is empty, her daughter has suggested that you could all live there for a week or so, whilst you sort yourselves out.'

The prospect of moving into poor Grace Blake's home with the woman barely in her grave was a touch macabre, but, as Jack reminded me, it was not the first time we had occupied a house in similar circumstances—remember Spey Bay? So the children and I climbed into Mother's tiny car and Jack followed behind in a taxi with the inevitable mountain of luggage.

The late Mrs Blake (whom, I must point out, I had never met; I could therefore be forgiven for not mourning her) had lived in a bungalow in Angmering-on-Sea. Her daughter lived just round the corner. She had lit the fire to welcome us, and I was most grateful.

'It is really very kind of you to let us stay here,' I forced out through my chattering teeth.

'That's all right, my dear. Seems a pity to leave it empty when you are homeless.'

Once again, we were back to the status of refugees. There was little doubt that our nomadic existence offered more than its fair share of contrasts in living styles.

To be truthful, Mrs Blake's bungalow could have been a lot worse. A two-bedroom bijou residence built in the 1930s, it was long overdue for a spot of modernisation, but at least everything was neat and tidy and in its place. There was not a spot of grease in the tiny kitchen, nor a speck of dust on any one of the miniature Goss china souvenirs that ornamented every spare piece of shelf space— tiny little white teapots, jugs and bowls, all bearing the crest of towns presumably visited by the owner.

'Don't touch, children—they are not for playing with.'

It was a relief to learn that Mrs Blake had died in a nursing home; just the same, I was dreading our first night in her less-than-double-size bed. Already I could picture my six-foot-plus husband's feet sticking out from underneath the candy-pink, satin eiderdown.

Was it Mrs Blake's ghost coming to haunt us, or was it simply the fact that the house had been unoccupied for most of the winter that made the place feel so cold?

'Cold? Nonsense,' said my mother briskly. 'It's just that your blood is a little thin. You'll soon get used to it. What you need is to get some meat on your bones.' During our two years in the heat of the tropics I had lost a good twenty pounds.

The first items on my shopping list were warm hats, coats and jumpers. The children, accustomed to running around practically naked, protested loudly when I forced their unwilling little bodies in winter clothing, complaining that shoes hurt and collars rubbed. Next morning, to my horror, I beheld my daughter disappearing down the road dressed in nothing more protective than a pair of underpants. The temperature outside was barely above zero.

Going back to being an ordinary housewife took a lot of adjustment. After two years of being spoilt, I had almost completely forgotten how to decorate a dinner plate with anything more substantial than a lettuce leaf. My family were unimpressed by my lack of culinary skills. 'Why can't you cook chips like Ah Moy?' the children wailed. But then Ah Moy did produce the most wonderful chips I've ever tasted. Countless times she tried to show me how she did it. 'See, it easy,' she would laugh as she spooned yet another pile of golden perfection out of the old saucepan. Her chips were never soggy or burnt nor undercooked but always golden and crunchy on the outside and gorgeously white and fluffy inside. It would have been wonderful if I could have packed Ah Moy along with the rest of our baggage. Mind you, the poor girl would probably have frozen to death: it really was a bitter spring.

Jack had already received his next appointment—back to good old *Ark Royal*, not with a squadron this time but as one of the team in charge of organising and supervising the ship's flying programme. Unofficially, his title would be 'Little F' ('F' for 'Flying'). This was not as bad as it seemed from the point of view of family life: the aircraft carrier was in the dockyard undergoing a massive refit, and so it would be some time before she went to sea. We were entitled to occupy a married quarter in Plymouth, but first it was off to Scotland, where the children and I would stay until we had sold our house in Fochabers, knowing that Jack was unlikely ever to serve at Lossiemouth again.

Back we went across the border, still driving our wonderful American wagon. Even though she had spent the past two years in mothballs, she was back on the road, as good as new. In Scotland, it was nice to see old friends. 'Ach, Mrs Worth, you're back. 'Tis good to see you and the bairns.' When I explained that I had only come back to sell the house, they looked genuinely disappointed. I had to feel sad that we were leaving such a friendly community. It is difficult to feel as if you really belong somewhere when you are always moving on. But my husband kept ringing to say how lovely it was down in Plymouth and to hurry up and find a buyer. Easier said than done! The market was dead.

April, May and June passed without an offer. I couldn't understand why. The house was looking bonny, the garden first a mass of daffodils and then of roses, but it seemed that the housing market was at an all-time low. If oil had been discovered off Aberdeen a lot earlier, I am sure the house would have gone like a hot cake; as it was, it was as hard to shift as a mouldy bun. Then, just as I was thinking that I would have to rent it out again, along came a young couple who made an offer for £4,000—two hundred more than we had paid four years earlier in 1964. We accepted with almost indecent haste. When all the bills were settled, we had made a profit of exactly twenty shillings and ninepence!

There was nothing isolated about the married quarters in Plymstock. Situated in the heart of a network of residential roads, it would have been difficult to tell where the join began and where it ended if it hadn't been for the uniformity that makes service family housing so instantly recognisable. As Jack turned the car into Campbell Road and stopped outside the first pebbledash-fronted semi, I knew we were there.

Our married quarter held few surprises. One is very much like another. They may come in many different shapes and sizes, but, once inside the front door, I knew exactly what to expect, from the metal-framed windows to the oak, draw-leaf dining-room table. In those days, the size of the house you were allocated was strictly regulated. It would have made no difference if we had had ten children or none at all: as the family of a Lieutenant-Commander, we were entitled to a semi with three bedrooms, one bathroom, two reception rooms and a solid fuel boiler in the kitchen that not only heated the water but also a single radiator in the dining room, thereby justifying the claim that the house was partially central heated.

The house, of course, came fully furnished, so when the removal van arrived with the contents of our Scottish home we were faced with a major headache. Whilst the proportions of the rooms of Number One Campbell Road were not ungenerous, they were never designed to accommodate two three-piece suites, two sideboards, and so on. When Jack asked very nicely if some of the furniture already *in situ* could be removed so that we could have more space, the Married Quarters Officer told him sternly, 'Absolutely not.' There was nothing in the rule books that permitted such flexibility. For days our house looked like a second-hand furniture emporium. Fortunately, one thing our house had was empty roof space. I suspect the Quarters Officer would have had a fit had he known how many items on his inventory we managed to squeeze through the hatch.

Our biggest headache was what to do with Big Bertha, which had come out of storage still churning and spinning the household wash as well as the day she was built. It was a matter of pride to preserve her at all costs: to have sent her to the scrapheap would have been a sin—or so my husband said. He considered her unique, which at least was true. She was also a pain. Far too large and bulky to fit into our kitchen, she sat outside in the garage whilst we tried to determine her fate.

In the end, there was only one place in the house where there was sufficient space to plumb her in close to a water source. We found two strong men to help

'And what, may I ask, is a washing machine doing up in your bedroom?'

haul her up the stairs and positioned her beside the wash handbasin in our bedroom. With her inlet pipes firmly secured to the hot and cold taps, the waste-pipe hooked over the basin and her transformer plugged into the electricity supply, we were back in the laundry business. That was, until the day the Married Quarters Officer dropped by on one of his routine inspections, when Bertha chose to go into overdrive.

'What on earth . . .?'

He stared up, horrified, at the vibrating ceiling.

'Um.' (With sinking heart.) 'Well, since you ask, that's my washing machine.'

'And what, may I ask, is a washing machine doing up in your bedroom? Have you ever thought what would happen if you had a flood?'

Actually I had, which is why I kept fit rushing up and downstairs to monitor her progress and why I had this recurring nightmare that one day she would come crashing through the ceiling waving her hot and cold and wastepipes behind her like an airborne octopus. Secretly, I was rather relieved when we were ordered to remove her forthwith and decided to replace her with a more conveniently sized model. I was sad to see her go. No, I wasn't. I can't tell you what bliss it was to be able to get out of bed in the middle of the night without stubbing my toe on her unyielding metal frame.

Very quickly we decided that we liked living in Plymstock. With easy access to Devon's glorious countryside, its many beaches and its miles of magnificent moorlands, we were spoilt. It was like being on one long holiday. Domestically, life was so convenient. There were shops just round the corner and a frequent bus service into Plymouth. The children went to schools within walking distance and there were plenty of friends for them to play with.

A married patch is a community where friends are easily made. We were hardly inside the door before a neighbour came a-knocking with an invitation to a charitable bring-and-buy sale, and within the week I had been invited to one lunch and two coffee parties.

The Hutchings lived next door in the other half of our semi, though for an unknown and somewhat eccentric reason their house was deemed to be situated in the next road and was known as Number One Carpenter Road—leading to much confusion amongst meter-readers, postal delivery men and strangers. Jenny and Bob were great neighbours and our friendship was to continue after we had gone our separate ways. They had one son, Stewart, who was the same age as Russell. Unlike me, Jenny was the original archetypal homemaker: everything in her house was always perfect and in its place. The cakes she donated to the bazaar bake-stall were beautifully decorated, unlike my lopsided sponges. Spring cleaning was her favourite pastime. She made me feel almost guilty when I turned a blind eye to the accumulation of dust and sneaked off on my bike to enjoy to the delights of the Devon countryside. Well, almost guilty.

Early 1970 was the beginning of a period of industrial discontent. First the dustmen left stacks of black bags of rubbish piled high on the pavements and then there was the dock workers' strike that triggered panic-buying, emptying the shelves in the local shops. A bag of sugar became an object of desire; queues formed for a loaf of bread; fruits such as bananas and oranges were almost unobtainable. The news of a delivery of toilet rolls passed through the married quarters' grapevine faster than a bar of chocolate laxative.

It was some months before *Ark Royal* came out of dry dock and then she was only at sea for brief spells whilst carrying out trials, so my periods of grass widowhood were short and family life was close to normal. Jack was able to take leave over the Christmas period, so we all drove over Worthing to take Robin, who had been with us for the holiday, back to his school. Seeing how happy he was to be reunited with the staff and other children made us realise how grateful we were to my mother for finding such a perfect environment for him.

We spent the next couple of days staying with my mother. On the morning of our departure, Jack was outside packing the car ready to drive back to Plymouth and I was in my mother's living room, scanning through the newspaper, when suddenly there it was—my husband's name in print. I think I screamed; in fact I know I did. It was such a surprise, but then we had both forgotten that it was the last day of December, the day when the broadsheets publish a list of names of those Naval officers who have been selected for promotion to the rank of Commander in the following June. If we had been in Plymouth, Jack would have heard of his good fortune through official channels, but because he forgot to leave a contact number he had to put up with a hysterical, incoherent wife flapping a copy of the *Daily Telegraph* in his face. We drove all the way back to Plymouth wearing silly grins on our faces and found that in our absence the news had quickly spread. Needless to say, we welcomed in 1970 with more than normal merriment.

So where to now? Actually, nowhere. We stayed in Plymstock for almost another year, *Ark Royal* having recommissioned and become operational, and spending most of the time at sea. The only noticeable change that occurred was that, in recognition of his promotion, Jack was referred to as 'Big F' instead of 'Little F'.

More often than not, the Royal Navy reward their newly promoted Commanders with a spell behind a desk. Few relish the thought—my husband certainly didn't— but when the almost inevitable appointment to the Ministry of Defence arrived, there was nothing he could do but accept that for next two years he would be churning out plans and policy papers. The next problem was where to live. Should we rent a house in the London area, or buy? If so, where? This is how we ended up like two fish out of water, house-hunting in commuter land. It had been my job to sift through the piles of estate agents' bumph that had dropped through our letterbox, which was pretty depressing as most of the houses were either unsuitable or unaffordable. Hopes of living close to London were soon forgotten: we were forty-five minutes down the railway track from Waterloo before we arrived in our price bracket.

'What do you know about Fleet?'

'Nothing that I can think of.'

The blurb at the bottom of the page described Fleet as a small, pleasant town surrounded by natural woodland, in the north of Hampshire. It boasted of good schools and shops and an excellent, twice-hourly train service to Waterloo. It sounded good. We arranged to leave the children with Jenny and dashed up to investigate over a long weekend in August. However, the first two or three properties that we looked at, we hated. Compared with our married quarter, they looked like the 'ticky-tacky boxes' so well portrayed in the song by folk singer Malvina Reynolds.

By lunchtime we were already flagging. We went into The Red Lion for a pick-me-up lunch and got talking to a nice Mr Price, who told us he was a builder by trade. When we said we were house-hunting, he said, 'Now I might be able to help there. I'm in the middle of building a select development in a quiet little cul-de-sac. All have four bedrooms and a good bit of garden.'

Conveniently, he just happened to have a brochure in his pocket.

'I could run you over there now if you would like to look.'

Mr Price was busy 'developing' land where once a large house had stood in a couple of acres, providing him with sufficient space to cram in seventeen detached houses. Whilst the footings were in, only one home had been finished and was occupied. The couple in residence, Marion and Jimmy Clements, seemed happy enough to let Mr Price use their home as his unofficial showhouse.

Marion, with her immaculately coiffured hair and designer jeans, fitted perfectly into her equally immaculate 'Ideal Home' with its acres of seamless, beige, fitted carpets, draylon-covered lounge suite (very popular at the time) and brass bedsteads. Her kitchen gleamed with stainless steel gadgets and the garden had already been tastefully landscaped with a costly collection of plants and shrubs.

'How wonderful,' I breathed with genuine admiration, knowing in my heart that we would never be able to keep up with the Clements. If we mortgaged ourselves to the hilt, we might just be able to afford the house, but of fitted carpets and new squashy couches there was not a chance. Undeterred, we enquired as to which plots are still available.

'You could have the one on the end,' he said, pointing to an outline of footings. The garden was a churned-up, muddy wasteland with a row of very tall pines at the bottom. That was in the summer. We did not see it again until the day we moved in just before Christmas.

'Well, did you find anywhere to buy?' Jenny asked when I delivered my thank-you-for-looking-after-my-children potted plant.

'Oh yes. We've put down a deposit.'

'My goodness, that was quick. You've only been gone a day and a half.'

'Oh well, you know Jack. He hates shopping.'

When I showed her the brochure, Jenny said she thought we had done well. Personally I had a nagging worry that we had overspent. Nine thousand three hundred and fifty pounds sounded a fortune. Little did we know lucky we were; we bought the house in the nick of time. The housing market, having been static for several years, suddenly took off in the spring of 1971, and by then, thankfully, we had already got our feet back on the property ladder.

— 13 —
Town and Country

I N early December we took possession of the keys of our new home. Ours was one of the few houses ready for occupation, and every morning we woke to a chorus of hammering and banging as Mr Price and his merry men endeavoured to finish another house before the Christmas deadline. As soon as the last tile had been nailed into place, yet another removal van would negotiate its way through the piles of bricks and copper piping and begin to disgorge its contents.

Built before the age of the neo-Georgian and neo-Tudor epidemic, the houses in Frensham Avenue were conventional red-brick, four-bedroom semi-chalets with open-plan gardens at the front. The cost of the houses was either £9,150 or £9,350. After hours of brow-furrowing arithmetic we decided we could just about afford the house with the slightly larger floor plan and a bigger back garden. (We weren't to know that, fifteen years on, the extra £200 would have grown into thousands when we came to sell!)

What set the small development apart from the other estates in the location was the cul-de-sac itself. It was situated where once there had been two large gardens, and many of the original trees and shrubs had been left undisturbed. Instead of taking a decade to blend into its surroundings, even before the last bulldozer departed the road looked established.

Inside the house it was warm and welcoming, thanks to the luxury of gas-fired central heating—something we were unaccustomed to. In my new dream kitchen there were thermoplastic tiles on the floor, Formica worktops and a stainless-steel sink—all the height of fashion at the end of the 1960s, as was the wooden parquet flooring downstairs and magnolia wall paint. The bathroom suite was primrose yellow and the four bedrooms each had a built-in wardrobe. The dining room had French doors that opened out on to what we hoped one day would be a garden, although at the moment this was little more than a heap of mud, sand and builder's rubble pockmarked with beer cans.

Fears that we would find our new neighbours difficult to get to know soon disappeared. Arriving from all parts of the country with a medley of different accents, everyone was happy to make friends. Most, like us, had young children. The cul-de-sac was a safe haven where the children could ride bicycles and play old favourites like hopscotch and tag. Televisions were rarely switched on. It really wasn't a great deal different from living in married quarters, apart from the lack of navy-speak.

Christmas was a good time to get to know each other and we were inundated with invitations to house-warming parties combined with festive celebrations. That year we had a proper white Christmas. The piles of debris abandoned by the builders disappeared under snow like nicely iced cakes. Potholes and puddles turned into mini skating rinks and the Basingstoke Canal froze solid enough to be walked across in safety.

With the arrival of the thaw, out came the spade, the fork and the wheelbarrow. A considerable amount of site clearance was required before our mud patch could become our Garden of Eden. A load of turf was ordered and duly laid, and for a couple of weeks it looked perfect but then it curled up at the edges and died.

'What you need, m'dear,' said the old boy who lived in the bungalow at the end of our garden, 'is muck. Lots and lots of muck and a load of topsoil and some fertiliser. Didn't you know that where your house stands now there used to be a pond?'

No, we didn't. That was something that Mr Price had forgotten to mention.

Nothing daunted, we planted a variety of plants and shrubs and became enthusiastic gardeners. Friends came to visit, bringing plastic bags overflowing with herbaceous offerings from their prospering gardens. Unfortunately, most of them took an instant dislike to the acid soil.

'Azaleas and rhododendrons. That's all you'll grow hereabouts,' said my pipe-puffing sage.

He wasn't totally right. Moss grew beautifully, especially on the lawn, as did too many tall trees around our boundary. Silver birch and pines that had grown to a height of twenty feet blocked out the sunlight. Next door had an oak tree complete with preservation order—a glorious thing, had it stood in the middle of a park instead of in a sixty-foot-long garden!

It took a while for the family to adjust to life in Commuter Country, what with the journey to work by train for the breadwinner and to school by car for the children. In Plymouth the school had been near enough for the children to walk to, but in Fleet the only primary school at that time, an old-fashioned Victorian building already bursting at the seams with the influx of new arrivals, was more than a mile away in the middle of the town.

Running the Naval air training desk at the Ministry of Defence was not an appointment that Action Man Worth relished, but he knew that it was a necessary evil from the point of view of his career—he had to grin and bear it, at least knowing that his sentence would last only two years. I was hardly more enthusiastic about my rôle as unpaid taxi-driver. No sooner had I dropped him off at the railway station than it was time for the school run. The trips to the station were especially awful. The mornings were bad enough, but at least the stream of vehicles dropping off the breadwinners kept moving; in the evenings, finding a parking spot where we could await the arrival of the puffer was a nightmare, with a *dramatis personæ* of ladies in large, shiny, new cars trying to back into spaces designed for nothing wider than supermarket trolleys.

My solution to the problem was to buy Jack a bicycle—a second-hand one, of course (a new one would have disappeared from the station yard before he'd bought his ticket). I scoured the local paper as soon as it arrived on the mat, searching for a bargain model suitable for a six-feet-something man. It didn't take long to learn that second-hand bicycles were like gold dust. I became less and less fussy; provided the machine advertised had two wheels I was prepared to view it, the age and pedigree unimportant. All I was interested in was, 'Was the bicycle still available?'

At last I struck gold. Well, not exactly gold—more a heap of rusty metal, a sit-up-and-beg museum piece hiding at the back of pile of junk at the local auction. When the auctioneer hammered it down to me for a tenner I was triumphant. Jack took one look and roared with laughter.

'The tyres are good,' I said, hurt. 'And think on the positive side: no one's going to pinch it.'

He agreed. My Jack has always enjoyed a challenge, and a few days after a considerable rebuild had got under way it was pronounced roadworthy and fit to pedal to the station, provided the weather were clement.

Fleet was a convenient place to live, with plenty of shops and the direct railway link to Waterloo. At the end of our road there were woods to walk in and the Basingstoke Canal to stroll alongside. On paper it sounded perfect, but, sadly, what had once been a quiet country town was having its heart ripped out by too many builders and property speculators. Daily, older properties were bulldozed and replaced by a dozen cheek-by-jowl little boxes, each with its own tiny plot laughingly referred to as a garden. Fleet was rapidly developing into a typical commuter town. However, a house bought in late 1970 was a fantastic investment. During the following year we watched the value of our property shoot up overnight with the explosion of the housing market that began in the spring. Who could have forecast that first, terrifying escalation of prices leading to first-time buyers forming queues outside estate offices and the coining of the word 'gazumping'?

* * *

After living in Frensham Avenue for over two years, in late 1973 Jack was appointed to be Commander (Air) at the Royal Naval Air Station at Yeovilton. This was great news for Jack and for his family too, as it meant that we would live in the rather upmarket tied house that went with the job.

During the following weeks we did a lot of soul-searching concerning the children's education. I hated, really hated the idea of sending either of them to boarding school, but, taking into account our nomadic existence, in the end I was forced to admit that they would benefit from stability—not an easy decision for any parent but especially not for a mother! By the time we were due to move, both children were settled in their schools in Sussex.

We were now entering an era of exeats and journeys to and from school with a term's worth of paraphernalia.

'Why don't we buy a motor caravan,' Jack suggested, 'and save ourselves a fortune in hotel bills?'

The mobile home we bought was no Winnebago; in reality, it was a brown and cream coloured bread van—a tasteful conversion, you understand, with a retractable roof that looked like a big yellow accordion when it was raised, a stainless-steel sink unit, a calor gas stove, pine louvred doors and room enough to sleep five at a pinch. The loo was strictly 'porta' and had its own tent. Before my husband could stand up straight we had to open the roof—a two-man job, or, rather, one for a man and a woman. Bearing in mind the considerable differences in our heights, this was not an easy task.

'For God's sake get your end up.'

'I'm trying,' I would gasp, perching tip-toe on the bumper.

Inside the van, my lack of inches was not necessarily an advantage. Small tufts of red hair clinging to the woodwork bore witness to my numerous painful encounters, with sharp corners positioned exactly at the right height to ambush anybody five feet four. I lost count of how many times I banged my head on the overhead locker above our bed. Perhaps I should have slept in a hard hat.

Driving the camper showed that the vehicle was still a van at heart, built for delivering bread rolls but not steaming down a busy two-lane highway. After years of driving our fully automatic American wagon, I had almost forgotten how to change gear, let alone how to double-declutch. The approach to a roundabout was frequently accompanied by the scream of grating metal and the crash of sliding cooking pots. Never mind—even if it wasn't very pretty, it was unique and no one tried to steal it. I can't imagine why.

The date to make the move to Somerset was approaching fast. The requisite estimates had been obtained from three different removal firms. The letting agency had found a nice family who wanted to rent our house. Everything was going to plan when the 'phone rang: there had been a change of plan.

The incumbent Commander (Air) on *Ark Royal* had been selected for promotion to the rank of Captain. A replacement must be found pronto. Ah. Worth. That's a good name. Who could blame Jack for being delighted? It was another 'pier-head jump' as well as a career jump, but to be Commander (Air) of an aircraft carrier was the height of any aviator's ambition—although, of course, it did throw our arrangements into confusion.

'Hello. Is that the removal firm? There's been a change of plan. We are no longer moving to Yeovilton. We are going back to Devon.'

'Where are you going to live?' I was asked.

'We've been offered a married quarter in Crapstone.'

'Really!' My neighbours thought the name very amusing.

In reality, Crapstone turned out to be a peaceful village on the edge of Dartmoor, far enough off the beaten track to be missed by passing tourists. We thought it rather a good place to live, and so had Drake. His drum is still on show just down the road at Buckland Monachorum. What was not so pretty was the married quarters complex. The enclave of whitewashed houses surrounded by an eight-foot-high whitewashed wall would have looked more at home in Andalusia than in Devon's rolling countryside. It really did stand out like an ugly, bleached scar on the green landscape.

The houses had only just been built. We were the first occupants and had everything new—carpets, furniture, cups and saucers, the lot. We even had central heating, though the door from the boiler cupboard interlocked neatly with the back door and the door leading to the hall jammed with that of the larder. In theory, it would be quite possible to lock oneself out the kitchen completely. Once again I was left wondering why it never seemed to occur to the Ministry of Defence that the best man for the job of designing the interior of a house is a woman.

From our back door you could walk straight out on the moor, complete with ponies. What could have been more idyllic? When the children were on holiday from school we would pack a picnic and climb down a steep, rocky trail to the valley where the young River Tamar rushed between huge boulders and hunt for fool's gold amongst the rocks. If we were lucky we would see otters swimming and running along the bank.

We lived in Crapstone for just a year, during which time *Ark Royal* had a refit in the dockyard and was in and out of the Sound, on sea trials, so Jack was home for some of the time. We had a couple of memorable official outings during those twelve months—one to Leeds, a glorious hat occasion in October when *Ark Royal* was granted the Freedom of the City in the presence of her patron, the Queen Mother, and one to Bath the following February that was not so glorious.

The morning of our little expedition on that occasion dawned foggy and damp. Jack had a meeting about flight-deck night lighting to attend and I went along for the ride, looking forward to a day exploring the city of Bath. We set out in the

Comet station wagon for what should have been a two-hour drive, little knowing that this would be the last time we would ride in her. Out of the fog, overtaking a line of lorries, came a red sports car speeding straight for us. It hit us head-on. There was a ghastly bang and then a terrible silence.

For a moment we sat, incredulous, watching the steam rising from beneath our bonnet before climbing out of the car. Jack had blood pouring down his face from where his forehead had hit the steering wheel. The young man at the wheel of his now very battered sports car leaned out of the window.

Unbelievably, he said in a mournful voice not 'Sorry' or 'Are you all right?' but 'There goes my no-claims bonus.'

I was incensed.

'To hell with your no-claims bonus. Thirteen years my husband has looked after that car, and now look what you've done.' At least, thanks to the account given by a witness, he was convicted for dangerous driving.

Fortunately the damage was mainly to the cars (though for a few weeks Jack wore an interesting row of stitches across his forehead that made him look almost Machiavellian), but the accident marked the end for our beloved American import. The astronomical cost of returning our faithful friend—valued at £80 by our insurers—to the road was unrealistic, and the last time we saw her she was languishing wrecker's graveyard. It was heartbreaking, although perhaps it was a blessing in disguise: keeping her on the road had been a challenge as spares were difficult to come by.

The children were very upset when we broke the news that the Comet was no more. Her replacement, a jolly red Mini Traveller, certainly did not have the same kudos, although in truth it was a lot more practical. This was the year of the oil crisis, when, for the first time since the war, petrol was rationed not by legislation but by self-inflicted deprivation caused by media-generated panic queues at the filling stations. The price of petrol leapt up overnight: soon we were paying fifty pence a gallon (we had just entered the age of 'decimalisation'). At the time, we thought this was a fortune.

Ark Royal sailed in and out of Plymouth on sea trials, but her programme would soon take her to further shores. I intended to follow whenever practical. By now the children were both away at boarding school and I was free during term time, but what I needed was to earn some money to finance my travels—a temporary job to help defray costs and fill in the time that hung heavy while they were all away. It was spring, and the fields around Crapstone were full of daffodils. I marched round to the nearest nursery, enquired whether they needed another picker and was taken on for the princely sum of £1.50 an hour.

Next morning, feeling a little nervous, I reported for work wearing gumboots, expecting to be sent out into the fields. Instead I was directed to the packing shed, where a group of ladies was busy sorting the freshly picked, budding flowers for dispatch to market. Momentarily, unused to outsiders, they broke off from their chatter to stare curiously at the new recruit. Who was I and where had I come from? The Naval married quarters? Well, I never! Whatever next! I might as well have said Mars.

A lady called Peggy was assigned the task of teaching me how to arrange the blooms into bundles of ten (more decimalisation.) For the rest of the morning I worked my unskilled fingers sore expanding rubber bands. This was not quite what I had expected. I wanted to be out in the fields, picking and plucking, not tearing the skin off my fingers.

My time with the flower-growers of Devon was brief but glorious. Never had I understood how many varieties there were in the family of the narcissus. My fellow workers soon forgot that they had an outsider in their midst and resumed their chatter. For years the same ladies had gathered at daffodil time to pick and dispatch the harvest; they were all old friends and had much gossip to catch up on as they worked at the bench. Everything was covered, from the wisdom of the choice of that year's May Queen to whom was suspected of being responsible for the missing underwear from the schoolteacher's washing-line. By the time the last daffodil had died back there wasn't much I didn't know about their village life.

After a day or so I could bundle as fast as the rest of them, but there was no doubt that I was happiest when I was out into the fields, filling my arms with the long, sappy-stemmed flowers, their buds still tightly closed. My job lasted three weeks. On my final day I staggered back to the quarters with arms full of flowers generously donated by my employer and called upon my neighbours distributing bounty. The cheque I paid into the bank did not add much to my travel account. Another temporary job was needed. A friend suggested I apply to be a market researcher.

'You mean standing in the street with a clipboard?' I wasn't keen.

'It doesn't have to be like that. I've been doing it for years. It's quite a nice little earner. They send you to London on an all-expenses-paid course for three days. Then you're in the business.'

It sounded very tempting, but, even so, I hesitated. Nevertheless, when I was recruited—no doubt through the intervention of my friend—I succumbed and found myself on the train, London-bound. My room was booked in a creaking old hostelry in Bloomsbury.

School turned out to be quite an eye-opener. I hadn't realised what was involved in the market research business. You couldn't just ask any person to complete your questionnaire. First of all you had to ask intimate questions about private lives and fit each subject into a category—'A1', 'B1', and so on. I found it all very embarrassing. What business was it of mine what their age was or their income?

When I protested at the intrusiveness of the questions, my instructor patiently explained the necessity of obtaining a fair cross-section of public opinion.

Still, it didn't help me on my first outing. I had to visit houses on the outskirts of Plymouth to find out how much trouble the occupants were having paying their rates. My first encounter was not encouraging.

'Yus?' He was big and burly and didn't look as if he had been long out of bed. Showing my credentials, I explained.

'I wonder if you would like to answer a few questions on how you spend your leisure time?'

He looked at me with deep suspicion.

'You from the Social? What I does with me time is my business.'

The door slammed in my face. It was not a great start. There was no reply next door, although the curtain twitched. At Number Six the lady seemed glad of an excuse to leave her dusting. She gave me permission to go ahead and interrogate her. Now I came to the bit I had been dreading. I needed to discover her social status, in the hope that she would turn out to be a 'B2' or, even better, the 'C1' lady I badly needed for today's quota.

'Um. Do you mind if I ask you what your husband's occupation is?'

My first encounter was not encouraging.

'As a matter of a fact, I do,' she responded with a sniff. 'Let's see what you're giving away first.'

'Well, nothing,' I admitted.

'No thanks then,' she said brusquely, closing the door in my face.

I had better luck at the next house. An elderly lady was obviously thrilled to have an unexpected visitor and invited me in for a cup of tea. No, dear, she didn't play any sport. Did I take one lump or two? Now, if I wanted to hear about her cat . . . It took me quite a while to extricate myself.

I stuck at the job for three months, exploring the community's preferences when it came to lawn mowers, instant coffee and chewing gum, but when I was asked to interview women and check out what sanitary towels they used I decided that market research was all too personal and it was time to quit.

In September 1974, having successful completed her trials, *Ark Royal* was deemed fit for duty and sailed for the Mediterranean. She was not due to return to Plymouth for a year, so, much as I loved Devon, and now that the children were away at school in Sussex, I knew that there would be little point in rattling around in a large married quarter on my own. Conveniently, the tenants of our house in Fleet had handed in their notice, so reluctantly I told the Quarters Officer that I would be vacating and, sadly, packed up the house on Dartmoor.

— 14 —
Lows and Highs

I WAS about to enter what I call my 'blue' period. Jack had sailed away on HMS *Ark Royal* and was likely to be absent for a year, and during term-time the children were at boarding school. For the second time in my married life I was going to be on my own, and I wasn't looking forward to it.

I drove Russell and Deborah back to their schools in Sussex and stayed with my mother for a few days, taking the opportunity to see Robin before reluctantly taking the road back to Fleet. I was not relishing returning to an empty house on my own. I turned into a Frensham Avenue that looked the same and yet was unfamiliar. The Frensham Avenue I had left had been alive, full of people coming and going and waving a friendly greeting. Now there wasn't a soul in sight.

The tenants had left our house clean and tidy, but there was that musty smell that is inevitable when a house has been locked up for a while. I wandered from room to room, throwing open windows and checking furniture that had that well-used look. It was all rather bare and forlorn. Even the garden, once my pride and joy, had gone to seed. Later that afternoon the removal firm delivered our baggage and I began to unpack, but my hat stayed in its box. It seemed highly unlikely that I would need it during the coming months. My social calendar was blank.

The next few weeks were not the merriest I remember. Life in Frensham Avenue had definitely changed. Gone were the coffee parties and companionable shopping expeditions. It had become an alien, grey-suited world where all the women felt unfulfilled unless they went out to work. During the week the cul-de-sac was like ghost alley. It was rare to hear a front door bang before teatime. At least in married quarters there had always been somebody else in the same situation to chat with. Here, much of the time, there was no one at home but me. It was all too easy to wallow in self-pity.

During term-time the house felt horribly empty and I was left twiddling my thumbs, wondering what to do with my days. There was no mess to clean up, no mountains of food to prepare; the house stayed neat and tidy and a cottage pie lasted a week. Only school holidays brought relief from the tedium of cooking for one. It didn't help that the news was full of gloom—miners' strikes, power cuts and the imposition of the 'three-day week'. Television screens blacked out right in the middle of a favourite programme and the radiators cooled. The winter of 1974/75 was not a lot of fun for anybody.

I needed to find something productive to help me pass the time. Perhaps I could get a job? That was easier said than done. Once I confessed that I didn't want to commit myself to working full time when the children were home for holidays, I was as good as written off their books. Temporary work was at a premium. My office skills were out of date, there were no daffodil fields in Fleet and I definitely wasn't going back to market research. The only jobs advertised in the paper were helping to erect marquees or change tyres at the local garage, and I didn't think that I was physically up to either.

Even at the local dramatic society I was considered too unreliable to be given a speaking part. Instead, I stood for hours hiding behind the curtain, waiting for my cue to rattle a thundersheet. I soon got bored with that. Voluntary organisations turned me down. 'I'm sorry, my dear, but we must have continuity,' I was told when I offered my services as a dog-walker. Really, would Rover be that upset if I deserted him for a week? Apparently the answer was definitely 'Yes.'

Meanwhile *Ark Royal* was sailing to waters new, first to the Mediterranean and then across the other side of the Atlantic, operating along the East Coast of America and in the West Indies. At least during term-time I was able to take the opportunity to catch up when she dropped anchor. First there was an idyllic two weeks in Malta in October, and the following March another two weeks in Florida. I think we can legitimately claim to having had another home on both occasions, even if only for a short period.

In Malta kind friends, Joan and Bertie Bloomer, loaned us an apartment in their house overlooking Dockyard Creek. This was a dream location, where I could sit eating my breakfast on the small balcony, watching the world below, entertained by the cries of the local water-taxi men plying for custom from their traditional, brightly painted, wooden *dghajsas*.

Bertie kept a magnificent old square-rigged yacht moored opposite the house, and the day *Ark Royal* was due to arrive in Grand Harbour we boarded *Sea Urchin* early and motored out into Grand Harbour to greet her. It was a perfect morning. The sea was glassy smooth, a mirror reflecting the image of the imposing Fort St Angelo flooded with the golden-apricot light of the early morning sun. Then, over the horizon, appeared the carrier, some of her aircraft up on the deck, the Royal Marine band playing and the sailors in their best square rig uniforms lining her side. We waved, and figures up in Flyco waved back. How romantic a memory is that?

The following March *Ark Royal* visited Jacksonville in Florida and her squadrons disembarked to the Naval Air Station at Cecil Field. On hearing that Mrs Worth had come out to join him, Jack, as the Air Group Commander, was offered the use of the Admiral's quarters at Cecil Field for the duration of his stay. This was a tremendous privilege. The apartment was quite a showpiece. The furniture, heavy and solidly built of darkest mahogany, had come from the Admiral's cabin on board the aircraft carrier USS *Intrepid* when she had decommissioned. The walls were bedecked with photographs and wooden crests commemorating the ship's history. I don't know how many eminent guests had slept in the king-size bed before us, but I hope they slept as well as we did.

Two particular memories come to mind from that visit. The first was escaping for a weekend up-country to the Okefenokee Swamp in south-eastern Georgia for a blissfully peaceful interlude in an otherwise hectic schedule. We hired a small boat with an outboard motor and chugged off to explore a tiny part of the 600 miles of wetland wilderness where the water is the colour of tea from the tannic acid of the swamp vegetation and the cypress, bay and gum trees are festooned with streamers of Spanish moss. Occasionally we glimpsed an alligator sunning itself on the bank or a pair of white ibis gliding at tree-top level, or disturbed a couple of ducks feeding, but mostly we just drifted along gently, enjoying the peace and tranquillity.

The second memory is quite the opposite—a barbecue party thrown by 892 Squadron aircrew to which a number of our American hosts had been invited by way of a 'thank you'. Apart from the ubiquitous steaks, baked potatoes and salad, the boys had laid on a barrel of oysters which were consumed at an incredible rate by those who were lovers of the mollusc and then they laid on some entertainment, performing the West Country Flurry Dance in silly hats and, for some reason known only to themselves, white thermal underwear issued to be worn under immersion flying suits. The Americans guests were totally bemused, not knowing whether to laugh or applaud politely.

Just before Christmas Jack had written to say that in May the ship would be going to South America to operate with the Brazilian Navy and then go to Rio de Janeiro for the debriefing and a seven-day visit. Almost by the same post came a change-of-address card from Dick and Darlene Corbett, old chums from Californian VX-4 days.

'We are in Rio for a three-year assignment in the US Mission. Why not come and stay?' When they wrote, they never really believed we would come!

The only thing stopping me flying out to Brazil was the little matter of cash. I had no idea what an air ticket to Rio would cost, but when I rang the travel agent I gulped. Where was I going to find that kind of money without selling something? My gaze fell upon the camper van that had sat unused since the day it had returned from Devon. It was never my favourite choice of vehicle, and I would be delighted to see the back of it. I placed an advertisement in *Exchange & Mart*, and was surprised at the interest. The leading cellist in the London Philharmonic Orchestra bought it, explaining that it was just the right size to carry his instrument. Two weeks later I sent a telegram to *Ark Royal*: 'Will be waiting for you in Rio.'

The Corbetts met me at the airport and took me back to their palatial apartment in Leblon, up a hill so steep that we could see the famous Ipanema Beach from the balcony. What a perfect place to adjust and get over jet lag in the company of good friends before we went to greet the fleet! Nestling between tall mountains and deep sea, Rio seemed to stretch almost languidly along the shores of the Atlantic Ocean. But languid she was not: the pulse of life was as strong and compelling as the rhythm of the samba, reflected by the exuberance of the happy-go-lucky people on the sun-kissed beaches. Rio was a superb spectacle.

Ark Royal dropped anchor out in the bay, just a liberty-boat ride away and a magnificent sight for all to admire. I joined the handful of wives gathered on the quay. The excitement grew as we waited for the boats to take us out to be reunited with our loved ones. It was, I have to say, all too romantic—the lights of the famous bay, the giant floodlit Christo figure high above the city, and then, as we scrambled up the ladder, sailors in their tropical white uniforms welcoming us on board. It was hard to swallow the lump in my throat.

Of course, greetings had to be kept very low-key to avoid embarrassment; we didn't exactly shake hands, but it was almost like that. There he stood, looking bronzed and gorgeous, but protocol dictated that it was 'hands off'—at least until we were alone some hours later in the privacy of our bedroom in the Corbett's apartment.

* * *

In June 1975 *Ark Royal* returned to Plymouth and we were all there to watch her stately progress up Plymouth Sound. Of course, there was much rejoicing as families that had been separated for many months were reunited. We had been lucky to be given an empty married quarter in Plymstock for two months whilst 'The Ark' was back in the dockyard. The house was identical to that in which we had lived three years earlier—the same furniture, the same carpets, all the rooms with the regulation borders of linoleum round the edges. I had hardly been *in situ* a week when a man from Works and Bricks came to visit, a big beam on his good-humoured face. He was, he said, the bearer of good tidings. From now onwards all married quarters, not just those occupied by commanders and ranks above, were to have fitted carpets.

'Perhaps you would like to choose the colour?' he suggested, dumping an armful of sample books in my hall.

116

We deliberated and we cogitated and we finally made our choice, and a week later, when he returned, we placed the order for matching vanilla, sixty per cent wool throughout.

'A wise choice, Madam,' he assured me.

'When will they be fitted?'

Well, he couldn't say—but soon. I didn't really expect to see the new carpet during the short time of my stay, but I was in for a surprise. Incredibly, a few days later there was another knock and there stood three more jolly Devonians in green overalls.

'Come to lay you new hall and stair carpets.'

Now this was really impressive, but what about the rest? They shook their heads, mystified. Just the hall and stairs—all they were authorised to fit. Oh well, it was a start. But there must be some mistake. I didn't order red. And this carpet wasn't wall to wall. There was still space for the regulation border of linoleum.

Bill, the senior carpet-layer, looked perplexed.

'Perhaps you'd better call your boss,' I suggested.

'No 'tis quite right, me love,' he told me with a shake of his head, and showed me his triplicated work sheet.

It took a while for the penny to drop. This was not my choice at all. According to the date on the worksheet, a previous tenant had ordered the red carpet three years earlier. When I suggested that it was a waste to lay this new carpet only to have it ripped up before it had hardly been worn, Bill gave me what my mother would have described as an old-fashioned look.

'Maybe your other carpet will be delivered soon and maybe it won't. I'm more inclined to favour the latter. In the meantime I'm told to carry on and lay this carpet, if it's all right with you, even though. as you say, 'tis a terrible waste.'

Needless to say, he was right. I hope the next tenant, or maybe the one after that, approved of our choice of colour.

Once more celebrations were in order with the announcement of the award of another stripe. In January 1976 Jack would be promoted to the rank of Captain RN. When *Ark Royal* sailed again, I returned once more to Fleet to await further instructions. 'If you go abroad again, I'll scratch your eyes out,' remarked a friend. I was careful to keep my season's greetings low-key when I added, as a footnote to her Christmas card, '. . . and by the way, I don't know if you have heard, but we are off to Italy!'

Six months on course at the NATO Defence College in Rome followed by two years in Naples sounded pretty good to all the family. There was always the question of where we would live, but that problem was soon solved when a letter arrived from Lavinia and Alistair Anson, asking if we would like to take over their tenancy.

'We live on the top floor of an apartment block on the Piazza Lante, overlooking the Apia Antica,' Lavinia wrote. 'There is a lot of space—three bedrooms and plenty of room to entertain, especially in the summer when we use the roof garden.'

A roof garden! How exotic! I read on, fascinated.

'The apartment belongs to *Signora* Brusasca, the wife of a Christian Democrat Senator. She seems to like having British tenants—you will be the tenth RN family to live here. There is a maid called Giulia, a real treasure who comes to clean twice a week and is a useful source of local information.'

All very well, but I didn't speak Italian. The best thing I could do was learn, but there was to be no messing about at adult education classes. I was going to do this thing properly. I looked in the local paper. There was only one advertisement offering private classes in Italian, so I rang the number.

A lady who answered introduced herself as Mrs Roberts. In spite of her surname, I was encouraged by her Italian accent and arranged to meet her in her house in Aldershot. The following week, armed with notebook and sharpened pencil, I knocked on the door of a small semi next to the local primary school.

Mrs Roberts ushered me into her living room and rushed off to make some coffee. I perched nervously on the edge of a sofa overflowing with satin scatter cushions and waited, my gazed riveted on rows of ruby-red Venetian glassware winking in the firelight. Tray in hand, Mrs Roberts, or Maria as she insisted I call her, was soon back with coffee, which she poured with great ceremony.

'I wouldn't like you to think I have always lived like this,' she apologised looking around the room in disgust. 'No, I must tell you that I am used to something better.'

It didn't matter that I was lost for a response, for there was no stopping the flow and soon there was little I didn't know about Maria. Her husband had been in the British Army—a Major, she stressed—but a year ago he had died of a heart attack, and then, to add to all her woes, her house had burnt down.

'And now look what I am reduced to—a tiny little house—me, who grew up in a grand villa in the hills beyond Verona. Such a come-down in the world,' she sighed.

I offered my condolences, though I was unsure what she was more upset about, her change in circumstances or the loss of the Major.

By now we were half an hour into my lesson and not a word of Italian had crossed my lips. During the following weeks I learned very little Italian though a lot about *Signora* Roberts, who had so many problems to share that my tutorial frequently remained unopened. Her life was a constant drama zone that she felt she needed to discuss in detail. By lesson two she had confided that the headmaster of the primary school next door, also her lodger, had asked her to marry him and that she had said yes only because her ten-year-old son thought it was immoral to have an unattached man living under the same roof.

'Mrs Worth—Jeel—what do I do? I really don't think I want to marry again.'

Sometimes I wondered who should be paying whom, as our lessons turned into a counselling session and I wasn't the one on the couch. Eventually she rang to say that she was too sick to teach me that morning.

'It is my heart,' she said.

Alarmed, I asked if she had seen a doctor, but she hastened to assure me.

'It is irrevocably broken. Mrs Worth, I do not love this man. I cannot marry him.'

'Then, Maria, don't.' I was doing my best to hide my weariness.

'But I've ordered the cake and the honeymoon is paid for,' she wailed.

She didn't marry her schoolmaster though they did go on the 'honeymoon', chaperoned by her ten-year-old son. Thus my lessons came to an abrupt end and I departed for Rome, conversant with the verb *amare* but barely able to order a litre of milk.

— 15 —
When in Rome

WE arrived in Rome in February 1976 in our brand new Fiat Mirafiore, having survived the journey relatively unscathed apart from driving through France in a snowstorm with a broken windscreen and getting caught up in a blockage on the autostrada caused by striking lorry drivers. *Sciopero*, the word for strike, was to become one of the most dreaded words in our Italian vocabulary.

Our first impression of the apartment block on the Piazza Lante was one of mild disappointment. We had imagined somewhere more picturesque—somewhere a little more 'Mediterranean', with window boxes overflowing with geraniums and brightly painted shutters instead of black security grills. Admittedly it was February: perhaps it was a little early for geraniums, even in Italy. It was also raining, which didn't help; neither did the abundance of aggressive graffiti sprayed across the wall. We sat in our car contemplating a large red hammer and sickle, reluctant to move.

'You go and see if she's up there.' My husband was referring to our landlady, *Signora* Bresasca. 'I'll stay here and look after the luggage.'

Of course, he was right. Our car was packed to the gunwales with everything we would need for the next six months. We had been warned never to leave it unattended. There didn't seem to be a soul about, but who knew who was watching?

'Anyway, you're the one who speaks Italian.'

He had to be joking. Six quick lessons with the charming but somewhat dizzy lady in Aldershot had prepared me for nothing more demanding than buying a loaf of bread.

Reluctantly, I climbed the steps and pressed the bell marked 'Six'. The intercom crackled into life and a female voice shrieked '*Avanti!*' I had to throw my weight against the heavy security door before it would open.

On the gate of the tiny lift there hung a sign, '*Non functioni.*' I didn't have to be a linguist to understand the implications. Ahead of me were six flights of winding marble stairs to be climbed on foot.

'*Signora* Worth. *Buona sera. Come sta?*' *Signora* Bresasca, our landlady, not a hair out of place on her immaculately coiffured head, stood waiting to greet me as I arrived, gasping, at the top. '*Mi dispiace.* I am so sorry.'

She waved a flawlessly manicured hand in the direction of the defunct lift. Being able to apologise in English seemed to be the full extent of her grasp of the language. From then on she reverted to her native tongue. No time to waste, neat little feet twinkled from room to room as she escorted me round her apartment, switching lights on and off, opening doors and peering into cupboards, all to the accompaniment of a stream of rapid-fire Italian of which I understood not a word. On and on she rattled, whilst I kept nodding and saying '*Si*', praying that all would become clear in the fullness of time or that, at least, Lavinia had left behind a comprehensive list of do's and don't's in English.

Thrusting a huge bunch of keys in my hand, *Signora* Bresasca shot off to some unspecified appointment, leaving me to climb back down to the bottom and break the bad news to my husband that every single piece of luggage would have to be hauled to the top by hand. It was quite dark by the time, exhausted, we dumped the last bag in our tiny entrance hall and unlocked the door and looked around.

'Lights?'

'Over here.' I pulled aside a floor-length, red tartan curtain to reveal a battery of light switches. I clicked the nearest.

'Aaah!' On the opposite wall, a pair of life-sized ceramic masks lit up, the eye sockets and gaping mouths glowing red. Spooky. I tried another switch, and eventually I had an array of lamps glowing dimly. The *pièce de résistance* was an enormous chandelier glittering with crystal dingle-dangles. For one dazzling moment the whole confection blazed in an amazing display of luminosity, and then with a bang all the lights went out and we left in total darkness. Now what? We didn't have a torch or candle. Outside in the passage all the lights were on. The power failure was obviously confined to our apartment, so with a little help it should have been restorable. Someone was going to have to go and talk to the concierge.

'I know, I know—I'm the one who speaks Italian . . .'

Timidly, I knocked on her door. A pleasant, round-faced *Signora* in an apron answered.

'*Si?*'

'Giulia?'

'*Si.*' She looked puzzled, and then the lira dropped. 'Ah, *Signora* Vort?' At least we were expected.

She shook my hand warmly, chattering away incomprehensibly. By now my brain had gone into total paralysis. Somewhere from the depths of my inner dictionary I dug up the words *'lucci'* and *'non functioni'*, waving my arms skywards. Fortunately, Giulia understood. Up the stairs she ran, giggling. At the top she opened the door to a fuse box and peered inside and nodded.

'Signora, too much *elettricatà*,' she advised, and rushed around turning off all but two table lamps. Then, with a flick of a trip switch, power was restored. '*Capisce, Signora?*'

I nodded. Now I knew what our landlady had been trying to tell me as she beetled round turning the light switches on and off.

'*Bouna notte, Signora. A domani.*'

'*Bouna notte, Giulia.*'

The apartment, we agreed, was different—not quite what we had expected. The tour, though brief, was full of surprises. 'Wow! Just come and look at this.'

In the living room there was a proper wood-burning fire. Moulded on to the wall above, flanked on either side by the illuminated masks, there was a vast plaster sunburst on a background of heavenly blue surrounded by the twelve signs of the zodiac.

I thought I would never get to sleep that first night in Rome. It was February, and, even in Rome, February can be chilly. It didn't help that we were in two single beds and that the squashy mattresses were stuffed with feathers that ebbed and flowed and parted like the Red Sea as I tossed and turned trying to get comfy. In the street below, the Roman traffic roared on unabated; across the room a portrait of the head of a blood-stained Christ gazed down reproachfully from the wall. Back in England our tenants were sleeping peacefully in our king-size bed. How I envied them.

In spite of taking for ever to get to sleep, I woke early the next morning. A night on the *Signora* Brescaca's feather mattress had left me far from rested, but outside I could hear church bells ringing. I shook my slumbering partner, determined that we were going to make the most of the one whole day of being tourists before he had to report to the Defence College.

Over breakfast we consulted our guidebook.

'We might as well begin at the beginning,' I said turning to Chapter One of Georgina Masson's excellent guide to Rome. The Capitol and then, maybe, take a look at the Forum? I couldn't wait to be a tourist. We were so lucky. Not for us a three-day 'See Rome and expire' tour: we had six months to explore and get to know the city.

'There's only one snag. It's raining.'

'Raining? It can't be! Not on our first morning in Italy!'

'Well, it is. Just look out of the window.'

Jack was right: it was chucking it down. Water was streaming off the roofs, the streets below were awash and, judging by the colour of the sky, the only sightseeing I was going to do concerned the inside of our apartment.

There was a good-size sitting and dining area, a large kitchen, small bathroom and three bedrooms, though one of these was little bigger than a cupboard. The furniture was classic Italian—dark and heavy, built more for style than comfort. Most of it was huge and required a great deal of muscle power to move. The décor was bizarre.

The tiny entrance hall was decorated with tartan wallpaper. Perhaps our landlady had a love affair with things Scottish. The ceiling-to-floor curtains were made of dark wine-red velvet, edged with matching fluffy bobbles. The windows had heavy shutters, designed to let in as little light in as possible. No doubt during the heat of a Roman summer we would appreciate the shade, but on a rainy midwinter day the lack of daylight was depressing. Even the six-foot mural over the fireplace did little to relieve the gloom. At least there was a reasonably efficient central heating system, shared with the rest of the apartment block.

Our landlady had left many of her personal possessions in place. Silver-framed photographs hung on the walls between the reproductions of early Renaissance religious works. Large family groups smiled stiffly into the camera. There was a triptych of a pretty little girl in a gauzy ballet *tutu*, a white communion dress and then a wedding gown that I guessed might be a photographic record of the life and times of our landlady. In a glass-fronted display cabinet a collection of ornate Capodimonte figurines gathered dust. I shuddered to think what would happen if we broke one. For all we knew, they could be priceless antiques.

Potted plants were growing in some of the most unlikely places. Variegated ivy twisted and turned and intertwined itself round a standard lamp, clambering over the shade. Some judicious pruning with a pair of nail scissors was required to reveal the on-and-off switch. In the kitchen, another 'triffid' had grown to Jack-and-the-Beanstalk proportions, clinging to the door and window frames as it continued on its relentless journey round the kitchen. Over the gas cooker it had acquired a yellow and sere look and dropped its leaves, although once over the sink it had become completely revitalised. The kitchen itself, with its painted white furniture and walls devoid of religious paintings, was the most cheerful room in the flat. From the window we could see across into the neighbouring block, count the empty wine bottles on the balconies and listen to the twitter of house martins nesting under the eaves. Indubitably the best feature of our apartment was the roof garden, furnished with a mass of potted oleanders and bougainvillea and a canopied, swinging sun lounger. On a good day you could see for miles across open countryside to the avenue of stiff umbrella pines that lined the Apia Antica.

Once we had unpacked, there wasn't much left to do. Frustrated, we kicked our heels, our only form of entertainment a crackling, static-ridden broadcast from the BBC World Service gleefully informing us that River Tiber had overflowed its banks and two people had drowned. Somehow this was not how I had envisaged spending our first day in Italy.

I browsed through the neatly typed set of housekeeping instructions left by Lavinia and her predecessors, listing where to buy the best fresh pasta and the days Giulia came to clean the flat. Underlined in red was a dire warning: 'It is very easy to overload the power system. Never use the iron without first unplugging the refrigerator or you will trip the system. Three lights are the maximum you can have on in the living room at any one time.' Now she tells us.

The rain continued to teem down all day, accompanied by thunder and lightning. In the evening we ran across the piazza to the local restaurant and drowned our sorrows in a carafe of Chianti before retiring to our feather mattresses early. He snored whilst I lay awake, listening to the hooting of the traffic in the street below. On the opposite wall the portrait of the blood-stained Christ continued to gaze down at me, His eyes fixed on my pillow. If I were to sleep in peace He would have to go. Next morning I made Jack lift the heavy frame down and we hid Jesus in the back of the wardrobe. Two days later, however, He was back, looking even more judgemental. For the next two weeks Giulia and I fought a silent battle. Every time I took the picture down she put it back. Had my command of the Italian language been better, I might have put my foot down, but as it was I took the easy way out and re-hung the picture on the mornings she came to clean.

On Monday morning the sun shone fitfully as we drove to the ultra-modern extension to Rome built by Mussolini and known as EUR in search of the NATO Defence College. We toured the main piazza several times before we found it, not located in some kind of university building but discreetly tucked upstairs on the second floor in an office block. There we met some of the other members of Course 48 and their wives. This was our first experience of serving with a multi-national force. That first morning a bystander could be forgiven for thinking he had arrived at the Tower of Babel. For the next six months, fifty-four senior service officers and diplomats from fourteen NATO countries would spend their days together, discussing and debating the current state of regional and world politics, military dispositions, science and economics. Unofficially they were setting up a kind of old-boy network throughout the countries of the North Atlantic Treaty Organisation. It is so much easier to converse with opposite numbers in Oslo or Brussels when the voice at the other end of the 'phone is that of an ex-classmate.

The students were divided up into committees representing not only different countries but different services as well. The American committee comprised the US and Canadian Forces and Jack, who, having served on exchange, had been dubbed an honorary American. Our social life tended to revolve within the committee. We moved in and out of each other's homes for buffet and drinks parties and religiously sat down together at the same table at official functions. This way we got to know each other very well.

During the six months we met some lovely people, especially Lars Ostigaard, a Norwegian Navy Captain with a hoary goatee beard, and his friend Tor. Together we explored Rome and the environs, escaping at the weekend to Tivoli and Frascati to enjoy the beautiful countryside, lap up a bit of culture and try the local wine. Later, when their boys broke up from school, Aril, Lars' beautiful ash-blonde wife, came out to join him.

Although, strictly speaking, the academic course was intended for the men, there were educational opportunities for the wives. Twice a week we could study Italian. When I was asked if I would like to attend the Wednesday art class I laughed, imagining that I would be expected to sit at an easel in a smock: I couldn't convince myself that being in Italy would bring out the Michelangelo in me. I had misunderstood. I was being offered the chance to learn to appreciate art in a city where art abounds.

The subject of the Wednesday-morning lectures was 'The History of Art from the Greeks to the Renaissance'. Our lecturer was a bearded Canadian called Edward, who had lived in Rome for so long that the Canadian side of him had long since rubbed away. Edward was a great authority on his subject, and we all looked forward to his classes. Unfortunately, sometimes he was absent on account of ill health induced by over-indulgence in the local *vino*, but as long as he was sober Edward's lectures were inspirational, as were the field trips he arranged to such places as Subiaco and Orvieto.

Living in Rome was wonderful, but it was never relaxing. You took your life in your hands every time you visited the Centre. It was the law of the jungle out there, with cars driven down one-way streets in the wrong direction, motorists slaloming round pedestrians on crossings and the pavements used as parking lots. The noise and congestion in the narrow mediæval streets of downtown Rome made it impossible to hold a civilised conversation.

Driving was hysterical and best avoided. On the whole, the golden rule was 'If possible, don't take the car.' There was an excellent bus service provided the drivers were not on strike, in which case a ride into the heart of the capital only cost only 100 *lire*—no more than the equivalent of ten pence. Fares were paid into a machine, which was fine as long as you had a coin. Coins, however, especially those of the 100 *lire* denomination, were as rare as a decent cup of tea. Rumour had it that the high silver content encouraged the Japanese to smuggle them out in large quantities for putting into the backs of watches; more likely the shortage was caused by hoarding. Under many a bed lurked a jar of *specile* put by for a rainy day. So the economy managed without, and it was quite normal to be handed a rose, toffees or an egg in lieu of change at the supermarket.

It took a while to acclimatise to living in Rome. Much to my surprise, I discovered that few of the local traders spoke English, and my limited grasp of the local language could therefore turn a shopping expedition into a bit of a nightmare. I frequently misunderstood what had been said: it was illogical that *caulda* meant hot, not cold, and I got *ova* mixed up with *ouva*, leading to some very strange looks from the stallholder as he meticulously weighed out ten grapes instead filling a box with eggs. As for the currency, it was months before I got the hang of all those noughts.

The everyday task of withdrawing money from the bank was a chore I dreaded in those pre-cashpoint days. Every time I made the journey to the Banca d'Italia in EUR, I held my breath. Would the buses be running or would they be *sciopero*, and when I got to the bank would I find the dreaded word *chiuso* stuck on the locked door? They changed their hours of opening to suit themselves.

A visit to the Banca d'Italia was an intimidating experience. The interior was like a marble temple to the goddess of wealth, with a six-foot-wide counter behind which a battery of clerks dealt with their customers in the correct pecking order—i.e., male customers first. A woman trying to cash a cheque was rarer than an armed robber and someone to be ignored if possible.

'*Si, Signora?*' At last I would catch the attention of a clerk. Slowly and carefully, I would do my best to express my need to withdraw a modest sum from our account. For a full five minutes the young man would study my chequebook and then take it away to show a colleague. They would confer, throwing the occasional furtive glance in my direction, and then one would go to check my file. Eventually he would return wearing something that could pass for a smile and hand me a form to be completed and passed to clerk at the next position who would stamp and staple with a flourish before directing me to the cashier who would count out a wad a notes and hand them over with a sigh as if parting with funds were both painful and sinful. I never went to the bank if I was short of time.

'Please teach me how to make them pay attention to me,' I begged Gabriella, my latest Italian teacher. 'How do I say "It's my turn"?' *Tocca a me* was a phrase that worked well, especially when it was uttered in unison with moving my elbows. When in Rome . . .

There were other important lessons to learn. How did one fend off the advances of an Italian male? It wasn't only the young and pretty who got propositioned. Standing too close to a Latin lothario on the bus was to be avoided unless you enjoyed having your bottom pinched. I believe that, these days, bottom-pinching is no longer the national sport, legislation against sexual harassment having spoilt the fun, although I bet there are still some men who cannot resist taking a liberty.

Carrying smart leather purses was not recommended. A plastic shopping bag was safer, and money was best kept tucked in one's bra. Tourists were the targets

For a full five minutes the young man would study my chequebook . . .

for every rogue in Rome. It was predicted that, by the end of our six months in the city, at least one in four of us would have fallen prey to crime in some shape or form. This turned out, unfortunately, to be an accurate prediction. It was best to look as little like a tourist as possible—by wearing heavy shades and designer jeans, concealing maps and guide books within the pages of *La Giornale* and looking at the Parthenon out of the corner of one's eye, as if it were part of the everyday scenery.

Our six months in Rome were passing all too quickly. In July the course at the NATO College was due to end and we would be moving down to the Naples area and needing yet another home. In April we drove south to spend the weekend with old friends Bruce and Genevieve Thomas. They were due to return to England in August and they thought that we might like to consider taking on the lease of the house they were renting.

It would have been hard not to have liked the sun-kissed villa. Butter-yellow stucco walls, a flat roof, a flower-filled garden—it was like one of those houses featured in up-market glossy holiday brochures, one that cost a fortune to rent. Apart from the spacious accommodation, acres of marble floor, four bedrooms and two bathrooms, the view from the long balcony across the beautifully blue water to the Isle of Ischia was something to die for. Of course we wanted to live there.

As we have so often found, however, nothing is that simple. We tried to contact the owner before we left, but although he lived in Naples he remained infuriatingly elusive and we had no choice but to return to Rome, leaving Bruce to arrange a tenancy for us. Negotiations dragged on for weeks. First we were told that we could have the villa, then we learned that the owner had changed his mind—the house was no longer on the market. Then, one happy day, an envelope arrived. It contained pages of the finest flimsy parchment covered in beautiful handwritten script, but in such formal, stylised Italian that it made little sense. Fortunately it arrived on the day of my Italian class, so Gabriella was able to translate for me. The house was ours if we still wanted it. The monthly rent was on the high side, but we pretended we could afford it.

At Easter the children flew out for their school holiday. As luck would have it, they broke up on different days, so arrangements had to be made with Grandma to escort them to the airport and hand them over to the care of flight staff as Deborah was only ten and Russell eleven at the time. There was great excitement as one small girl appeared, holding the hand of the air stewardess and wearing a familiar grin on her face. She'd made it. Two days later it was back to the airport to collect her brother and then, for a short while, we were all together again—though not for long.

Twice during the course the military men went a-travelling. After Easter the whole of Course 48 took to the air with their instructors and disappeared across the ocean to America, leaving their dependants alone in Rome. Fortunately it wasn't difficult to keep the young entertained. Russell became an instant expert on things Roman and we spent hours down in the crypts exploring underground tombs and wandering round the forum, breathing in the world of Julius Cæsar. When visitors came to stay, he became a self-appointed guide: with a child's ability to memorise and assimilate, he could bring the world alive. I bought the children little books showing 'Before and After Rome'—the earliest form of virtual reality available. With these we were able to reconstruct from the ruins what the city must have looked like in Roman times and started a prize-winning project, illustrated with numerous postcards purchased during our tours.

Perhaps the visit best remembered, and the one written up with the greatest glee, was that to the Church of Santa Maria della Concezione, where we went not to pray but to look at the macabre Capuchin Cemetery, where, in a series of caves, the bones of 4,000 monks are on display. In one chamber, hundreds of skulls were stacked against a wall, their countless black eye-sockets returning our gaze. In another, ribs and pelvic joints were fastened to the walls and ceilings in weird, swirling patterns. Elsewhere, niches contained whole skeletons of some of the most devout brethren, enveloped in their monks' robes and standing in grotesque poses, the faces staring out from under their hoods.

Alas, the holiday sped by all too quickly and I was putting the children back on their flights to London. By May, Rome was heating up in more ways than one. The roof garden became my delight, with its swing *chaise longue* and rows of potted oleanders; I was happy just swaying and reading. We planned a big party out on the terrace, imagining how romantic it would be to dine by moonlight. The invitations were issued, the guests accepted and the menu was planned.

The party was to be held on a Friday evening in early June. On the previous Monday morning, I woke to the sound of knocking.

'*Signora. Signora* Vort,' Giulia and two grinning dungaree-clad workmen stood outside the door.

'*Signora. Questi sono gli uomini che sono venuto lavorare al terrazzo. D'accordo?*'

Baffled, I scratched my head, trying to understand what she had said.

'*Lavorare?* Work?' What work was she talking about?

'*Si, Signora,*' and off she went into a stream of incomprehensible, idiomatic Italian.

'*Piano. Piano.*'

It was useless. Only one word in ten made sense. Eventually, exasperated, she marched past, leading the men out on to the roof garden and leaving me open-mouthed. What was going on? Why had I not been warned? But it seemed that I had: Giulia had told me days ago and I had failed to understand. Not for the first time, I was to regret my lack of ability to grasp idiomatic Italian. Now, too late, I discovered that this was the advance party who had been ordered by our landlady to give the roof garden a complete face-lift, all part of a massive restoration programme. Scaffolding was being erected and a tribe of workers from a mid-European country was swarming all over my beloved paradise. When all was finished it would be wonderful—a new marble floor, fresh paint, the whole structure reinforced for our safety. And when would that be? Giulia shrugged. Not for six weeks. Maybe more.

I hoped I had misunderstood her, but I hadn't. Without so much as a by-your-leave, our lovely landlady had transformed our little haven into a work site. From seven in the morning till sunset, we were to be subjected to banging and singing. Worst of all, I was denied access to my sixth-floor haven. I could have wept; in fact, I believe I did.

No amount of irate telephoning to the college helped. Shoulders were shrugged. It was a shame that no one had asked our permission, but then why would they? Sympathy was offered, but little else. Where was I to hold the beautiful moonlit supper party? Giulia said she would talk nicely to the workers, which is why twenty people sat at their tables surrounded by plastic sheeting within a trelliswork of scaffolding. The day we departed from Piazza Lante the workers were still crying 'Over to you, Alfredo.'

June gave way to July, and, as the mercury in the thermometer rose, Rome became like an inferno. With each passing day Piazza Lante grew quieter. Parking spaces in the square were easier to find as more and more of our neighbours escaped to the coast or sought the cooler air in the mountains. Our local shops only opened by rota: some days I was forced to walk half a mile just to buy a litre of milk. Soon it was time for us to leave too.

The College term ended in July, and, once the last farewell speech had been made and the medallions and diplomas handed out, we were ready to say our *arriverdecis* to Guilia and our Piazza Lante neighbours and join the exodus driving down the Autostrada del Sole.

— 16 —
See Naples and Survive

OUR first week in the Naples area was meant to be a family holiday, though it didn't work out that way for my husband. While we were waiting for Bruce and Genevieve to vacate the villa in Parco Azzurro, we rented a chalet at the Camping Averno Resort. With its swimming pool heated by natural volcanic hot springs, floodlit tennis courts and restaurant, the Resort was an ideal spot for the family to enjoy some rest and recreation—though, alas, Jack did not have much free time to enjoy the facility. His predecessor was impatient to hand over the reins and return to England. While the rest of his family were jumping in and out of the pool, therefore, Jack had to put on uniform and report for duty.

Not that the children and I escaped completely: we had but a couple of days to enjoy our holiday surroundings before Papa herded us into the car for our first visit to the Headquarters of NATO South. Identity photographs had to be taken, base passes applied for and our names checked into the medical system.

Driving on to the base was like entering another world. Outside the gates, the streets of Bagnoli were noisy, narrow and congested, full of local colour and character; inside it was all law and military order, the roads swept pristine-clean, the driving speed strictly regulated to a snail's pace. It was as if we had entered a totally different civilisation—one that had been scooped up and dumped in the middle of the southern countryside.

Beyond the obligatory mass of official buildings and a parade ground where, every morning, the ceremony of raising the flags of the Southern Flank countries took place were all the facilities provided for NATO families. There were schools, churches, a cinema and sports centres, clubs where families could socialise, have a meal and enjoy a swim, and a shopping mall selling all kind of goods from Parmesan cheese to postcards and from cameo brooches to coffee. Mothers could leave their children in the nursery and husbands could visit the barber or have their car serviced, all without having to battle with the local lingo. It would have been possible to have survived without knowing a word of Italian. Talk about being mollycoddled! I did, though, appreciate being able to use a bank where all the cashiers spoke English and the customers waited their turn in an orderly line!

There was also the British Store, a miniature supermarket supplied by the NAAFI where treats like fresh cream, pork sausages, Wiltshire bacon and traditional Christmas crackers were sold—items that in those days were unobtainable in the local markets. The Americans had a purpose-built hospital; we had our modest little medical centre staffed by one doctor and a nursing sister. Anything major had to be treated at the International Hospital. It was just as well that we were a healthy lot.

Next door were the offices of the British Services Support Unit. This was where the families could turn for advice and succour—and, believe me, there were times when we all needed our hands held. Life in Naples, whilst exciting, was frequently a bureaucratic nightmare. Certainly, during the early days I wondered if I would ever feel at home in what seemed to be a very foreign environment. It may not have taken us long to drive from Rome down the Autostrada del Sole to Naples, but, culturally, the two cities felt a world apart. The local dialect was practically unintelligible, the waving of the hands more frenetic and the traffic, if it were possible, even more chaotic. We could have been forgiven for imagining that we had crossed the border into another land.

Newcomers were issued with a bible packed with a wealth of information on everything from where to shop to how to protect themselves and their property in an area with a phenomenally high crime rate. On the notice board was a list of accommodation available for renting. We were keeping our fingers crossed that we wouldn't need to use it.

On day three we had an appointment with our prospective landlord at the villa. First we had to show proof of identity before Raffaèllo, the gatekeeper, would open the security gates so that we could drive into the *parco*. Up and up the road wound steeply to the top, ending in a cul-de-sac. *Dottore* Armando-Exceler, a silver-haired gentleman in his senior years, elegant and full of Latin charm, was waiting. Thankfully, he spoke perfect English.

'*Capitano* Worth and the good *Signora*.' He took my hand limply in his and held it for a moment longer than was absolutely necessary whilst gazing into my eyes. 'I understand you are interested in renting my villa?'

'*Si, Dottore*,' we nodded. He sighed gently.

'You know, I have been thinking of perhaps I should sell the villa rather than rent it out again.'

My heart plummeted.

'You see,' he continued, ' I built the villa for my wife. She likes to escape the heat of Naples in the summer, you understand, but now, well, she says there is too much traffic on the coastal road, too many people at the Lido, too many Americans living in the *parco*.'

Tactfully, he refrained from adding 'and British.'

'So, I am thinking that perhaps I should buy a villa in somewhere up in Abruzzi where the air is so much purer.'

There was a stunned silence as we waited to hear what he had decided. He must have seen the look of anguish on my face. Suddenly, he smiled.

'However . . .'

There was a pause whilst he inspected the hand-stitched buttonholes of his perfectly tailored jacket, checking to make sure that each one had been embroidered to his complete satisfaction.

'. . . as I hate to disappoint, I have decided to let my villa just one more time. But,' after another dramatic pause, 'it is most unfortunate, but I must raise the rent a little.'

Here we go again, I thought.

'You know how it is, taxes going through the ceiling.'

He raised his arms and shrugged his shoulders in an expression of deep sorrow, knowing that he held all the winning cards. Our desire to rent his house was all too transparent—and, more than likely, he knew to the nearest *lira* exactly how much we would receive in housing allowance. It was pointless to haggle.

Once the bargain had been sealed with the signing of the all-important *documenti*, the *Dottore* took his leave.

'*Arrivederci*. I hope you will be very happy living in Parco Azzurro,' he smiled, gently lifting my hand to brush it with a butterfly kiss before settling a pork-pie hat on his head and departing in his chauffeur-driven Mercedes. We never saw him again, not even on the day we vacated when our tour was over.

The children were already upstairs arguing over who was going to have which bedroom.

'If you don't pack it up, the pair of you will sleep in the cellar.'

'A cellar! Is there really a cellar?'

'Yes. The stairs go down from the garage.'

We descended a precariously steep flight of steps that led to the two rooms beneath the house. The walls were roughly whitewashed; the air smelt warm and fungal.

'Wow, what is that?'

We peered incredulously at a huge, ugly, cast-iron contraption that looked like a mock-up of Stevenson's rocket.

'That, believe it or not, is our oil-fired central heating boiler.'

'You're kidding. Who needs central heating?'

It was hard to imagine, on that melting-hot August day, how glad we would be to have the use of this antiquated installation when winter came. The house, with its marble floors and single-paned windows—which, as a precaution against earthquakes, were allowed to rattle freely in their frames—was not well insulated.

'Great! There's a ping-pong table in here,' Russell called from another room. 'And a lot of spiders.'

Miss Muffet made a rapid exit.

'So, do we think we will be happy living here?' Jack asked, as we re-emerged into the sunlight.

'Very!'

And why shouldn't we be? Compared with most houses we had lived in, Villa Ambra was a *palazzo*, with acres of floor space in the living area and four bedrooms up the shrimp-pink marble staircase.

The light and airy kitchen had a cooker fuelled from a hefty gas cylinder known locally as a *bombola*, a washing machine and an American-style refrigerator as big as a wardrobe. The walls were decorated with pastel-blue tiles and the floor was terracotta brown. Both bathrooms upstairs had been tastefully decorated with expensive ceramic tiles delicately painted with sprays of flowers. Admittedly, some of the flowers were standing on their heads, but this merely added a touch of Neapolitan charm, as did the fact that, from the prone position in the tub, you could see that the walls were not exactly perpendicular! Next day we packed up our chalet in the Camping Averno and moved into the Villa Ambra permanently.

Most visitors to Naples rented their houses unfurnished. To help us set up home, we received a one-off payment of just over a million *lire*—the only time in our lives we were likely to be millionaires. However, by the time we had paid Bruce and Genevieve for their pastel-green three-piece suite, the dining set, beds and chest of drawers, the lawn mower and the hundred terracotta pots of geraniums that stood on the patio, there was not a lot left in the bank account.

A shopping expedition to downtown Naples resulted in the purchase of an ultra-modern, glass-top coffee table and a few more *lire* were handed over to a persuasive door-to-door salesman who arrived late in the evening with a load of multi-coloured rugs and cushions to help cosy up our living room. The last of the cash was spent on a dishwasher bought from an American family who were going home. We had to visit the nearest *cambio* as the vendor had insisted on being paid in dollars. A lot of the American families claimed they never used *lire*: they did all their shopping in their local PX and Commissary. Everything from lettuces to loo paper, from calculators to clothing, was flown in from the States. A visit to the local market was a treat many of them passed up on. To us, this seemed incredibly unadventurous.

After travelling so much by bus in Rome, I had got out of the habit of driving. Now I had to bite the bullet and get back behind the wheel if I was to be mobile. We therefore spent the rest of our windfall on a second car, a battle-scarred Fiat

Seicento that had clearly survived more than one confrontation with the Neapolitan traffic. Solid as a rock, however, she was built to take the knocks.

The children christened her Arabella and she quickly became an important member of our family, treasured for her reliability. And reliable she had to be, too. The ascent to our villa was almost perpendicular. The map of the Parco Azzurro looked like a twisted tree branched with many small cul-de-sacs and crescents, and our villa was almost the last house on the twiggy bit at the top.

Arabella was a splendid little vehicle with a lot of heart. She was also very desirable, so Jack installed a secret anti-theft device. Under the driver's seat he hid an ignition disabler—an on-and-off switch filched from a bedside lamp—and wired it up to the car's electrical system. Crude by today's standards but effective, this simple little gadget worked like magic in a city where small Fiats went 'rollabout' almost daily, protecting her from being stolen. Once I came out of the supermarket to find that she had mysteriously relocated herself at the bottom of the hill, presumably abandoned by a would-be thief baffled by his inability to jump-start her.

My first solo in Arabella to the nearest shops in the tiny town of Arco Felice upped my heart rate to a dangerous level, but I made it, even finding somewhere to park. I felt as triumphant as if I had conquered Everest and Mars in one expedition. The following day, feeling braver, I promised to take the children to meet their father for lunch beside the pool at the club on the base. To reach Bagnoli, we could either drive down the relatively safe toll road (the *Tangenziale*) or take the slower, free route along the Via Domitiana. At any time of the day the Domitiana was one long traffic jam, vehicles constantly stopping and starting as they wound their way through the heavily populated port of Pozzouli and up the hill, passing the active crater of Solfatara, its jets of steam charged with sulphurous fumes stinking like bad eggs and spitting hot mud and mineral springs with carbonic acid gas. On this occasion it seemed sensible to settle for the more expensive if less adventurous route, in the hope that we would arrive looking as cool as my non-air-conditioned car would allow.

'Exit three, through two sets of traffic lights and you're at the gate,' my husband had instructed me. 'Shouldn't take more than fifteen minutes out of rush hour.'

Oh yes?

All went well until we reached the exit pay booth, only to find a queue of cars waiting behind the automatic gate that was stuck firmly down. Drivers were out of their cars and walking around, waving their hands in the air. A large, highly voluble man was banging on the collection booth, telling the lady behind the window that the automatic machine had eaten his expensive season ticket. *Mangare!* He had no intention of budging till the machine spat out his card or he was suitably compensated. There we all sat in the heat of the baking sun, stuck. An age later, authority appeared with the appropriate key to let us through, but by the time we arrived at the AF South gate we looked more like tomatoes than the cool cucumbers I had had in mind—as did my worried husband, who had been waiting with some agitation. When I tried to explain why we were late, he, knowing my penchant for taking a wrong turning, looked sceptical. A week later the same thing happened to him.

From the balcony of the Villa Ambra we looked west in an uninterrupted view over the roofs and semi-tropical, foliage-filled gardens to the mysterious hump of the Acropolis of Cumæ—a favourite picnic-spot and site for exploration during school holidays—and beyond to the island of Ischia on the northern edge of the Gulf of Naples. In the evening we would sit out on the balcony and watch some of the most spectacular sunsets I have ever seen. Here they lingered longer than in the tropics, the gold-etched clouds against a backcloth that gradually turned first pale green and then deepened to apricot and then crimson, lilac and purple. The warm glow reflected on the pale villa walls and on to our faces.

Above our cul-de-sac the land reverted to agriculture. Grapes ripened on the rows of vines in autumn between the groves of citrus trees. In February the air was saturated with the overpowering perfume of orange blossom and mimosa; in May the road surface was splattered with ripened fruit that fell from heavily laden apricot trees that hung over a neighbour's wall. Throughout the year bougainvillea, hibiscus and oleanders bloomed, uninterrupted by frost, and ivy-leaf geraniums tumbled over walls and balconies in cascades of salmon, vermilion and white. In the bed below the kitchen window, all the ingredients for traditional Italian cuisine—thyme, oregano, rosemary and aromatic sweet basil—grew non-stop in abundance amongst a profusion of hot-coloured zinnias that had seeded themselves from the previous year. Winter was very short, almost non-existent.

At the foot of the *parco* stood Raffaèllo's gatehouse, a small food store with a hairdressing salon at the back and a private *piscina* (swimming pool) area. The *piscina* boasted a music system powerful enough to relay entertainment to the rest of the *parco*. Day after day the air throbbed with whatever was the latest hit. The young folk who gathered by the pool liked their music sad. First it was a crooner sobbing how he missed Honey. I never did find out who Honey was or where she had gone. By the middle of August this unhappy ballad had slipped to number two in favour of an equally morbid lament from Eric Carmen who told us time and time again that he was 'All by Myself.' Personally, I wasn't in the least surprised.

On Sundays, in the middle of the summer the coastal road that passed the gates of the *parco* became one long traffic jam of tiny Cinquecentos crammed with happy Neapolitan families, iceboxes and blown-up lilos piled high on the roof, driving to and from the local beach. A journey that theoretically should take fifteen minutes could take an hour or more. You had to be mad to venture out and join them.

Our neighbours on either side were both Americans. On our left we had Bernie and Barbie from Missouri, who had been living there for years, and on our right were Betty and Rich from New Mexico, who were newcomers like us. The majority of the villas in the *parco* were rented to Americans or Britons, so was it any wonder that my ability to speak the Italian language made little progress?

One Italian couple lived three doors away, but they kept themselves very much to themselves and hardly spoke except for a polite *buon giorno* when we passed. On the other hand, their little dog was very friendly. Encouraged by my children, Willie, a sort of sheltie-cum-corgi with a Basil Brush tail, would drop in daily for a biscuit and a chat. Willie was a bilingual dog whose yowls almost made sense. When the breadwinner's car drove in the through the gate, Willie would bound into the kitchen singing 'Jack's back,' and after an absence of a week, when asked where he had been, he would sit himself down in the middle of the kitchen floor and bring me up to date on his love life in almost comprehensible dog-speak.

Driving in Naples was rather like taking everlasting rides on the dodgems, and he who could get his nose ahead was the undisputed winner. I used to wonder if there was an Italian equivalent of our Highway Code. If there was, it must have been a very slim volume. Italian drivers really were a law unto themselves. At night there were extra hazards, like road checks mounted by *Polizia* with guns. Usually we were waved through by an officer with a lollipop wand, thanks to the magic powers of the special AFI (Allied Forces in Italy) car plates issued to the members of NATO, but it was unwise to assume that this privilege was automatic— as a certain Naval officer, returning from collecting his maiden aunt from the airport, found to his cost.

'Shouldn't you be stopping, Alistair?' Aunty asked anxiously as her nephew accelerated away. 'That man seems to be shouting at us.'

'Don't fuss Aunty,' Alistair laughed, confidently. 'Cars carrying AFI plates are never stopped.'

It was doubtful if she heard him above the rattle of machine-gun bullets ricocheting off the car boot.

Fortunately, Alistair's back seat passenger emerged from the experience un-scathed, and, as she explained in an imperious tone to the *Polizia*, this was not quite the welcome she had expected to his country. After apologies all round, the party was allowed to proceed with no more than a warning. The car bravely bore its battle scars for the duration of its time in Italy, and probably carried them all the way home to England.

Many of the NATO wives, especially the Americans, refused to drive in down-town Naples or into the surrounding countryside. My neighbour Betty absolutely

'Cars carrying AFI plates are never stopped.'

refused to take her big Pontiac station wagon to anywhere other than the PX and American Commissary on the base. She would go straight down the toll road and back again for her weekly shop, never diverting so much as a yard from the route. She said she thought I was very brave to drive in such awful traffic on my own. What she really meant was mad.

'It's not so bad once you get used to it,' I promised. 'Why don't you come with me some time?'

A week later my husband asked me if I would pop to the Corso Umberto. No one popped to the Corso Umberto: such an outing was an adventure. I telephoned Betty.

'Why don't you come too?'

'Gee! Downtown Naples. That sounds like fun.'

'Pick you up at 9.30 sharp tomorrow morning.'

Next morning she was standing at the gate, looking pale and nervous.

'I'm not sure I should come. I've been sick all night.'

'Come on. It'll do you good,' I said, thinking she was just being 'chicken'.

Reluctantly, she climbed into the car, and as we drove along she clung on to the door handle, eyes closed, feet rammed hard on the floor, growing greener by the minute. Eventually I found somewhere to park Arabella. Betty opened her eyes and whispered weakly.

'Are we there?'

'Come on. A walk will help,' I replied, assuming that, once out of the car, she would recover.

We were barely half way up the street she announced that she could go no further.

'Maybe I've got a bug.' She did look rather a nasty colour.

I handed her the car key and told her to go and sit in the car. I would be back in a jiffy. Returning fifteen minutes later, I was puzzled to discover the car still empty, the doors locked. Naturally concerned, I walked up and down the street, peering into every shop, even into bars, though, frankly, Betty was not the sort of person to drop in somewhere for a quick snifter. Still, she had been feeling poorly. But Betty seemed to have vanished into thin air. Was she suffering from amnesia or, worse still, had she been abducted? It's amazing how the mind can play tricks with one's imagination. What was I to do?

'Did you get your errands done?'

I turned to see whence the voice was coming. There she was, sitting in the passenger seat of a white Fiat not unlike my own but a lot younger and less battered. It also had an anti-theft deterrent in the form of huge chain wound round the steering wheel.

'What are you doing in there?' I hissed.

'Why, what's the problem?'

'The problem is that this is not my car.'

'But your key opened the door.'

'I can't help that. Just believe me that this is not Arabella, and if you don't hop out smartish we'll be in a heap of trouble.'

The last thing I wanted was to have to explain to the owner in my broken Italian why a blonde, blue-eyed American lady was sitting in his car. My God, what if he thought she was propositioning him? I grabbed Betty by the hand and sprinted off round the corner to where the faithful Arabella sat patiently waiting.

'I'm sorry but all these little Italian cars look the same to me,' she sighed, pressing her hand to her fevered brow as I performed the fastest U-turn of my life.

Nought for observation, Betty. My little car was very distinctive since Deborah had given her a face-paint job. A pair of eyelashes curled, Disney-fashion, above her headlights, whilst from a mouse-like button 'nose' grew a fine pair of whiskers. As far as I was aware, there was not another like her in the whole of Naples, or indeed Italy.

With or without Betty, a visit to Naples by car was never relaxing. The traffic had long since passed the point of exasperation. On 19 September it was likely to be even more diabolical as this was a very important day in Naples—the day of the famous ceremony involving the liquefaction (or otherwise) of the blood of San Gennaro, the city's patron saint.

San Gennaro is the saint who protects the city against natural disasters. The saint's head (or, I should say, the skull) is kept in the cathedral, locked in a safe with a silver door in an ornately decorated chapel glittering with gold, silver and precious stones along with the phials that contain a hard brown substance, said to be his sacred blood that liquefies and boils three times a year. If the blood liquefies quickly, it is accepted that all will be well for the city; if it takes a long time, gloom starts to spread; if it fails completely, all manner of disasters will occur.

There are not many places in the world where one can make a date to witness a miracle, but, according to the local American radio network, this year's miracle would take place any time after 10.00 a.m. Rapidly I made a couple of 'phone calls and had no problem persuading two other British wives, Mary Biddiscombe and Lavinia Anson (the same Lavinia who had been my predecessor in the Roman apartment), to come with me to watch the spectacle. We decided not to drive; instead, we would catch the two-coach train that left from our local station at Licola. We bought our tickets in time to catch the 8.10, which left at 8.40. An hour later we disembarked at Montesanto and ran down the shiny, cobbled main street of Spaccanapoli, dodging cars, scooters and revving mopeds, and turned into the Via Duomo, too late for the religious procession that had taken place much earlier but still in time for a miracle. This is the area of pickpockets and the Neapolitan Mafia, an area irresistibly vibrant by day though one to be avoided at night. The streets were decked out in bunting and strings of coloured lights. Roadside stalls offered balloons, junk jewellery and toys, sticky toffee, nuts and yellow beans, and shiny red and gold busts of San Gennero looking like foil-wrapped chocolate Santa Clauses lined the street.

The interior of the cathedral was heaving with crowds, milling and jostling for a good vantage point. From the back we could just make out the distant figures of the red-and-purple-robed cardinals and priests. The atmosphere was tense; clearly, something was expected to happen at any minute. All around us people were chanting, calling out to the saint by name. The closer we elbowed our way to the altar, the thicker became the crowd. The heat was intense. Never mind the blood of the saint; I could feel *myself* beginning to liquefy.

We all agreed that what we needed was more elevation or we wouldn't see a thing. Enviously, we glanced at a group of swarthy-looking men of a gangsterish mien enjoying a bandstand view of the proceedings from the steps leading up to a marble pulpit. That was where we needed to be, but there was not much chance of our getting up there unless . . .

We both looked at Mary, who was the tallest of our trio.

'I'm game if you are.'

We nodded. Irreverently Mary put her foot on a convenient ledge and hoisted herself over the parapet of the pulpit and then hauled first Vin and then me up after her—to the astonishment of the male occupants, who, fortunately, were immediately distracted by the cries from the congregation. We had arrived not a minute too soon. The priest held up the circular reliquary in which the ancient phials were enclosed between two clear circles of glass, tilting it this way and that,

140

to show the ecstatic congregation that the dark red substance was indeed fluid. The good news was greeted with sighs of joy, applause and a volley of rifle fire. After a prayer of gratitude had been offered, the people rushed forward to kiss the relic. The choir burst into song with 'San Gennaro be praised.'

One of the Mafia look-alikes said something to Italian-speaking Vin, who consulted her watch. He sighed with relief.

'Sometimes,' he told her, 'you can wait all day for the blood to liquefy—and the cardinal will talk for most of it.' Was it really a miracle that the American Radio Network forecast was right on the dot?

We beat a hasty and undignified retreat. Disembarking from the train at Licola, we were greeted by the strong smell of grape juice. In the short time we had been away the small booking hall had been stacked with wine kegs, and outside, in the

We all agreed that what we needed was more elevation . . .

area normally reserved for parking, we found *Signor* and *Signora* Stationmaster, Nonna, Zio and Zia and all the *ragazzi* busy pressing the harvest from the family vineyard.

Delighted when we showed an interest, they offered us a glass of their latest vintage, and when we assured them that it was '*molto buono*' they hastened to top up our glasses not once but many times. Why not stay for a plate of pasta?

Somewhat later than expected, we rolled home each clutching a litre bottle of non-vintage Vino del Stazione after what had been a truly miraculous day!

— 17 —
Neapolitan Life

OUR days in Naples were never dull: there was always something going on. 1977 was the year of the Queen's Silver Jubilee, an occasion for some celebration. The British community held a garden fête in Carney Park, a vast, bowl-shaped crater in the centre of the local walk-in volcano that had been transformed into a massive recreational area for the Americans and their NATO friends and families to play anything from baseball to golf. The fête was organised and co-ordinated by none other than my husband, who was thenceforth known as 'Jubilee Jack'. On this glorious day the ground was dotted with stalls selling the inevitable jubilee mugs and Union Jack aprons, there was a mock-up of a British pub where one could quaff a tankard of ale drawn from specially imported kegs of Red Barrel, and a barbecue grilled an endless supply of British bangers.

The day started with a game of cricket—the British against the Rest of the World. The team representing the Rest of the World, comprising various outcasts and vagabonds from the United States, Denmark, Canada and other far-flung corners, were the outright winners beating Great Britain by 56 runs. Some observers were heard to remark that the better team won; some said that the umpire had been got at; and the players themselves blamed the mixture of champagne and beer forced upon them every five overs by three delightful dolly birds bearing silver trays.

Other entertainment included a troop of Scottish dancers who performed reels, a knobbly-knee competition, and a display of belly dancing. Topping the bill was our very own Gracie (Fields), over from Capri with husband Boris to help entertain the troops. The glamorous seventy-nine-year-old treated the audience to a lusty rendering of songs, including 'Sally', and then led the community singing until it was time for God Save the Queen. The day raised £6,000 for the Jubilee Appeal.

Of course, there was also the inevitable Wives' Club activity, including lunch at the Officers' Club once a month at which attendance, though not obligatory, was encouraged. The food was usually a national dish from whichever country was hosting the occasion—moussaka, kebabs, pasta and so on—and whilst coffee was served the hostesses provided a cabaret. The Greeks imported traditional dancers, the Turks whirling dervishes, the Italian wives sang from Verdi and the Americans showed us films. In 1978 the British wives held a fashion show—not your slink-down-the-catwalk-parading-designer-wear-from-a-smart-Neapolitan-boutique type of show, more a bunch of amateurs wearing yesterday's faded glories. It was amazing what we found lurking on the rails of the base charity shop; there was even a wedding dress. So our show was 'themed'—a wedding with bride, brides-maids, best man and all. I don't remember volunteering to be the commentator, but somehow I ended up with a microphone in hand, and 'just the thing for the bride's mother' accompanied Mary twirling gracefully across the stage modelling an emerald green ensemble that had once belonged to the Commodore's wife.

'*Solo due cento lire*, ladies!'

The audience expressed their appreciation with loud applause.

There was always plenty to laugh at in Naples, most of it bizarre. Our in-house magazine, *Voice*, was full of accounts of experiences enjoyed (or otherwise) by readers. We aimed to fill the pages with everything from where to go and what to see to survival tips such as where to find a loo if caught short in downtown Naples, awarding cleanliness and comfort points according to a scale of one to five 'crossed legs' symbols. The anecdotal columns were the most popular. Everyone loved a story to which he or she could relate, especially if spiced with a little poetic licence, such as the tale of the Naval wife who took a visiting friend to the local market.

'So what do we want to buy?' she asked. The friend confessed she had no idea: she just wanted to browse and stall-shop.

The Friday market along the sea front at Pozzouli was in full swing, the choice of goods on sale overwhelming. Sandwiched in between the racks of designer dresses and a booth selling sheets and textiles they came to a stand heaped with ladies' undergarments—petticoats and frilly panties, girdles and flesh-confining corsets. Ladies of all dimensions were catered for.

'How about buying one of these?' suggested the Naval wife, pointing to the line of shoestring brassières fluttering like bunting in the sea breeze overhead. 'Some of them are really very pretty.'

The friend giggled. 'If I knew my size in Italian maybe I would.'

Unbeknown to her, the moustached lingerie vendor understood English. Eager for a sale, he was quickly by her side.

'*Signora* that is not a problem.' Then with the merest murmur of a '*permesso*', he stretched out his arms and firmly cupped the relevant part of her anatomy in his hands. '*Quaranto-otto!*' he announced confidently. '*Si*, forty-eight will do nicely.'

Aghast, she backed away as he turned to reach down towards a lacy little number. 'This one will fit. Only one thousand lire. A bargain. *D'accordo?*'

'Quaranto-otto!' he announced confidently.

Recovering her composure with admirable speed, she fixed him with a steely eye. 'And what if it doesn't fit? Will you change it?'

'Si, *Signora,* but'—with a twinkle in his eye—'believe me, I am never wrong!'

There were numerous contributions concerning the art of driving in Naples. The Italian manager of the British Store, Mr Cuccerre, chipped in with an article called 'Sex and the Italian Driver' in which he was happy to laugh at the expense of his own countrymen. 'Never forget that manhood is involved in even the most casual traffic encounter.' He was absolutely right. Beware the lady driver who thought she could overtake an Italian male without incurring his wrath and rage. It was probably just as well that she did not understand the meaning of his hand gesture as he cut her out at the next set of traffic lights. From Mr Cuccerre's article I quote: 'In Italy there are, as elsewhere, laws about streets, maximum permissible speeds, which side of the street you drive on, and so forth. However, these laws exist only as test of character and self-esteem. Stopping at a stop sign, for example, is prima facie evidence that the driver is, if male, a cuckold or, if female, frigid and barren. Contrarily, driving through a stop sign is proof not only that you are virile and fertile, but that you a person of consequence.' Bearing all this in mind, we all learned to drive like maniacs, which was fine until we entered the base, where failure to obey all the rules could lead to serious trouble, as I discovered to my chagrin when I was pulled over for failing to obey what seemed to me to be a totally unnecessary stop sign. Protesting that there wasn't another car in sight failed to sway the US military policeman from his duty. My husband was not amused when he received a citation informing him that four traffic points had been awarded against him for a traffic violation. Indignant as only a man can be, he swiftly returned the disposition form pointing out that it was his wife who had been at the wheel, not he. The form was returned with an apology and a note to the effect that the points assessed had been transferred to his wife's driving record. The amended citation was pinned on the back wall of the downstairs loo for his chauvinistic friends to smirk at.

Half the fun of living in Naples was that we never knew what would happen next. Even the weather could take us by surprise. There were many thunderstorms, especially in the summer, and, when it rained, the rain was more often than not tropical, resulting in damage to the fragile infrastructure. The electricity came and went and roads could disintegrate before one's eyes—as I discovered one June day whilst driving to Bagnoli through a river of muddy water. Suddenly, from out of the rain-sodden gloom, a small man waving his umbrella materialised. At first I thought he was just trying to cadge a ride and I kept my foot firmly on the accelerator. Then he started to run beside me thumping on my roof and crying 'Signora, stop.' I braked in the nick of time. Horrified, I was staring into a forty-yard crater that had appeared in the middle of the Domitiana. Some say it was possible to see the ruin of an ancient Greek temple far below, but I cannot verify the story.

What I do remember is that for the next six weeks a stretch of our only road to the base remained closed. All the coastal traffic was forced to use a diversion along pot-holed back roads, adding hours to any journey. As always in Italy, however, there was a way round every obstacle. Word got about that a track through a field had been discovered that allowed us to circumnavigate the hole. After all the rain, the track was somewhat bumpy and squelchy and had to be negotiated with care, but it was better than using the lengthy diversion. At first just one or two cars were using the trail, but by the end of the week the line of AFI traffic resembled a refugee convoy. One morning we found the exit manned by an extraordinary, rotund, Giles-like grandma figure, swaddled in many layers of sweaters, with a man's cap perched on a halo of bleached frizz and demanding the payment of a toll. Who she was and, more relevantly, what right she had to be there no one knew, but one thing was for sure—she had no intention of letting any cars through unless the drivers first handing over 200 *lire*. By the end of the week she had her business down to a fine art, collecting our coins with one hand whilst with the other directing the traffic through the gate as skilfully as a policeman on duty in

Piazza Venezia. Those of us whom she recognised as her *regulare clientèla* were blown a kiss. A week after the Domitiana reopened we heard that our *Signora* was neither the landowner nor even an impoverished Countess from Pozzouli (as had been suggested by some romantic) but just a little old lady who had spotted a chance to earn some money.

The temporary loss of electricity was something to which we grew accustomed. One clap of thunder, and out would go all the lights. Fortunately, power was usually restored within an hour. Some people were not so lucky. Those who defaulted on the payment of their bill could return home and find that their supply had been cut without a word of warning; getting it restored could require a good deal of patience.

Anxious to avoid such a disaster, I was quite prepared to pay our bill on time. There was only one problem. Owing to the reluctance of the meter man to climb our hill, six months into our tenancy no demand had been received. Should we let sleeping *carne* lie or should we try and sort things out? Rightly or wrongly, we opted for the latter. Sometimes I wonder why. In England, such problems could be cleared up on the telephone; in Italy, an expedition to the offices of ENAL was the only way. Jack set off, accompanied by the gorgeous Giorgio, one of the Italian Naval officers who worked in the same office as Jack, to act as interpreter, armed with the up-to-date reading of our meter.

The tiny office was overflowing with customers waving their bills, as agitated as a bunch of backbenchers on Budget Day. Some had fistfuls of money in their hands (cheque books were distrusted), others just bills they wanted to dispute. It seemed that half the queue had stories of mishaps to relate to the bored official behind the counter. It looked as if they would be there for hours. Eventually they arrived at the cashier's window, only to be elbowed aside by a short, thick-set customer, his clothes reeking of garlic and cigarette smoke. He thumped the counter and ranted and raved. Georgio explained afterwards that it appeared that ENAL had cut off his electricity six months previously and that, although he had paid his bill, his supply had not been restored. And now, to add insult to injury, they had billed him for electricity he had been unable to consume, threatening him with a trip to court if he did not pay up. Thanks to Georgio, our bill was sorted out within an hour—quite quickly, all things considered—and a payment made on account. From then we received bills regularly, though they were always estimated, presumably because the meter-reader could never find our villa. In retrospect. I am sure we could have left the country without paying ENAL a *lira*, but at least we never had our electricity disconnected.

Obtaining any form of official documentation was a nightmare. Hours were spent queuing and filling in forms. A visit to at least two windows if not more was essential before the requisite number of stamps was obtained. Members of NATO

147

were entitled to drive one car free of road tax and to buy special petrol coupons, provided their car had the special AFI number plates. These were obtained at the offices of ACI, the Italian equivalent of the AA. This privilege was not dispensed without considerable delay, however. It took Jack three visits—the first to obtain a form, the second to submit it completed (in Italian) and the third for a re-write—before the plates were allocated. Of course, there were ways to hurry up the procedure: I wouldn't say that the system was corrupt, but the gift of a carton of Marlboro cigarettes worked wonders. Prized because they were considered superior to the locally manufactured product, American Marlboros were happily accepted as currency. A carton represented a week's wages for the gardener, and one packet slipped to the parking attendant guaranteed exemption from a ticket. It took a little time to adjust to the idea, but, when in Naples . . .

After six months in Rome we were already very security-minded. Even in the *parco* we never left the villa without closing every *persiana* (the heavy slatted wooden shutters) and locking every door. When going shopping it was unwise to carry a handbag. Yet one had to carry cash—cheques were rarely welcomed, and in those days credit cards were almost unheard of. I would go into Naples with my money hidden in my bra, even though it meant performing a kind of striptease act in the middle of the flea market. Some shops in downtown Naples actually provided changing rooms for this very purpose.

It was a long time before I could confidently calculate the correct sum of money that was required. Long strings of numbers, even when spoken in English, tend to leave me performing mental arithmetic acrobatics. Said fast enough, the price of even a modest slice of cheese could sound like the national debt. I did most of my food shopping at the local supermarket, where it was so much easier to sneak a look at the till to discover what you owed. Only if I had time to spare would I venture into one of those wonderful scented caverns where long, sausage-like nets of salami, hams and strings of garlic hung from the ceiling, or visit the fish market by the harbour at Pozzouli for fresh-out-of-the-sea sardines and anchovies.

Shopping in small shops required infinite patience. Even a quarter of *prosciutto* could take for ever to buy if there were other customers in the shop. Nothing was purchased without first holding a discussion about the result of last night's football match or the latest scandal from the political front. Purchases never left the shop without first being immaculately gift-wrapped. All this took time.

Nothing emphasised the changing of the seasons more than the choice of vegetables and fruit on sale at our local stall. Everything Pietro sold came from his gardens; nothing was imported. From January to May there were cabbages, cauliflowers both white and green, celery, and huge white bulbs of aniseed-scented fennel. Then, overnight, these vegetables would be unavailable and not be seen again until Christmas. Ask for an orange after June and Pietro would look at you as if you were mad. The disappearance of melons in early November heralded the approach of winter, and chestnuts and walnuts featured in the autumnal displays—but just try and find a grape in December! Strawberries came in May, beautifully arranged in little, hand-woven baskets, which we saved to make baby dolls' cribs for the Christmas bazaar, but always there were mountains of fresh salads and huge chains of garlic—and, of course, tomatoes (without which the Italian nation would disintegrate) in all kinds and shapes and sizes, always full of sun-filled flavour. Demi-johns of raw, drink-up-quick 'plonk' pressed from the grapes that grew on the vines behind the shack were on sale from mid-September. Judging by the rich magenta colour of the feet of the family, the grapes must have been pressed in the good old-fashioned way.

We soon learned about seasonal shopping. All summer the exteriors of the shops were strung with blow-up dinghies, lilos and snorkelling gear, but come the first week in September you could not buy a beach ball for love nor money. I wanted a kettle in August, but the shopkeeper looked at me in amazement. He never stocked kettles until the autumn, and it was at least another month before he was expecting a delivery. The same applied to clothes. By September cool print dresses were no longer displayed at the travelling street market. Even if the temperature was in the eighties, stall-holders filled their rails with fake furs and leather jackets. It was no use trying to buy a pair of sandals, but the choice of leather knee-high boots was infinite. In October the shutters were removed in Ski Alley to reveal the latest fashions in skiwear, although it was unlikely that a single flake of snow would fall in the Abruzzi until New Year.

As soon as the feast of Ferragosta was over, the endless procession of beach-bound Cinquecentos, their roofs piled high with *chaise longues*, cold boxes and wine jars, was reduced to a trickle. At last we could change up from first gear as we drove down the Domitiana. From September all the *piscine* were emptied and at the beach the concessionaires packed away the parasols. We were able to go to the beach free. The sea was empty. No self-respecting Italian would so much as dip a toe for fear of catching some terrible malady. The drawback was that, once the beach was free, the shacks that during the summer sold cola, pizza and *gelato* assumed an air of dereliction and no one came to clean the sand. Soon the flotsam and jetsam thrown up by an unexpected storm piled high, and it remained there until the start of the following season. It would have been hard to find a bigger contrast.

Christmas came and went relatively quietly, but the birth of the New Year was celebrated with a huge display of pyrotechnics as a million rockets and firecrackers exploded in one gigantic percussion of pops and crackles, filling Naples Bay first with blinding illumination and then with a cordite-scented fog which finally enveloped Vesuvius. We drove home in the small hours of the morning, slaloming through an obstacle course of broken furniture, saucepans and china that had been thrown out of windows for good luck.

There was little time to sleep off the effects of the night of revelry. We were all invited to work off our hangovers by competing in an inter-*parco* hockey match. The invitation read, 'No ability or knowledge of the rules of the game required, the only obligation being to wear fancy dress. All the family invited to participate.' At ten thirty sharp the two teams appeared, dressed bizarrely in whatever garments they had managed to scrounge from the family closets—straw hats and wigs, lace tutus, caftans, shawls. Anything would do. Normally sober army officers stuffed inflated balloons beneath T-shirts and tucked up their petticoats to reveal size twelve tennis shoes. Boys wore their sisters' frocks; girls decorated their sports wear with tinsel. The game rules were flexible, the number of players in each team varying from ten to thirty, depending on the stamina of the contestants. The game was played with whatever weapons could be found—brooms, walking sticks, umbrellas, even (somewhat more conventionally) hockey sticks. A pair of rolled-up socks was, wisely, substituted for the ball. The task of umpiring fell to a United States Army colonel, who had promised to be entirely impartial. Parco Azzurro lost the toss and was condemned to spend the game battling uphill to the goal. There was no half time, nor were there any winners. We just fought on until the beer and sausage rolls ran out.

In January we planned our first assault on the ski slopes in the Abruzzi mountains. First, however, we needed the kit—the snowsuits, the hats, the boots and so on. The skis we would hire when we got there. The cheapest place to shop for bargain-priced skiwear was down in Naples, in Ski Alley. The group consensus was that the best way to travel to the centre of Naples was by train, and we duly met up on the station platform of our local branch line.

The journey into the city was as smooth as silk. Wandering between the rows of brilliantly coloured waterproofs, bobble hats and masks with full face-wrap was bemusing, but finally we were lured into the cubby-hole of one *Signor* Alberto, supplier of the latest designer gear to the top professionals. Rubbing his hands with glee, he soon had the children kitted out from top to toe, while for me there was an outfit in pillbox red that made me look like Michelin woman ('Gosh, Mum—at least we'll be able to spot you in a snowdrift!'), but Dad was not so easy. Alberto wore a worried frown. Neapolitans do not grow to the height of six foot one, and the longest pair of *salopettes* he had in stock was a good six inches too short. Refusing to be beaten, he added a further two inches by means of a pair of detachable braces. '*Alora!*' Looking very pleased with himself, he produced a pair of matching snow gaiters. The result was not exactly *chic*, but at least Jack would be able to keep the snow out of his boots.

Loaded with plastic bags, we struggled back to the *stazione*, only to discover that, without a word of warning, the train drivers had gone on strike (as was their wont) and there was nothing for it but to pass on the savings we had made in our bargain hunt to the taxi driver, who took us for a very expensive ride home. Win some, lose some—that was life in Naples.

On the Sunday morning the family were out of bed and in the car by six o'clock. We had a two-hour drive ahead of us, convoying behind our friend's car. Of course, everyone from Naples was on the road too. The Neapolitan traffic jam had moved up the mountain. By the time we parked it was nearing ten.

We piled out of the car, eager to get started: better make haste or there wouldn't be any skis left for hire. Actually, I got the last pair. What a relief! Never mind that they were as long as the QE2, or that the boots were excruciatingly uncomfortable— I was determined that, by the end of the morning, I would be zigzagging down the mountainside with the rest of the family. If only.

'How am I meant to control these things?' I gasped as for the umpteenth time the giant skis slid away from beneath me.

I finally managed to stay upright for about ten yards before ending up in an undignified heap in the middle of the queue of skiers waiting for their turn on the lift and having to be helped to my feet by a dashing *signor*. I was whacked. The rest of the family were itching to be gone.

'Why don't you buzz off and have fun?' I suggested wearily. 'I'll have a wee rest and enjoy the view.' Perhaps people-watching was more my style.

Much of the charm and chaos of the streets of Naples was duplicated on the slopes of the Abruzzi. It was most important for young Romeo or Giulia, and even their Papas, to be seen wearing the latest trend in snow-wear: no one wanted to be spotted in last year's gear. Even on the piste it was all about the pursuit of *la bella figura*. Mama was happiest parading her new fur coats and taking photographs of her *ragazzi* behaving like embryo Ferrari drivers on their toboggans, oblivious to the fact that they were causing an obstruction.

That night we stayed in a sort of hostelry, sleeping in rows of double bunks and steam-heated to boiling point. Next morning I woke feeling as if every bone in my body had been welded together. The snow outside had turned to sheet ice.

'No thanks,' I said. Somebody had to be fit to drive home.

One of the glorious things about being posted to a country like Italy was that one is never short of somewhere to go for an outing. School holidays were spent visiting as many of the multi-starred tourist attractions as there was time for. Even if one's children were unimpressed by mighty works of art and architecture, Pompeii and Herculaneum never lost their fascination. Out-of-season visits to anywhere along the breathtaking Amalfi coast were popular, as was taking a ride to the top of Vesuvius on the chairlift with feet brushing through the tops of the wild broom that grew in such profusion. On Boxing Day we drove some twenty miles south of Naples to Pæstrum and sat eating our turkey sandwiches on the honey-coloured steps of what is arguably one of the finest Greek temples anywhere in Europe.

We had access to many fascinating sites often missed by less fortunate tourists on package holidays. Just down the road was Pozzuoli, once Rome's chief trading port with the East and still a busy little seaport. We would sit and drink an *espresso* on the waterfront and watch the world go by. Time had changed little. Maybe the young wore jeans rather than togas, but it was not hard to imagine what it was like in Roman days.

Close by the Phlegræan Fields, still bubbling with volcanic activity, stood one of the best examples of a Roman amphitheatre but, like so much in and around Naples, hopelessly lost in the city's modern sprawl. Clustered upon the cliffs to the south-west, one could see all that remains of the once famous spa of Baiæ. Anyone who was anyone in Roman history came here to escape the heat of the capital—Marius, Pompey, Julius Cæsar, Tiberius and Nero had all built holiday villas. Most of the ancient city is now under water, a victim of the same earthly upheavals that have affected the area during this millennium. Here we snorkelled, floating just a few feet above what had once been a grand Roman harbour, stood on the tops of submerged pillars, our heads just above water, and duck-dived for shards of barnacle-encrusted Roman pottery. Valueless they may have been, but to the children they were priceless treasure.

A cycle ride away from where we lived stood the Acropolis of Cumæ. Here the children played happily where wild thyme, wood sorrel and clover sprouted amongst the cracked paving stones. The ancient city has long since vanished, but the Acropolis remains, a tall, romantic hill with temples on the summit and a honey-combed labyrinth of passages below, leading to the eerie hall where once the Sybil was said to have prophesied the future of Claudius. Nearby is Lago d'Averno, the supposed entrance to Hades, a spooky mysterious place over which it was said to be impossible for a bird to fly without being swallowed up. Certainly I never saw birds there, but the more likely reason was that they been shot by a local. This was a sport considered very 'macho' by some Italian males, who can easily be recognised by the bandolier of shotgun cartridges they wear slung across their chests.

There was a price to pay for living in such a beautiful corner of the world: I can't remember how many Saturday evenings we spent at the airport, waiting for the cheap, late-night flights to arrive from London. At first we played the rôles of host and hostess with zeal. It was lovely seeing all our friends of course, but pretty soon the novelty of slogging round the tourist circuit palled.

'Not Pompeii again' I would groan. 'Wouldn't they like to climb to the top of Vesuvius on their own?'

Thus we started lending our visitors maps and guidebooks, and even the keys to our car. I would wave them goodbye with a 'Have fun and take care', never letting them leave without first stressing the importance of looking after their personal possessions. Most of our guests returned home unscathed, but the luck ran out for some chums from Fleet. They had hired a car and gone for a drive along the Amalfi coast. They had a lovely time, and had stayed the night at a perfect hotel at Positano but, returning home, had somehow missed the turning for the *Tangenziale* and had ended up lost in the centre of Naples—not a good place to be in the middle of a hot afternoon in July, or at any time of the day when you are a stranger.

A man wearing an official-looking uniform complete with regulation white top hat poked his head in through the drivers' window. Were they lost? Where did they want to go? The *Tangenziele? Si.* Gratefully, they listened to his instructions on how to get back to the toll road. He even held up the traffic to let them through, but not before he had surreptitiously taken the opportunity to scan the contents of the car, checking on the accessibility of the ladies' handbags whilst applying an overdose of Neapolitan charm. He hoped the *signore e signori* were having a wonderful holiday. He apologised for the terrible traffic. And all the time his eyes were wandering.

Ten minutes later, all smiles, they spied the arrow pointing to the *Tangenziale.* Their relief was short-lived as, seconds later, a van pulled out in front, blocking the slip road. Frank leaned on the horn. Nothing happened, so he hit the horn again, this time for longer. Distracted, the girls never saw the motorcycle that drew up alongside, never saw the brick the pillion rider had in his hand until it came crashing through the window, barely saw the hand that deftly snatched their handbags from their laps. It all happened so fast that the motorcycle and their possessions were gone before the reality had sunk home. Only then my friends remembered that they had forgotten the cardinal rule: always hide valuables under the car seats.

Slowly and sadly, they continued on their journey, picking the glass out of their clothes. Fortunately none of them were physically hurt, but their holiday was spoilt. Apart from the loss of money, passports and cameras, they were deeply traumatised. It was a miserable way to end what had been up to then a wonderful break.

Such assaults were not uncommon, unfortunately. It was all too easy for the thieves to pick out tourists. Hire cars were recognisable by their licence plates. Whilst chatting up the ladies, the 'helpful guide' in Piazza Stagione had needed only one glance inside the car to spot easy pickings. By the time our friends had reached the slip road, the message had been passed along the grapevine to the modern-day highwaymen, who were ready and waiting.

In October 1978 we were due to return to England. Our last months in the sunshine were a mixture of happiness and sadness at the thought that we would soon be leaving this maddening, frustrating, yet addictive part of Italy. Even the prospect of a protracted holiday *en route* did little to quench our sense of loss. Rome and Naples had provided a wonderful and quite extraordinary experience, and one we would remember for a very long time, as we would the number of good friends to whom we would have to say goodbye (though, we hoped, to some only temporarily).

Although the number of British servicemen by comparison to the Americans was tiny, we could not have had a better bunch to serve with if we had hand-picked them ourselves. Friendships made then have endured to this day.

The inauguration of the Va Bene Club took place one evening while we were seated around a Formica-top table in our local *pizzeria* in Arco Felice, where some of us used to gravitate when we wanted to let down our hair. At Marco's you could get a carafe of wine and a cartwheel-size pizza for 2,000 *lire* a head. Half of the group were leaving Naples soon, having come to the end of their tour. Someone said, 'We must meet up again when we get back to UK. Why don't we have an annual reunion?'

'Absolutely!'

The idea was greeted with enthusiasm. *Va bene* means 'all goes well', or 'very good', and was an expression that even the poorest Italian speakers amongst us used a good deal, so it seemed an appropriate name to choose. Unbelievably, once a year members of the Va Bene Club still meet for lunch in the autumn—which says a lot for an idea that was born nearly thirty years ago.

Still, there we were, another tour of duty coming to an end. Once more our possessions were boxed up and the rooms at the Villa Ambra emptied. We could not hand the house on to our predecessors as the good *Dottore* had carried out his threat and sold his villa to an Italian family. Poor Betty wrote that, for months after we left, the noise of destruction and reconstruction was something un-believable.

We took to the road and slowly wended our way back to England. Jack's next appointment was Deputy Director Air Warfare. It sounded very grand, but it meant another spell of duty in the dreaded Ministry of Defence in London and, for the family, a move back to our home in Fleet.

— 18 —
London and the Surrey Hills

BY the time we returned to Fleet in October 1978 the trees that lined our avenue had long since shed their leaves and winter was well on its way. The skies above were leaden; as we turned into our cul-de-sac it began to rain. There was no sign of life—no balloons or festive banners, nobody there to welcome us back. This was hardly surprising as most of the houses were now occupied by total strangers, many of our original neighbours having sold up and moved on. We knew virtually no one.

There were different curtains at the windows of the house across the road, but that was not unexpected. I knew that Val and Mike had emigrated to New Zealand and that Mary and Noel had moved back to the Midlands. Elaine and David were still living next door; though in their Christmas card they had warned us that they were house-hunting, so presumably sooner or later even they would be gone. We had returned to stranger-land.

Shivering, we let ourselves back into Number Five and wandered from room to room. Although our tenants had left things clean and tidy, the house looked tired and shabby. Not really too surprising after three years' absence.

'A lick of paint will work wonders.'

'Maybe,' thinking it would take more than a tin of magnolia to make the house feel like ours again. How wrong you can be? Once we had unpacked and made the acquaintance of some of the newcomers, *la dolce vita* faded away into just one more happy memory. This didn't mean that we planned to stay in Fleet for ever. Frensham Avenue had been a happy place to live when the children were small, but now we had outgrown open-plan living. Sooner or later, when our Navy days were over, we would wish to move and put down roots. But first we had to find a *pied-à-terre* in London—somewhere with enough space for me to join Jack during term time.

Knowing that the hours Jack would be working in the MoD would be long, we had agreed that commuting was not an option, but finding even the humblest lodging within our price range was not easy. We studied the evening paper, highlighting anywhere that looked even vaguely promising, but, when he went to view, what he saw filled him with horror—over-priced, dank holes, most of them. Then Jack found an old friend beavering away behind one of the many desks in the Defence Department who told him that he and another Naval officer were sharing an apartment with the lady owner. Mary, he said, was happy to have members of the Senior Service as her tenants. He thought Jack would be welcome to rent the empty spare room and agreed to organise a viewing.

The flat was conveniently situated in Victoria, on the third floor of a five-storey terraced house at the back of Westminster Cathedral. Built in Edwardian times, the houses in Cardinal Mansions with their imposing red and white brick frontages and steep steps leading up to their porticos had been designed as homes for well-to-do, upper-middle-class Victorian families but now, like so many properties in London, were divided into flats. Jack agreed to rent the funny little wedge-shaped room at the back.

The room was furnished with a single bunk bed above a chest of drawers, a small wardrobe and a shiny horsehair sofa to which Jack chivalrously decamped when I invited myself to stay. The view from the one small window was of a feral pigeon nesting on top of the drainpipe. She was still sitting there when Jack moved out six months later.

I have no idea what the neighbouring flats were like inside as I never entered any of them, but I do know that Mary's was long overdue for modernisation and redecoration, especially in the non-designer kitchen where the exposed wiring dripping from the ceiling in skeins would surely have made the hair on the head of a health and safety officer stand on end. Cupboards and drawers overflowed with a collector's treasure trove of ancient pots and pans and gadgets, and the gas stove was a museum piece. Little light filtered through the solitary grimy window—which was probably just as well. What the eyes don't see . . .

Apart from the kitchen there was a large reception room that served as the living-cum-dining room with dusty, floor-to-ceiling, burgundy velvet curtains, squashy sofas and standard lamps with silk fringed shades decorated with Christmas-card scenes of coaches and horses and inns with tiny cut-out windows through which a dim light beamed faintly. On the narrow wrought-iron balcony overlooking the road, a very dead Christmas tree forlornly lifted its needle-less branches to the sky, begging for a decent cremation.

The bathroom, with its bad-tempered geyser that spluttered indignantly into life when asked to fill the above-average-size tub, had probably not had a face-lift since before the war, but at least there was plenty of room to stretch out and enjoy a soak after returning from a foot-slogging day on London's pavements—with the added bonus of a serenade from our famous neighbour, the actor Andrew

Cruickshank (alias Doctor Cameron), who lived on the other side of the partitioning wall. Everyone had good-sized bedroom except Jack, who, being last man in, was stuck with his little wedge-shaped room at the back.

Our landlady Mary and her three Naval gentlemen lodgers lived in happy harmony. There was really only one house rule: to avoid kitchen chaos it had long ago been agreed that, Monday to Thursday, the flatmates would take it in turn to produce the evening meal. Pinned on the notice board was a duty roster.

The provision of this meal was taken very seriously. This was no thrown-together picnic, but a three-course meal served with wine, fit to grace a restaurant table. Commander M—— would return from the weekend struggling under the weight of cold boxes filled with foiled-wrapped dishes prepared by his wife. On the other hand, Captain D—— liked to do his own cooking. His speciality was curry, and very good it was too. The drawback was that he liked to prepare the dish before he went to work in the morning, leaving it simmering in the communal slow cookpot all day. By seven o'clock the aroma of frying garlic heavily laced with Oriental spices had permeated every corner of the flat, seeping under the door into my bed space. Yuk!

Jack had never shown any interest in cooking—bacon and eggs was about the sum total of his culinary skills—and so having to provide dinner for four was to prove quite a challenge. During term time I would come to his rescue, driving up to London with my apron and shopping basket, but during the school holidays he had to manage on his own. I have no idea how he would have coped had there not been an open-all-hours convenience store round the corner. Mr Khan's chill cabinets were well stocked with foil-wrapped, ready-to-pop-in-the-oven meals, his shelves were crammed with cans of soup and his freezer overflowed with ice cream. Perfect! All Jack had to do was synchronise the oven and the boiling water for the frozen peas whilst serving up the contents of the cans of soup for the starter course, and he had cracked the problem of how to serve up, if not banquet, then at least a feast for four.

Meanwhile we continued to search for somewhere more self-contained for both of us to stay, and when, after six months, Jack received a 'phone call asking if he was interested in renting a small ground-floor flat in Dolphin Square he said 'Yes, please' without hesitation.

We were so lucky. Dolphin Square, looming with art deco grandeur behind its impressive arched entrance, sits between the Thames to the south and Pimlico to the north. It had over a thousand flats, complete with a well laid out garden, an indoor swimming pool and a restaurant. There could have been no more desirable place to live.

The accommodation is divided in thirteen 'houses', each named after a famous navigator or Admiral. Jack's modest flat, really just a bed-sit with a bathroom and a doll's house-sized kitchen, was on the ground floor in Keyes House. He had been grateful for the six months in Victoria, but having his own front door was a joy, as was the freedom to eat when and where he liked. We furnished the flat with bits and pieces brought up from home and a stove and a pull-out sofa bed that we found advertised on the communal notice board. The rent was phenomenally low and all the hot water arrived free of charge courtesy of Battersea Power Station just across the river.

Dolphin Square was a really handy place to live, as many MPs have found. During term time I would catch the National Express bus up to London on Tuesdays and stay until Friday, having a whale of time visiting museums, going to the theatre and spending a few hours helping Anne Murray, the secretary in the office of the Fleet Air Arm Association in Piccadilly. Time passed all too quickly.

That year we had the moving bug. Almost the same week we were given the key to the Dolphin Square flat, we moved from Fleet. We had spent many weekends scouring the countryside from east Sussex to west Hampshire, in search of a new home to buy. We saw some pretty awful places, learning quickly that phrases like 'has plenty of potential' meant that a great deal of time and money needed to be spent to make them habitable. We were in one of those discouraging periods of 'property drought', when estate agents shook their heads and said, 'Nothing on the market—at least, nothing at your price.' We knew we could sell our own modern conventional home at the drop of a hat, but what we couldn't find was a house with character to replace it. For six months we searched every leafy village in the southern counties, with no success.

When the particulars featuring a picture of a red-brick cottage at Hindhead on the Surrey/Hampshire border dropped through the letterbox, I was amazed. Four bedrooms, one of them twenty feet long, a study and a third of an acre of garden backing on to National Trust Land—all for £45,000 (which, even in 1979, sounded cheap). There had to be a snag, and of course there was: the A3 passed right by the front door. Anyone who has driven along the road that runs from London to Portsmouth with traffic lights at Hindhead knows what I'm talking about when I say the road is very busy.

'You'll fall in love with the place once you're through the front door,' the agent assured me, 'and there is talk of building a bypass.'

When? Well, he couldn't really say for sure. Common sense said tear up the details, but instead we made an appointment and drove over on a Saturday afternoon in May. We parked on the opposite side of the road and looked across at what was admittedly an unusual cottage-style house, with leaded light windows, clematis climbing over the porch and roses blooming in the front. Unfortunately, the line of vehicles drifting up to the traffic lights continuously blocked our view.

'There is absolutely no way we are going to live here,' Jack said.

I agreed. It would be sheer madness.

'Let's make a quick get-away. We can telephone from home to apologise.'

'We can't. The lady of the house is standing on the doorstep, waving.' We both knew how dire it is to get a house looking spick and span for viewing and then have nobody show up. 'The least we can do is go and take a look.'

So we took our lives in our hands and threaded our way between a double-decker bus and a van and passed for the first time through the portals of the dwelling that was destined to become our future home. Once the front door closed, we knew that the house was exactly what we had been looking for—a cottage-like interior with bags of character and space. It even had an outside loo! At the back, the garden, informally planted with rhododendrons and azaleas, had a view to die for along the valley as far as the South Downs.

Next door stood Undershaw, the house that the author Sir Arthur Conan Doyle had built at the turn of the century. Our house had once been his gardener's cottage but had been sold and in 1920 had been extended so that what had once been a two-up-and-two-down dwelling was now a spacious four-bedroom home of character. We were shown a living room with a wide bay and leaded-light windows and a twenty-foot-long dining room. Behind a pine door in the kitchen, a flight of stairs led to the upper part of the house where, before the extension had been built, there would have been two tiny bedrooms with eyebrow windows on either side of the bricked-in chimney. Now this area was lined with cupboards. Beyond, we were taken into a huge room which could sleep six without difficulty.

The Little House was definitely the character home we were looking for. Apart from the road, it was perfect. As an investment, common sense told us that its location would pose problems. Every house has at least one wart; admittedly, this wart was more like a carbuncle, but it was this very carbuncle that brought the property within our price range. Joy and Jimmy, who owned The Little House, assured us that there was a very good chance a bypass would be built in the near future. Plans had been on the drawing board since 1930. In reality our gamble has paid off, although it has taken another twenty-five years for the Government to give the thumbs-up to a tunnel that will take the heavy traffic away from the village and leave the glorious acres of National Trust property on Hindhead Common and the Devil's Punchbowl traffic-free.

So we made an offer, which was accepted. Many a time during the coming months as we were waiting to exchange contracts I awoke in the night in a cold sweat. We had to be crazy even to contemplate living there! Yet Jack remained steady in his resolve. The only reason he could see for backing out of the deal was if planning permission to build a drive and garage was refused. Eventually we beat the bureaucrats and we got our way, and so the final obstacle was removed.

The house in Frensham Avenue was sold and we moved house once more, although we knew it would not be for the last time. Already we were thinking about Jack's next appointment, which was almost certain to be as the Commanding Officer of an Air Station; he had Yeovilton firmly in his sights. We were still unpacking our boxes when Jack received a phone call from the Naval Secretary that changed everything.

Jack asked me what I knew about Pretoria.

Not a lot, I had to admit, other than it was the capital of South Africa and that it was somewhere in the north of the Republic.

'Why?'

'I've been asked if I would be interested in going there as the Naval and Air Attaché. The First Sea Lord wants to get a Naval officer back down there.'

I had to sit down for a minute. 'And are you?'

'Interested? I might be. This is a difficult one.'

As far as I was concerned, Pretoria won hands-down, but this was not my call. It didn't take long for Jack to make up his mind. Influenced by having spent two exhausting years preserving the EH.101 Merlin helicopter project, amongst others, from being axed, he believed that, with all the cuts being imposed on the Navy by Minister of Defence John Nott, Yeovilton would not be the job it should have been. Pretoria offered a much-needed change of environment. The unforeseen Falklands War would of course change everything, but we were not to know that.

I must admit that I was somewhat surprised that the job attracted Jack, who had always said that he would refuse a diplomatic post, the reason being too much 'cocktail circuit' and not enough action, but, as he explained, South Africa would be different. Owing to the worldwide boycott of South Africa because of her apartheid laws, many countries were not represented, seriously limiting the Attaché social scene. Moreover, the embargo on the sale of defence equipment meant that there would be no sales to worry about. There would be a major requirement to 'snoop'—which he found far more attractive.

So we were off again, not to Somerset but to the Southern Hemisphere and a part of world I had never dreamed of inhabiting. But that was the way our life had always been—full of the unexpected. That's what made it so interesting.

Fortunately for us, it would be another twelve months before we left, giving us time to sort out the new house and time to plan what we would need to take with us for what would be a totally new experience. Taking full advantage of our staggeringly generous allowances, duty-free concessions and diplomatic discounts, we had a wonderful time shopping for china, crystal and silverware to grace our table so that we could entertain in a manner expected of an Attaché. At least we were spared the chore of stocking up on consumables such as toilet rolls and tins of butter as recommended in the *Attaché Wives' Good Guide to Survival* for families sent to postings classified as 'Hardship.' There was also time to wade through the thousand-odd pages of James Michener's *The Covenant*—a history of South Africa told in an easy-to-read, fictional format.

Although English is widely spoken in South Africa, we were sent on a course to learn Afrikaans. One-to-one lessons took place in a sparsely furnished room at the back of Selfridges. Marika, our teacher, was a charming coloured girl from the Cape. Jack took his studies very seriously and passed his course with distinction; I, on the other hand, was relieved to hear that I was not expected to take a test—which was just as well as I doubt whether I would have passed. Not that it mattered much. Most Afrikaners automatically spoke to me in English, and I very quickly forgot how to say anything more ambitious than *Bia Dankie!*

When not struggling with my classes, I was shopping. Going out to South Africa as the wife of an Attaché was a great excuse to top up my wardrobe. For the first time in my life I bought not one but three dresses at a go without feeling guilty. And, of course, I was bound to need another hat. From the huge range in the millinery department I selected a cartwheel of a creation made of silky tan-coloured velour embellished with wreath of pheasant feathers. The hat was enormous, as was the price tag, but I bought it.

'Shall I wrap it up for Madam?'

'No, I'll wear it.'

In my eye-catching ensemble of well-worn anorak and million-dollar hat I made my way down the escalator to the underground. By now it was rush hour. The tube was packed with six-foot-tall commuters. The feathers on my hat were about on a level with their noses. A space appeared around me as if by magic.

If I was not up in London I was busy in Hindhead sorting our new home. The first thing we did was change the name. 'The Little House' sounded just too twee. Below the garden was the Nutcombe Valley so we tried Nutcombe Cottage. No good—that had already been taken, as had Nutcombe Almost Everything Else—so we settled for Charnwood, where Jack had spent his boyhood.

Then the inevitable tribe of workmen had to be organised to attend to the roof, the drains and the electrics and to build a garage. Before we moved in, the mortgage company insisted that we had the property sprayed by Mr Woodworm, which meant lifting and then re-laying all the carpets. Tiles on the roof needed replacing, and my new next-door neighbour recommended just the man for the job. His name was Sean, and, yes, he was Irish—very. He was also drunk most of the time he worked for us. One day he was so sozzled that he put his ladder through one of the leaded-light windows. He tried to mend it as if it were a jigsaw puzzle and in the end I told him to forget it and called in a glazier.

The garage arrived as a flat pack and the drive was built by Mr Worman from Headley—and a very good job he made of it too. The ancient electrical circuits were

A space appeared around me as if by magic.

re-wired by Mr Smith from round the corner and the drains were sorted out by two merry lads from Liphook. It all took a while, as these things do: it was probably six months before peace reigned.

The news on the South African domestic front arrived in a letter from the Naval and Air Attaché incumbent, Group Captain Gerry Peasley. There was a house to go with the job, so there were no house-hunting worries. In the garden there was a swimming pool and a fascinating thatched structure referred to as The Barn—photos enclosed. It all looked very impressive.

Six months later, on 8 March 1982, we stepped off the aircraft at Johannesburg and began what was to be our last foreign posting.

— 19 —
Upwardly Mobile

SOUTH Africa. The very name conjures up romantic images of vast stretches of breathtaking scenery, flat-topped mountains, rugged coastlines and national parks rich in wildlife, all lit by an eternal sunlight. If I imagined that life was going to be one long safari, however, I could not have been more wrong. Of course, I knew that we weren't going to be living in the middle of the bush with wild animals on our doorstep, but I did not expect Pretoria to be quite so pristine or so modern—so many high-rise office blocks and American-style shopping malls; the streets broad and lined with jacarandas; the houses in the residential areas more Ascot than Africa. Not a grass hut in sight. If you wanted to see a lion then you went to the zoo.

As we drove north up the modern highway from Johannesburg Airport to Pretoria, the view from the car window was urban. Where no doubt in days gone by mighty herds of game had roamed, the sun-baked veldt was now pockmarked with clusters of boxy houses and billboards announcing the grand opening of a new hypermarket, and the only animals grazing were of the domesticated variety. Apart from the blazing sun, we could have been booming up the M1. Well, perhaps not the M1, but at least the autostrada.

We were travelling in tandem. Jack and I were riding with the Peasleys (Beryl and Gerry) in the Naval and Air Attaché's official car, a past-its-best-sell-by-date Ford Cortina, the worn leather sticking to our sweating limbs. At the wheel sat our official driver Zach, a big grin on his amiable black face. Our thirteen pieces of luggage plus one large hat box travelled behind in an even more ancient Land Rover, driven by the Army Staff Sergeant, a member of the small Defence Section team attached to the British Embassy.

'I thought the best thing to do was to go straight to the house.' Beryl said. 'Then I can introduce you to Violet.' Ah, yes—Violet. The maid-in-a-million, of whom Beryl had waxed so lyrical in her letters. 'After that we're having lunch with the Military Attaché and his wife, and then this evening we're all invited to a reception at the South African Defence Department, so we'll need to pick you up from your hotel at six-thirty.'

I gulped. After thirteen hours of travel I was feeling far from sociable.

'I'm afraid the next two weeks will be action-packed,' she told me happily. Beryl obviously enjoyed a party. 'But things will probably quieten down after we've left.' I wasn't sure what to read into that.

Our two vehicles proceeded slowly down Charles Street, a long, straight, tree-lined thoroughfare that runs east from the city through the strangely named suburb of New Muckleneuk. On either side large houses crouched behind screens of tropical shrubbery. There was a playing field where small, predominantly white boys were playing cricket. It was all very colonial.

The car turned into Number Seventy. Nervous butterflies fluttered in my stomach: like it or loath it, this would be our home for next two years.

My first impression as the car crunched up the shingle drive was of a large, white, two-storeyed house with square, metal-framed windows and a green tin roof that gleamed in the sun—a facsimile of the kind of house that my children drew during their first year at school. In front of the house was a sun-browned lawn the size of a tennis court and beds of flaming orange cannas lilies. On the step in front of the heavy wooden door a solitary figure in a pink overall, dilapidated tennis shoes and an unseasonable woolly hat waited to greet us with a shy smile on her dusky face.

'Welcome Madam,' she giggled and then dropped me a curtsey.

Heavens! Who did Violet think I was—royalty? Trying to appear suitably regal, I thanked her graciously and followed Beryl indoors to tour my palace. Unfortunately there the fantasy ended, for there was nothing majestic about Number Seventy. There was no gilt, no glitter, just a plain, four-bedroom property with large echoing rooms—a 'nothing' house, immensely practical but short on character. With a sinking heart, I knew that my hat would have to work very hard to make this barracks block feel like a home.

The house was rented from Mr Johan Voster, the incumbent South African Ambassador to Taiwan; the British Embassy supplied the furniture. Both house and furnishings were in need of a serious make-over, with top priority given to the kitchen with its cracked stone sink and antique cooking stove and to the replacement of the pygmy-sized double bed lost in the vastness of the master bedroom. The chintz covers on the settees were faded and the carpets worn. We were told that the landlord had promised to redecorate and renovate and the that the Embassy would refurnish. Of course that was good news. Alas, my enthusiasm was tempered by a feeling of *déjà-vu*: it did seem that where'er the Worths went a tribe of workmen was bound to follow.

Then I saw the back garden and immediately forgot my disappointment. How stupid I was being. Wasn't this the land of the great outdoors? Why grumble about the house's lack of character when we had a luxuriously large swimming pool and a forty-foot thatched summerhouse in our back yard.

The Barn, as the summerhouse was known, was as big as a bungalow. At one end stood a bar with a long counter, at the other a huge open fireplace built of rough stone and a matching tropical fishpond complete with dribbling fountain. The bar, the tall stools, the table and chairs were all fashioned from rattan. The cushions and curtains were colourfully cheery. The ghosts of many parties past lingered in the atmosphere. In the middle of a squashy cushion, a black and white cat lay sunbathing.

'Say hello to your new owner, Snuff.'

Snuff yawned and went back to sleep.

The tour was fast and furious as we were already late for our first social engagement—lunch with the Military Attaché and his wife.

Lisa and John deCandole lived further up Charles Street. We sat outside and ate quiche *al fresco* in a garden that was a riot of tropical colour. The setting was so paradisiacal that if it hadn't been for the endless flow of shoptalk I might have believed that we were on some exotic holiday rather than at the beginning of a two-year tour of duty.

There was no doubt that what I was hearing was a briefing, even if it was a light-hearted one. Names were dropped into the conversation, many heavy with Afrikaner inflections—General Van That or Mrs De The Other. I learned that one should wear kid gloves at all times (metaphorically speaking), especially when talking with members of the South African Military Intelligence Department—officially our hosts—whose job it was to keep the Attaché Corps in order. They were especially suspicious of the British. This was not really surprising, considering that Jack and John were here to monitor and report back on what was going on in their country militarily, on their capabilities, and about who, if anyone, was breaking the embargo. In short, Jack would be a spy—a rôle he would relish. In those days there was not a lot of love lost between the respective governments, and sometimes we would be walking a very thin line. None of it sounded terribly comforting.

I had arrived in South Africa armed with a little handbook entitled *What Every Good Attaché Wife Should Know*, lent to me by the wife of an ex-Attaché to Athens. But Athens had little in common with Pretoria. Thanks to the apartheid laws, South Africa was a country diplomatically boycotted by more than half the world. An Attaché in Athens or Paris attends a cocktail party almost every night of the week. In Pretoria the cocktail party circuit hardly existed, simply because there were few embassies and even fewer Attachés. Teams of visiting arms salesmen would not be sleeping in our guest room because there was an embargo on the sale of defence equipment. Of course, we already knew this—it was one of the reasons why Jack had agreed to do the job—but it did sound as if we had entered a social wasteland.

Not so, I was told. Jack would be much in demand as an after-dinner speaker, especially with the ex-servicemen's veteran associations. And wheresoever my husband went, I would go too. I would be amazed at how many famous victories there were to commemorate, how many wreaths there were to lay. It sounded as if a black hat would have been more in keeping than one with a cocky feather.

The Attaché Corps was small. There were only fifteen in all—three Chileans, three Taiwanese, one Argentinian, one Paraguayan, one Portuguese and one from France, *Monsieur* Molinié, whose wife, Ann, was a lass from Lancashire. That just left the United States officers representing the three branches of their armed services.

'Well, at least it will be easy to get to know them all.'

'Oh, you'll certainly do that. We see plenty of each other, especially when we're on tour.'

'On tour? It sounds as if we are part of travelling circus.'

'You could say that,' Lisa laughed. 'The South African Defence Corps organises trips for the Attaché Corps to visit various parts of the Republic where there are military installations. Of course, it's really organised for the men, but families are invited to tag along. It's somewhat heavy going, especially for those whose first language is not English, but the odd treat to a local tourist sight is usually thrown in as a sweetener. You'll find out what it's like soon enough: we are all off to the Cape next month.'

During the next few days we shook hands with many people and dined at a diversity of venues, sometimes with pomp and at others with a lack of ceremony. I never knew what to wear. At the Pretoria Club, where we ate steak baked to a crisp beneath the gaze of rows of glassy-eyed stuffed trophy heads of gnu, antelope and buffalo, I sat next to the wife of the Taiwanese Naval Attaché stunningly gift-wrapped in gold lamé. Beside such glory the little dark blue number I had purchased with such glee from our village boutique looked dull and dowdy, but when I wore it to meet the elderly ex-pat members of the Royal Air Force Association in Johannesburg, where we ate pork pie and ham sandwiches in a building reminiscent of Boy Scout's hut, I felt positively overdressed. I couldn't win.

There was hardly time to catch our breath before it was time to put on my travelling hat again as we were booked on to a flight to Cape Town. Years ago the Naval Attaché had been permanently based in the Cape, but the Chiefs of the South African Defence Forces relocated to Pretoria and all the Naval Attachés had to follow. Regular visits were sanctioned during the summer months, however, when the official government was in residence in Cape Town, so at least we were promised the occasional sniff of sea air.

So round the buoy we went again on another programme of 'nice-to-meet-you' parties. Fortunately, we were able to snatch a little tourist time and go for an exhilarating drive along the stunning coastline to Simonstown and watch the waves crashing in as the brilliantly aquamarine sea was whipped into frenzy by a strong south-easter. We drove into the hinterland to Stellenbosch, the oldest settlement in South Africa, a lovely University town with broad streets lined with oak trees and gleaming, whitewashed houses, and then it was on to lunch at Lanzerac beneath the vines of the old Cape Dutch homestead. This was the life. We had to forget that tomorrow the Peasleys would be flying back to England, Jack would officially become the Air and Naval Attaché in Pretoria and I would have to face up to the job of unpacking the stack of crates waiting in Charles Street.

Once more Zach was at the airport to meet us. Smart in his grey uniform and peaked cap, he held the door respectfully, stowed our bags in the boot and then climbed into the driving seat and turned the key in the ignition. Nothing happened. He tried again and was rewarded with a faint whirring noise.

'Oh my, oh my.' He pushed his cap to the back of his head, exasperated. 'Don't worry, Sir. Give it time.'

'Is this normal?'

'Oh yes, Sir. It always works in the end.'

Sure enough, at the sixth attempt the engine caught and we were under way, Zach happily chatting about himself.

'Yes, Sir, I've worked for the British Embassy for nearly ten years now. Yes, Sir, I'm very happy in my work.'

And why not? He probably had one of the best-paid jobs in town.

'Mr Peasley—he says we will soon have a new car?' There was a question mark in his voice.

Jack agreed that he had also been told the good news, but unfortunately the date of delivery was still in the distant future. At the moment having an official car, whatever its age, was still a novelty: hitherto Jack had considered himself lucky to have been allocated his own parking space, never mind an official set of wheels.

On the domestic front, Violet was awaiting our return. Had Madam enjoyed her visit to Cape Town? She had heard that Cape Town was very beautiful. How she would love to go there. The furthest Violet had ever travelled was twenty miles to her homeland and back.

The long living room was stacked ceiling-high with wooden crates and there were new chintz covers on the sofas and armchairs.

'The lady from the Embassy said you were to have all new stuff.'

Really? Well, that was amazingly quick. I was used to waiting patiently for months, if not years. Upstairs a new king-sized bed was already *in situ*. I was delighted. Not to worry that none of our sheets fitted—that was not an insurmountable problem.

For the first time since I arrived I had the opportunity to look around the house on my own. Such a large dining table and so many chairs! Would I really need all of them? It was hard to imagine how I was going to make such a vast reception room look cosy. At one end was a ceramic stove that Gerry had said they never lit because it smoked. (Later we were to discover the decaying corpse of a large bird, possibly a crow, blocking the chimney. After that it worked superbly during the winter months.) On either side of the stove were two empty, glass-fronted cupboards—the only built-in feature in the long room.

Bit by bit the house began to look a little more like 'our place' as we hung pictures and arranged books and ornaments. Word filtered down from the Embassy that our landlord was expected home on leave and would be dropping by to discuss a few renovations he had in mind. We sharpened up our pencils and put down some of our own ideas on the subject.

The list was long, starting upstairs in the bathrooms and ending up in the hellhole of a kitchen. The sight of the ancient gas stove and the unhygienic crazed stone sink made me shudder. How could I be expected to cook out here? I soon discovered that I wasn't. Violet did the cooking. She did the washing up, the laundry and the ironing too. She also cleaned the house from top to toe. Domestically I was redundant.

Nor was I expected to work in the garden, where Frans ruled the flowerbeds. By day he would cut the grass, prune the roses and clean the swimming pool. Frans was a recent addition to the staff at Number Seventy. The Peasley's gardener—an absolute charmer when sober—had helped himself to the contents of Gerry's whisky bottle once too often and been given his marching orders just before we arrived, so John deCandole had offered to share the services of his gardener, the pint-sized Frans. This arrangement worked perfectly provided Lisa and I made sure we held dinner parties on different nights, for, when we had guests to dinner, Frans would swap his fetching ensemble of pseudo-leopardskin vest and white solar tope for a crisply starched, oversized white mess jacket and a pair of white gloves to hide his soil-worn hands and help Violet wait on table.

Tell a friend that you have a built-in staff and chances are their response will be 'lucky you.' I did not always see it that way. It wasn't that I missed doing the chores: what I really hated was my loss of privacy. In her worn tennis shoes, Violet could move around the house so softly that I would never know where she and her broom would pop up next. 'Sorry Madam,' she would giggle wildly when she walked into the bedroom and caught me *in puris naturalibus*.

'Violet, I wish you'd knock.' But she never did.

Only during the afternoon could I be sure of a brief spell of solitude, if not peace and quiet. Violet was very sociable. Between the hours of two and four, she entertained, maids from the neighbouring houses congregating on her doorstep to catch up on the local gossip over cups of tea. But as long as the chorus of female prattle interspersed with shrieks of hilarity continued to float in through the open windows, I had the comfort of knowing that she was unlikely to pop up from behind the sofa.

My feelings were far less tolerant when the party re-grouped on Sunday morning. Jack had disappeared to the golf course and I was stretched out on my sun-lounger reading the newspapers. Sunday was Violet's regular day off, so I suppose I shouldn't have been surprised when Jesse and Bella arrived, each trying to out-shriek the other, shattering the morning peace. Perhaps they had only just dropped by for a minute, I thought optimistically, but an hour later Katie and Lulu came too, and judging by the clatter of pots and plates it was picnic time. Obviously this was Violet's normal routine. Too 'chicken' to go round and ask them to drop the noise by a few decibels, I took myself out for a walk.

Was this what every Sunday was going to be like? Fortunately, Violet solved my problem for me.

'Would Madam mind if I went home this weekend?'

'Of course not,' I said, trying not to sound too delighted. 'In fact I don't understand why you don't go every weekend when you live only a bus ride away.' Beryl had told me that Violet came from Ranhuwa, a black township to the north of Pretoria.

Violet looked at me in disbelief. 'Re-eally Madam? Are you sure you won't need me?'

'Yes, I'm sure,' I said firmly.

'Oh Madam, that will make me very happy.'

Not half as happy as it made me as we sat out on the terrace the following Sunday morning with only the twitter of the weaver birds disturbing the peace as they disagreed over the choice of site for their hanging basket-nests.

The weavers were an endless source of entertainment. The cock was the nest-builder. He started with a single loop of grass or palm at the end of a branch, on to which he interlaced and knotted further grasses. Having woven a coconut-shaped structure, he would then seduce a female by hanging upside down, calling and fluttering his wings. She would enter through the tiny aperture at the bottom and perform her inspection. If she was happy with his handiwork she would take up residence, but she could be very picky. 'Not good enough, not good enough,' she would twitter, and, patiently, he would tear apart his handiwork and start all over again. He must have been happy in his work, for, once he had Wife Number

One installed, he would build another nest to entice another female, and so on until he had a harem, each nest with its own living quarters—a colony of beak-woven rustic dwellings dangling in my tulip tree.

Once we had established a routine, Violet and I got on like a house on fire. I was more than happy to hand over the early morning frying pan; cooking my husband's breakfast of bacon and egg had never been my favourite task. Whilst she performed her daily onslaught on the non-existent household dirt, I went out.

'Going shopping, Violet.' I would call. 'Anything you need?' Together we would make a list.

'Just some mealie-pap, Madam.' Mealie-pap, a kind of porridge made from maize, was Violet's staple diet.

The deal was that as well as paying her wages each month I also topped up her store cupboard with mealies, tea, sugar, jam and her favourite brand of peanut butter (it was most important that it was the crunchy type). Such items were cheapest bought in bulk at the hypermarket, which is where I drove once a week. The rest of the time I would visit the local shops, where most goods and services were available. There was even a Woolworth store, though, oddly, the clothes bore the 'St Michael' label.

Within walking distance of the house was Ginsburgs, an emporium the history of which harked back to pioneering days. Here a shopper could purchase anything from peas to paraffin. Upstairs were racks of clothes more practical than fashion-conscious, and equally sensible shoes. Across the road were the seven concrete tennis courts that belonged to the New Muckleneuk tennis club. Ladies' mornings were Tuesdays and Thursdays, 8.30 sharp. I dusted off my tennis racquet and applied for membership.

My first morning was intimidating. These were no other ladies from the diplomatic corps or from the defence forces waiting to play. I was on my own with twelve Afrikaner-speaking ladies. I wished I'd tried harder in my language class.

Somewhat out of practice (I couldn't remember the last time I had picked up a racquet), I walked on to the court in fear and trepidation. My partner was none other than the leader of the group, a statuesque lady called Elise Coetzee who hit with such power that I was amazed that there was any felt left on the ball. I was glad to be on her side of the net, though I don't think she reciprocated my pleasure. She liked to win, did Elise, and with me as her partner she was on a hiding to nothing.

'Gosh, these balls are heavy,' I grumbled, my first two serves having barely reached the net.

'At altitude we have to play with special balls,' Elise explained patiently. Perhaps that was why when I tried to toss my ball it stuck to my fingers, although more likely it was just nerves. As play progressed, my toll of double-faults mounted.

Volleys shot out of court, my racquet handle slipped in my sweaty grasp, blisters appeared on my unconditioned heels. I lost the match with a sweeping backhand that cleared the fence and landed in the clubhouse.

I crept off the court expecting to have my membership card torn up, but Elise's bark was worse than her bite. Yes, I was perhaps 'a little rusty, but with practice . . .' Play finished for the day and we all congregated in the clubhouse, where tea was served by a Violet look-alike—same woolly hat, same pink overall. The ladies of New Muckleneuk had much to discuss over their teacups, most of it incomprehensible. Even their English was spoken with a clipped accent that made them sound cross.

Over the coming weeks my tennis improved. Goodness knows it should have: I had enough practice. With so much free time on my hands, I played almost every day, either with the ladies of New Muckleneuk or at the Ambassador's residence with Irene from Australia, Vanessa from Holland, Vera from Austria or Spring from Vietnam. I'd really caught the tennis bug. It was just as well. With no housework to do, I was much in need of exercise.

— 20 —

Pretoria

NO sooner had the young arrived for their Easter holiday than we departed to Cape Town on our a package trip. This was to be our first experience of what it was like to travel courtesy of the South African Defence Tours. There we all were at the crack of dawn, waiting to board the aircraft scheduled to take us to Cape Town along with the other members of the Attaché Corps, their wives, their children and various members of the South African Defence Force who had come along as our escorts.

The aircraft waiting for us to board was a C-130. We travelled Troop Class (which is to say, uncomfortably). The Hercules was ponderous and noisy, the frame vibrated and the basic seating consisted of narrow canvas benches designed for the bottoms of paratroopers and other military personnel. There were no windows to look out of and the toilet facilities were portable. But hey—who was complaining? The trip was free and the atmosphere was almost holiday-like as we scrambled aboard clutching our brown paper bags of army rations and strapped ourselves in for take-off. The flight took over three hours, but at least there was space to walk about and an invitation to join the aircrew on the flight deck, from where we had a spectacular bird's eye view of the vast areas of bush, veldt and desert across which we were flying.

Before we disembarked, copies of our programme for the next few days were handed out. One glance at the printed schedule soon destroyed any illusions I might have had that we were on a 'jolly'. Our itinerary was action-packed, starting at the crack of dawn the next morning with a half-hour ride in a transport aircraft to Saldanha Bay, followed by a lot of climbing in and out of buses to visit various military installations and listening to lectures heavy with political innuendo. The only bright spot in the programme for the children was a ride in a crash boat round to one of the offshore islands where jackass penguins were nesting.

On Tuesday morning we were on the bus by 6.30. A rowing regatta was taking place at Simonstown and we were there to cheer the lads on. As a rent-a-crowd we were pretty useless, however: few of the ladies had the least idea what was going on and, frankly, it was so cold we didn't care who won or lost.

It would have been a good idea if we had been warned that the next item on the agenda was a tour of *Proteus*, a survey vessel. Scrambling up and down narrow iron ladders in pencil-tight skirts and stiletto heels proved tricky if not dangerous for our fashion-conscious South American ladies. Another boat ride was promised but a gale blew up, much to the relief of those prone to seasickness. Instead we had a talk about Simonstown and its history, delivered in a dull monotone by the padre and illustrated with ancient slides. By now the younger members of the party were growing restless, but fortunately the after-lunch trip to a nuclear plant was men-only and wives and children escaped to the beach. In the evening, the gentlemen and their ladies were invited to the Castle for a seriously heavy dinner hosted by Afrikaner-speaking Army officers. By bedtime my head was spinning and my digestive system completely stressed out.

Wednesday was lecture-free, but we still clocked up a good many road miles sightseeing in a hard-sprung military bus. We drove along the coast to Chapman's Bay, stopping for photographic moments, and then across the peninsula, pausing along the wine route for a spot of tasting. By lunchtime we were all well and truly merry (and I'm not just referring to the adults). For two teenagers, the stop at the Taal Monument was one stop too many. How were they to know that the building that commemorates the acceptance of Afrikaans as an official language was almost sacred? It had been a long hot sticky day and they were fed up with 'behaving properly'. The sight of all that cool water was too hard to resist. Kicking off their shoes, they jumped into the fountain and ran splashing through the water. Herman, the young Army lieutenant assigned to be our guide and chaperone, was not amused.

April 2 was my birthday—and the day the Argentinians chose to invade the Falkland Islands. We were at a party in a marquee in the garden of Admiralty House, sheltering from a howling gale, trying to keep warm under an electric light bulb, when someone broke the news. Furious, I exploded with patriotic rage but was told to shut up and hold my tongue. We had a long evening ahead of us and had to carry on as if nothing had happened—which was asking a lot of someone who was probably as outraged as Margaret Thatcher herself. At least I was not asked to socialise with the doyen of the Attaché Corps, an Argentinian Admiral by the name of Ruben Chamorro.

What would happen now, we wondered? Having an Argentinian for our leader was going to be, not to exaggerate a point, tricky. The rest of the Attaché group watched with interest. Would it be pistols at dawn, perhaps? No such luck! Ruben continued to greet us with a cherubic smile as if nothing was happening. The advice from the Foreign Office was, 'Do what you think best.' The only 'best' we could come up was to carry our drinks to a Ruben-free zone.

The Sunday after we returned from Cape Town we attended a memorial service for the members of the Royal Air Force who had died in South Africa during the Second World War. Jack, dressed up in his best white uniform, gold aiguillettes, medals and sword, laid a wreath of poppies. This was the first of many similar ceremonies we were to attend during the next two years. A month later found us at the SAAF Monument near Swartkop Air Force Base. By now it was the middle of the Southern Hemisphere winter, and although the sun was shining the wind was bitter. We could have done with wearing thermals. By the time we had sat through an extended sermon from the padre and some choral renderings, I was in the early stages of hyperthermia. And there were a lot of wreaths still to be laid.

Twenty dignitaries led by the Minister of Defence, General Malan, filed up the steps and paid their respects, followed by representatives from various military organisations. Finally it was the turn of the Military Attachés. You could feel the buzz of expectation. Who would be the first to lay a wreath? Would it be the Argentinian or the British Attaché? Etiquette dictated proceedings and Admiral Ruben Chamorro went first. The press had a field day reporting this.

Throughout the Falklands conflict the South African Government wanted to be seen as impartial—which could explain why there was only very limited coverage on the South African Broadcasting Corporation's television news programmes and why most of what was shown was twenty-four hours out of date. So our best way of keeping up with the news was to sit glued to our radio, listening through the hiss, pop and crackle to the BBC World Service.

In June we celebrated the end of the Falklands conflict, toasting our boys with bubbly at a party held in our barn. Lisa and I made cottage pie for a hundred—my first attempt at mass catering. It was the coldest night of the year and it was freezing. The next morning the goldfish in the outside pool were tummy-up amongst the empty champagne bottles, though the cause of death was more likely alcoholic poisoning than hyperthermia.

Four months later Captain Nicolas Viejobueno relieved Admiral Chamorro and normal friendly relations with the Argentinian Attaché were restored. Elena, his wife, and I played tennis, and our children partied together. In Pretoria at least, bygones were soon bygones.

Everyone assumed that after we had said goodbye to Ruben he had returned to his homeland. Imagine my surprise when, months later, I bumped into the little bald-headed admiral browsing amongst the detergent packets in the hypermarket.

'Hallo, Jill,' he beamed, and kissed me enthusiastically on both cheeks as if I was his dearest friend.

'Ruben, what are you doing here?'

Craftily evading the question, he introduced me to the lady at his side.

'I'd like you to meet Marta. Marta—this is the charming wife of the British Naval Attaché,' he oozed insincerely.

Marta acknowledged my presence with a curt nod, making it very plain that she had no wish to be friendly.

Marta? Who, I wondered was Marta? Definitely not Mrs Chamorro. Mrs Chamorro had never crossed the water. A week or so later a picture of Ruben appeared in the *Cape Times*. The caption read, 'Wanted admiral lay low in South Africa for months.' Apparently he had been hiding out in Pretoria, too scared to go back to his homeland. Human rights lawyers in Argentina had filed a suit for his arrest on various charges, including illegal incarceration and the murder of detainees in the notorious concentration camp where he had been Commandant prior to being posted to South Africa. So much for the cherubic smile!

It was traditional to celebrate the Queen's Birthday with a party in the grounds of the British Embassy, but as a result of the war the entertainment budget had been slashed. Instead of employing the services of outside caterers, therefore, the wives were asked to produce finger-food. When asked to join the sandwich-makers I shuddered; sandwiches and I do not get along well together. Whilst others produce geometrically perfect triangles, mine ooze, drip and disintegrate. Anyone foolish enough to pick up one of my soggy sarnies was likely to end up with egg on his best bib and tucker.

Come the day, instead of with the traditional champagne the Queen's health was toasted with cut-price wine that bordered on the disgusting. Forewarned, Her Majesty's Defence Attachés had taken the precaution of hiding a bottle of whisky in the bushes for special friends. Eyebrows were raised when 'Don't Cry for Me, Argentina' blared over the music system. *The Citizen* reported, next day, that in his speech the Ambassador referred to casualties on both sides and asked for a brief silence in their honour, thus making up for the musical *faux pas*. It was also noted that the guests enjoyed the excellent snacks prepared and served by the wives and staff, making the whole affair more homely and intimate. I bet, if given the choice, our guests would have preferred the prawns and lobster served up the previous week at the Paraguayan Embassy's Independence Day celebrations!

Life settled into some kind of pattern. Invitations arrived in shoals. Weeks could go by with nothing happening, and then suddenly the mantelshelf would groan with embossed cards. Sometimes the invitations sounded like fun, sometimes they didn't. Nibbling *sushi* at a lunchtime reception held in the garden of the Japanese Embassy was enchanting, sitting for four hours under a broiling sun watching a military parade on the hottest day of the year (with hats a 'must') in downtown Pretoria was not.

Conversation at drink parties was often so repetitious that it was hard to stay animated. Even after we had been there for a year, I was still being asked, 'How many children do you have? And how old are they? How do you like living Pretoria?' Robot-like, I would reply diplomatically, assuring them that life was absolutely dandy. Well, what else could I say? Dinner parties varied. Some were relaxed and the guests like-minded, others had me fighting to keep my eyes open, longing for my pillow-time. Probably my worst memory is of finding myself seated between the Mayors of Roodeport and Krugersdorp. Their English was as terrible as my Afrikaans, and so by the time the soup plates had been cleared away we had run out of conversation. Thus, for the rest of the occasion, the two mayors chatted to each other above my head, incomprehensibly. It was a very long evening.

At least I was far too nervous to fall asleep at our own parties. My first dinner party is indelibly imprinted on my memory. I had spent days agonising over the menu, scanning through my recipe books until I decided that I would cook roast duckling with a grapefruit sauce. In my cookbook it looked scrummy; it looked even more appetising on the serving dishes that Violet and Frans carried round to our guests. Sadly, appearances were deceptive. I must have bought the toughest ducks in town.

'This looks absolutely delicious,' said the South African commodore on my right. Grasping his knife and fork in his large hands he attacked a leg with zest. Five minutes later he was still hacking and sawing as, mortified, I watched the mutilated joint slide across his plate and land moistly at his feet. Thank goodness he had a sense of humour.

'Frans,' yelled Jack from the other end of the table. 'Any seconds?'

'No, Sir,' Frans beamed proudly. 'All gone.'

I cannot say that I would put Pretoria at the top of my list of favourite cities. Aesthetically, with its shiny clean façade, it was a very pleasing place to live, but an entertainment capital it was not. It was too stuffy, too prim and proper; I could even add 'boring'. In Pretoria I felt like a fish far from water, whilst when we were down in the more cosmopolitan Cape I was in my element.

Had we been posted to South Africa before the Defence Department moved to Pretoria, we would have lived in Cape Town permanently in a fabulous, quint-essentially English house (complete with thatched roof) called Elphinstone. For six months of the year the seat of government was moved from Pretoria to Cape Town and our Ambassador and some of the lucky members of the British Embassy staff followed. This meant that two sets of Ambassadorial residences had to be maintained in South Africa, but unfortunately the move did not include Attachés and so all we were entitled to was the occasional flying visit. 'Our house' was now the official home of the First Secretary, though there were still furled anchors embossed on the gateposts and a naval crown atop the front door. We were invited to dinner one night and I felt quite envious. For the short time we were in town we stayed in the Serengeti Executive Suites, a block of slightly old-fashioned but spacious flats which became known, to us, as our 'second home'. The Serengeti was very conveniently situated within walking distance of most of the city's attractions, and so while Jack was away being dutiful I was free to stroll down Government Avenue through the cool, dappled tunnel of ancient oaks that led to the shops and museums.

Fortunately, there were plenty of opportunities to pack a bag and go travelling. The trips we made were nearly always in the line of duty; there were those that we organised ourselves, when we went and did what we chose, and those with the South African Defence Forces, when we didn't. The latter usually lasted about five days, during which time we covered many hundreds of miles.

We would not have been allowed to enter unescorted some of the parts of southern Africa we visited, like the camp on the border of the Angolan war zone or the specially built village at Omega in the middle of the Kavango Province where Bushmen who had been recruited for their superb tracking skills lived with their families. These visits could be very exciting—sometimes almost too exciting. Flying low-level to avoid enemy missiles is not the most relaxing form of travel, and trying to sleep in a caravan with a guard with a nasty cough outside our door is not easy. Being escorted round a hospital ward filled with wounded SWAPO prisoners glowering from their beds was just plain embarrassing.

More enjoyably, we flew across lakes blushing salmon-pink with flamingoes, drank cups of tea on the top of sand dunes in the middle of what is now the Namibian desert, were escorted to the bottom of a diamond mine (no souvenirs allowed) and were entertained by our own tribe of Zulu dancers in warrior kit. But we earned these treats. Lisa and I lost count of how many yawn-engendering lectures on weapons and war tactics we sat through. It was rather like being back at school with two classmates sitting in the back row being naughty.

'Are there any more questions?' Oh, no, we would groan. Please, John (or Jack)—don't put your hand up. But, sure enough, they did.

The Attaché tours were always highly organised and the timetables were inflexible. Personnel had to report early, their bags packed ready for onward transit. Every part of the day was mapped out with military precision. No one dared to be late, whereas the trips we made on our own were more relaxed. They were usually made by car, and, taking into account the size of the country, that could mean a very great deal of driving. For the first twelve months, these journeys were made in the ancient Cortina. The springs of the passenger seat sagged more and more and the seat sank lower as each journey was completed, until eventually it collapsed altogether and I could no longer see out of the windscreen. It was a joy when the car was replaced with a white Vauxhall Cavalier, although even this lacked the air-conditioning that would have been very welcome as we crossed the many burning miles of the Karoo Desert that covers two-thirds of Cape Province.

Our tours took us from coast to coast, from the top to the bottom of the Republic. There were few corners we did not visit. The beauty of the countryside was staggering—the awe-inspiring Drakensburgs, Durban's Golden Mile of coastline, The Big Hole at Kimberley and the famed Garden Route. Even the Karoo, with its endless miles of dusty dwarf vegetation unbroken apart from tabletop-hills in the distance, had its charm, although it was always a relief to see the line of the Outeniqua Mountains that form the barrier between the Cape and the rest of the Continent, as we knew then that we were nearing the end of our journey. The first time we drove the route it was autumn and the vines were turning golden, rose and burnt orange, providing a feast of colour after the hours spent contemplating desert scrub.

In our quest for the 'real Africa' we visited a number of National Parks, including the very visitor-friendly Kruger Park, where you could drive through the bush on tarmac roads and sleep in charming rondavels with running hot and cold water. In contrast, we spent an amazing ten-day leave under canvas in the Okavango Delta in Botswana. In those days, before the package-holiday market had got its act together, you could drive for hundreds of miles in the Delta, through the maze of lagoons, channels and islands, without seeing another human being. And drive we did, for many hours, bumping and lurching through the bush in search of wildlife. We were rewarded with the sight of herds of antelope, zebra and giraffe and a family of hippos bathing in a pool of strawberry-pink water at sunrise. The lions remained evasive until after dark, when a female dropped down from an overhanging bough on to the bonnet of our Land Rover and sat there glaring at us through the windscreen, her emerald eyes as bright as two headlamps. The creature had probably been in the long grass stalking us all day.

On the way back to camp, we found ourselves in the middle of a herd of elephants with young. The matriarch expressed her displeasure at our presence with a spirited display of trumpeting and dust-raising and then charged towards us waving her trunk in a most alarming fashion. 'Sit still and don't even move an eyelash,' hissed Dave, our big white hunter-guide. In fear of our lives we obeyed, silently praying that he'd got it right; it was well within her power to flip the Land Rover over. I think we were spared by the elephant's poor eyesight and by resisting the urge to drive on until she had returned to the herd.

Whatever adventures we had en route, eventually all roads led back to Pretoria and our home in Charles Street. 'Madam—it is so good to have you back!' I don't know if Violet was sincerely pleased to see me. Certainly Snuff, the cat wasn't. In fact he was downright miffed. In my absence he had invited the pair of stripy ginger moggies from next door to take up residence, and he couldn't believe it when I shooed them home. That night he took his revenge. I could hear the sound of scuffling on the landing. Our bedroom door slowly opened and there stood Killer Cat, eyes glinting with a small, half-dead brown rat hanging from his jaws. The next moment he had landed on the end of the bed and deposited his trophy at my feet. Woken by my scream, Jack surfaced and staggered, zombie-like, out of bed and jettisoned the 'kill' out of the window, swiftly followed by his assassin. Next morning Snuff turned his back on us with a reproachful look, clearly disappointed by our ingratitude.

It took six months for the landlord's workers to appear, but once they did I thought that they would never leave. The first destruction gang arrived on 3 November and removed a massive amount of plumbing and tiling from the guest bathrooms before departing, leaving the two empty shells to mature.

'When will they be back?' I asked the foreman, Bossman Villeon, a beanstalk-tall Afrikaner.

'Maybe Wednesday, when they have got over their hangovers.' There was a note of resignation in his voice.

What actually happened the following Wednesday was that we were jolted from our slumbers by the burble of Bantu banter, accompanied by the *thump* of a ghetto blaster playing Radio Zulu from somewhere beneath our bedroom window. I threw back the curtains to be greeted by three shining black faces wearing pearly white grins and grubby baseball caps. Hastily throwing on a wrap, I fled to the privacy of the bathroom.

When I complained to Johan Villeon he was sympathetic but appeared powerless, explaining that The Three Js (as Joseph, Jed and Jonah were known) had to start early as they did not like painting outside in the midday sun. The good news was that they should have the back of the house finished by the end of the week. So soon? My sarcasm was lost on him.

When I agreed to host the annual Attaché ladies' tea party to thank the wives of our mentors in the South African Defence Forces for all their help in our barn, I had no idea that the building work would not be finished. That was the day that the plumber chose to report back for duty after his alcoholic break and add the crash of his hammer to the scream of the tile-cutter's blade. Our neighbours, who had recently started building an extension to their house, contributed to the racket with an iron bar-throwing act whilst our house decorators pressed their noses to the barn windows like a bunch of hungry puppies, eyes fixed longingly on the generously heaped plates of homemade scones, chocolate brownies and milk tarts provided by the Attaché ladies.

'Thank you so much for having us—it was such fun.' Alice, the wife of Brigadier Deysal, pecked first my right and then my left cheek. 'Such delicious things to eat. I'm sorry we have not done it justice but I think you will have no problem finding a home for what is left.'

I threw back the curtains to be greeted by three shining black faces . . .

My 'boys' needed no second bidding. The platters were clean before the ladies had departed down the drive.

As the weeks passed, the noise levels rose in direct proportion to the increase in the size of the workforce. At one point we had ten lads knocking down the garage and rebuilding it. No one had told us that the garage was to be demolished, and, even more infuriatingly, the demolition work had priority over my kitchen and the guest bathrooms that still had no water supply.

Bossman Villeon promised that the kitchen would be started after Christmas. He even came up with a date. Bearing this in mind, a trip to the Cape was planned so that we could escape the worst of the disruption. Three weeks later we returned, refreshed and revitalised. I couldn't wait to inspect my lovely new kitchen, but, sadly, nothing had changed; even the revolting old sink was still *in situ.* I could have wept with frustration.

It was the second day of March before the new appliances were installed. The following week the men dug the kitchen floor up. In the garage a stack of rosy ceramic tiles sat waiting to be laid, but, yet again, the work was put on hold while the workers recovered from their payday hangover, and for a week we crunched across a floor as rough and gritty as a carpet of uncooked rice.

At last the work was done and I bade the gang farewell without a tear in my eye. The day they departed it was pouring with rain.

'Madam, isn't that your umbrella they are taking?'

I was so happy to see the back of them that I couldn't have cared less.

Flowers, Friends and Farewells

EVEN after all the modernisation, I never felt any great affection for Number Seventy Charles Street. It was too impersonal—too characterless a building. I would have preferred somewhere cosier, especially on a midwinter evening when the house was difficult to heat. Of course I loved The Barn, the swimming pool and especially the garden. No matter what the time of year, there was always some exotic shrub in blossom.

In early spring the heady scent from the tiny, lemon coloured pom-poms of the wattle or mimosa took my breath away, whilst the sweet-pea bush bloomed with a profusion of fragrant, pinkish-mauve flowers. I loved the Yesterday, Today and Tomorrow bush with it small, flat, five-petal flowers that turned from purple to mauve and then to pure white; at times the shrub looked like a collage displaying all three colours at once. Throughout the summer the showy red and yellow trumpets of the allamanda bloomed on a jack-and-the-beanstalk vine while the descriptively named bottlebrush displayed red spiky flowers and the gardenia double-white blossoms. The salmon blaze of bougainvillea all added to the feast of colour that we experienced in October, and poinsettias with fiery-red bracts, snowy frangipani, a bank of cobalt-blue hydrangeas and South Africa's national flower, the protea, also flourished in this mini-botanical paradise.

In common with almost every garden in Pretoria, we had a jacaranda tree. In October and November, when the jacarandas bloom, their violet-mauve bells clothe the city; from the hills above they appear like a mauve mist, with roofs and ribbons of tarmac between them. This was the time to climb up to Meintjes Kop or the Muckleneuk Ridge for a long, unhurried view of the wide valley between and the steep flowery streets climbing the hills.

During the long hot days of summer, the pool was an absolute blessing. The Barn could be put to good use at any time of the year. It was a superb venue for a party, and there was an unwritten rule that we volunteered to open the doors for group entertainment. In December the Attaché Corps used it to entertain their comrades in the South African Defence Force to a *braai*, or barbecue. Grills were installed in a row beside the pool; serving tables groaned under the weight of pots of beans, bowls of salad and baskets of bread. The Argentinian contingent provided the charcoal and the chicken, slabs of steak, and (of all the most unlikely food) sweetbreads. There was enough meat to feed an army—provided the soldiers had had good strong teeth. In its raw state the meat looked delicious, but the cooks thought that all meat should be served very well done, so, disappointingly, the end result was more akin to very chewy leather than to prime sirloin. Fortunately there was plenty of good South African wine to wash the meal down.

Wherever they are living, Christmas is a festival the British abroad do their best to celebrate traditionally. In Pretoria, as well as turkey and plum pudding, there had to be a pantomime and, midway through December, members of the British Embassy Thespian Society began rehearsing that year's production in our barn.

Transforming The Barn into a theatre caused much disruption. A temporary stage was delivered in sections, so the cast had to be careful not tread between the cracks. Our living room filled up with baskets containing costumes and props; crates of beer were stored wherever a free space could be found. The cast rehearsed almost nightly, the neighbours complaining to the Ambassador that we were indulging in non-stop parties.

For our first Christmas, the play was a variation on that old favourite Snow White that had to be renamed 'Nie-Blanke and the Four Dwarfs' as there was a shortage of miniature actors—not that it mattered, as the plot bore little resemblance to the original fairy story. In the Embassy version, the beautiful Nie-Blanke was reclassified as non-white and resettled in Bophotha Tswana. Here she encountered a group of demented diplomatic dwarfs and assorted deviants. Succumbing to the total onslaught of the wicked queen on her salary and index-linked pension, she was rescued by a handsome spook and they lived happily ever after in a redundant HMSO filing cabinet. Is it surprising that the young children in the audience went home baffled?

'Mummy, why did the wicked queen have a beard?'

'Don't ask silly questions, Jamie.'

Still, they loved the zebra. A zebra in Snow White? Oh well . . .

Our second-year choice was Skinderella, which was memorable for the lively exhibition of flash dancing executed by the girls from the Secretariat. Unfortunately, blinded by strobe lighting, one of the scantily dressed ladies missed her footing and fell off the minimal stage into the lap of our dishy ex-Rugby playing Ambassador, Ewen Fergusson. His wife Sara was unconvinced when assured that this move had not been choreographed. Naturally, the last-night party took place in our garden, and the next morning there was something very nasty floating in the swimming pool. There was huge relief when what I had thought to be the body of our puss turned out to be nothing worse than the wig worn by one of the Ugly Sisters.

We celebrated our family Christmas by diving in and out of the pool. What else is there to do when, according to the newspaper, the temperature is a sizzling 35 Centigrade? Pity the Ambassador all dressed up as Santa Claus, handing gifts to the children at the Embassy party! The heatwave had started in the middle of our first December in Pretoria. By Christmas the water at the Hartbeespoort Dam had fallen to 48 per cent of its normal level and there was little relief on the horizon apart from an isolated thunderstorm. We were experiencing a real African drought, and it was not pleasant. The countryside was turning brown and cracking; the maize crop was shrivelling on the stalk. An official day of prayer for rain was held and all the churches were packed. The local witch doctors performed their ritual dance, but the population had to wait a long time before the heavens opened. When it did eventually rain in April, the amount that fell was minuscule.

From Christmas onwards we had a stream of visitors escaping the English winter, including my mother, who came for a month. Most of the Embassy-attached children arrived for holidays, some of the older ones bringing friends or live-in partners, leading to consternation amongst the mothers. In those days when blatant promiscuity was still frowned upon, many refused to countenance bed-sharing, sternly enforcing the 'not while you're under my roof' rule, though one, more broad-minded mother was heard to confess that her 'sin-in-law' was coming for Easter.

After Easter everything went quiet. Without the children the house echoed with emptiness. Winter was coming and it was getting cold, especially at night. Some mornings, when I drew back the curtains, there was frost on the grass. It warmed up during the day, occasionally reaching seventy, but at night the thermometer plummeted and the house was freezing. For the first time since I was a child I wore a vest. Then the much longed-for rain arrived, and it lasted for days. Although it made the gardeners and the farmers very happy, it was pretty boring for the rest of us.

So what do on a wet morning in Pretoria when it is too cold for swimming and the tennis courts are flooded? I had long ago exhausted the list of museums and monuments in the visitors' guide book. Sitting reading a book for any length of time guaranteed a rash of goose pimples. Houses built to be cool in summer can be veritable iceboxes on a sunless day.

To the rescue came Pam Coetzee, the good-fun wife of Jack's golfing partner, who suggested that we could fill a rainy morning with a visit to the cinema. I had no idea that anyone went to the movies that early. How very decadent!

'On Golden Pond is showing at the multi-screen complex in the shopping centre,' she told me, tantalisingly. I was sold.

We carried our cardboard cups of coffee into the darkened auditorium and obediently sat down where the lady pointed her torch beam. At least there was no obligatory tall man sitting right in front of me; in fact, when the lights were turned up, we discovered that we had been the only ones in the audience.

'Hey, they didn't tell us we were going to a private viewing,' said Pam as we emerged, blinking at the daylight.

Sitting through a film in the middle of the morning might have seemed unnatural, but in Pretoria I did many things that seemed unnatural—such as being coerced into helping out at the annual Jumble Sale. Once a year the wives organised a giant sale in the grounds of the British Embassy. For weeks we collected donations. Every now and then, amongst the rubbish, someone would discover a gem.

'You should see what the Dutch Ambassador's wife has sent,' Lisa told me. 'It looks like a designer collection. Pity she isn't my size.'

The event, known affectionately as 'The Jungle Sale', was the highlight of the year for the maids, gardeners and drivers who worked for the Embassy staff. On the morning of the sale Violet was so excited that she served breakfast wearing her Sunday hat, ready to go.

'Oh, Madam, there is always such a queue. I must be there early. There will be so many people. You'll see.'

Already I was dreading the day, which was promising to be very hot.

The tables were set up and piles of clothes and household goods were displayed; there was everything from coats to rolls of carpet, although I was assured that by the end of the morning there would not be so much a pair of socks left. The Ambassador's size 14 shoes were attracting a great deal of attention. His chef and his driver both wanted them as a souvenir. In the end the judgement of Solomon had to be imposed and they happily settled for one shoe each.

I was on Ladies' Fashions with Joan Atkins, newly arrived from Britain. Ladies' Fashions were very popular—not only with the ladies but with the men as well. Big Jake, gardener at the Ambassador's residence, was right in the middle of the early scrum, buying up dresses ranging from petite to extra large. 'Must have a harem tucked away,' murmured Joan, *sotto voce*. Or a shop?

I knew many of our customers by sight as most of them worked for various members of the Embassy staff. They knew me too, and hoped for preferential treatment. Pattie, who worked at the Minister's house, held up a Laura Ashley print that I recognised.

'Who are you buying for?'

'Why me, of course.' She seemed surprised that I should even ask.

I could have explained that, while the dress had looked well on the Ambassador's wife, who was just a slip of a thing, on Pattie . . . well, let's just say that Pattie was comfortably roly-poly. Not that it would have mattered what I said. Where there's a will there's a way: Pattie would zip herself in somehow.

Violet was very pleased with the pink and mauve psychedelic number she found at the bottom of the pile.

'What do you think, Madam?'

'Very becoming,' I blinked, adjusting my sunglasses.

A week later the Dutch Ambassador's wife rang Lisa with near-panic in her voice.

'When did you say your jumble sale was being held?'

'I'm afraid you've missed it. It was last week.'

The Dutch Ambassador's wife groaned. 'I suppose there isn't a hope that my dresses went unsold?'

'Well, no. They went like hot cakes.'

'I'm not surprised. My maid gave you the wrong bag. Those clothes were meant for the dry cleaners!'

I cannot remember which organisation benefited from our efforts. There were so many good causes crying out for help in South Africa, and the British Embassy were keen to support more than their fair share. Diplomatic wives are nothing if not bountiful. Never a week went by when I was not asked to make a mountain of scones or a pyramid of Scotch eggs and sausage rolls, or man a giant teapot until my arms ached.

The Ambassador's size 14 shoes were attracting a great deal of attention.

Not all our socialising was undertaken in the line of duty. Once in a while we made the most of our capabilities to entertain personal friends in a style that we would never again be able to emulate. Our Taranto Night dinner was one of the most memorable occasions of our tour.

Every year in November, the Fleet Air Arm commemorates its famous victory at the Battle of Taranto, ranked as one of the most daring episodes in the Second World War, when twenty-one Swordfish aircraft from the aircraft carrier HMS *Illustrious* knocked out virtually the entire Italian Fleet, transforming the balance of maritime power in the Mediterranean. It is customary for both serving and retired members of the Air Arm to celebrate the occasion with a black-tie dinner. With a venue as wonderful as our barn, why shouldn't we do the same? There were as many as a dozen ex Fleet Air Arm couples living in the Pretoria and Johannesburg area who might come. Our invitations were accepted with enthusiasm.

Happily, I had a lot of help with the catering. Apart from the ever-reliable Violet and Frans, Deborah was living at home, having decided to spend her gap year in Pretoria. Unlike her mother, my daughter loves to bake, and once we had cracked the formula for baking cakes at altitude (her first sponge cake rocketed to the oven ceiling before flopping back to a lava-like pancake), she would spend hours patiently icing and decorating creations to grace our dinner table, so it was over to her for the 'pud'.

Come the night of the party, our company gathered, the men in black ties and their wives in posh frocks. It was an occasion for old chums to reminisce and to swap 'shop' stories. The gold and blue candles on the tables were lit, and twenty guests sat down to enjoy Prosciutto Taranto with melon flares, Beef Illustrious and Winged Victory Gâteau, Deborah's *pièce de résistance*. Then the toast was proposed 'To the men of Taranto' and the guests raised their glasses, just as they had done many times in bygone days.

Deborah found herself a clerical job in an attorney's office in Pretoria. Russell, who was only with us for the school holidays, had less luck earning pocket money, so he concentrated on learning to drive. Passing the driving test in Pretoria was a cinch. The most difficult part was probably the ten pages of the multi-choice, tick-the-box theory paper. Driving skills were not tested on the road, where the candidate might have had to deal with real traffic, but through a maze of streets in a purpose-built 'toy town' with prefabricated buildings, hump-back bridges, a pedestrian crossing with traffic lights (or 'robots', as they are called) but with neither real people nor vehicles. It was little wonder that a licence issued in South Africa was not recognised back home.

There was no escaping the artificiality of our lives. Many of the 'friendships' were superficial. We never kidded ourselves that the row of embossed invitations propped up on the mantelshelf was any guide to our popularity. However, there were exceptions. Every so often we would discover an ex Royal Naval acquaintance living in South Africa. Butch Barnard, an former Fleet Air Arm pilot, was one such character; Jack had known him when they had served in *Ark Royal* together. Butch, a tall commanding figure with a striking Boer beard, had taken early retirement after expressing his unwillingness to take his frigate on the Beira Patrol during the War of Rhodesian Independence. He had returned to his roots in the Orange Free State, taking his wife Anne and children with him. By the time we met up again, he was the proud owner of a cattle ranch of Texan proportions, where we were welcome to stay whenever we were 'passing'. It was an invitation that we accepted with pleasure on several occasions.

The first time we saw the Barnards' home, we were really impressed. The original farm house had been destroyed by fire, and it had taken them two years to transform the ruin into a beautiful classical Dutch Cape homestead with whitewashed walls and a high-pitched roof with moulded plaster gables. Inside, the floorboards and furniture were constructed from indigenous woods, the boards from yellow-wood that glowed and the heavy chests and tables of black stinkwood. Outside, the symmetrical sash windows were small-paned with shutters. The view from the front ranged across the many acres of farmland dotted with flat-topped kopjes, where cattle grazed on grassland watered by natural springs.

During one of our visits, Jack was able fully to appreciate the immense scale of the property from the air when Butch took him for an unforgettable ride in his bright yellow Beechcraft Staggerwing, a biplane that I understood to be a real collectors' item and one of two aircraft that he owned.

None of the bad things one had heard or read about the way white farmers treated their workforce could ever have applied to Butch and Anne. Their workers were looked after like family. They were provided with housing and the women came to Anne for their daily food supplies. There were times when Butch was forced to go to extremes to keep everyone happy. Recently, a death had left one of the houses empty, but the only way he could persuade any of his workers to accept vacant possession was to scrape the plaster off the wall, banishing the spirit of the late departed so that the deceased would no longer be able to haunt the property.

Butch specialised in Aberdeen Angus stock and had been President of the Angus Breeding Association. He had up to 1,600 head of cattle and two of the biggest bulls I have ever seen. According to Butch, the older one weighed over a thousand kilos and at two years old was still growing. The beasts were very docile, and were completely unconcerned when I stroked their heads. The cattle were not the only livestock on the farm. There was a beautiful golden-haired retriever and a very old and rather smelly bulldog called Attila the Hun. There was also a parrot that whistled and shouted whenever he thought he wasn't getting enough attention. I resolved never to own a parrot!

We will always remember the Barnards with affection. I wouldn't say the same of the Gerhardts–though they had me fooled for a while. Dieter Gerhardt, as Commodore of the Naval Dockyard at Simonstown, was on the official list of guests to be entertained by the Naval Attaché. We first met Dieter and his wife Ruth when we invited them to a dinner party in the famous Mount Nelson Hotel. They were so friendly, so chatty and so transparent. There was no holding back. By the time dessert had been served, I had heard how Ruth had met Dieter whilst skiing in Switzerland, how she had helped him pick up the pieces after the disastrous break-up of his first marriage, and all about their son, Gregory, upon whom they doted. Dieter also enjoyed talking–mostly about money. He boasted about his antique collection of furniture and his sailing boat, apparently financed by his dealings on the stock market whilst on courses in Britain in the era before the embargo. Jack reported on the many inconsistencies in their stories, which got immediate attention from Whitehall–with subsequent worldwide repercussions.

When we said goodnight, Dieter thanked us for dinner.

'Next time you are in the Cape, come and stay. Bring your children and we will go sailing.'

We never did go sailing or see the famous antiques, though I came quite close. The invitation to lunch from Ruth was waiting upon our return to Cape Town a month or so later. Dieter was away in the United States, but could we come anyway?

We arranged to go on the last day of our stay in the Cape. That morning the telephone rang early, probably at about seven. A small voice whispered down the line. 'This is Ruth Gerhardt. I am so sorry; I will have to postpone our lunch party.'

I said I was sorry too. Was she sick? No, not sick. She would explain later.

Replacing the receiver, I felt concerned. She didn't sound a bit like the normally upbeat Ruth. Had something awful happened? I was sure she wasn't alone. I had my answer the following day as we were on our way home driving through the Karoo.

Imagine being in the middle of nowhere, with no sign of human habitation and nothing much to comment upon, when suddenly a voice on the radio inter-rupts the music to announce that two people you had come to know quite well had been arrested. We listened with personal interest to the newsflash. The Gerhardts had been arrested and charged with spying for the Soviet Union. Ruth had been taken away from the house where quantities of equipment–cameras, false passports and the like–had been found and Dieter arrested as he re-entered the country. That certainly gave us something to talk about for the rest of the journey.

We were eventually to learn the full story. A meeting had been set up in Europe in 1973 between Dieter and Ruth, and, in accordance with instructions from the

KGB, they married and become a team. Dieter had remained a 'sleeper' as he worked his way up the ladder of naval promotion until he reached the crucial position in the premier military 'think tank' in the Ministry of Defence in Pretoria and had then become Commodore of the dockyard at Simonstown—having in the meantime had access to all the top-secret files.

The world was reeling, especially that of those who knew the couple personally. At his trial he was given life imprisonment (he was released in 1994 after the first democratic government elections in South Africa), whilst Ruth was put away for ten years. Their son, Gregory, who, we learned afterwards, was named after their Russian contact (as a cover), went to live with his grandparents in Switzerland. Even today I find it odd to think that we have been directly involved in a real-life spy exposure.

More pleasantly, Jack's popularity as a guest speaker increased four-fold once the Falklands War was over. Interested South Africans had been starved of first-hand news footage of the conflict, so when the members of military organisations and ex servicemen's clubs throughout the Republic heard that Jack had access to videos of BBC tapes through the Embassy, he instantly became the most wanted guest speaker in the continent. I lost count of how many miles we drove with Jack's travelling video show, or how many darkened rooms I sat in, listening to the voice of Brian Hanrahan reporting, 'I'm not allowed to say how many planes joined the raid, but I counted them all out and I counted them all back.' I could have done a voice-over: I got to know the commentary off by heart.

In December Jack was invited to Johannesburg to commission the new RNA Branch; I was invited to along to cut the cake. Jack got doled up in his best white uniform, ceremonial sword, medals and so on; I wore a dress that I hoped was suitable for the occasion. Zach dropped us off outside a rather dingy shopping arcade in one of the city's less prestigious streets. We had been invited for 7.30 p.m. and understood that we would be met and escorted to the function, but there was no one waiting to greet us so we were left shuffling from foot to foot, wondering if we had come to right place. Eventually, to our relief, a smartly turned-out petty officer with a row of World War II medals on his chest materialised.

'I'm afraid we're not ready for you yet' he apologised. 'Would you like to pop across the road to the Penguin Café and have a cup of tea? I'll come and fetch you when they are ready for you.'

So off we went: anything was better than standing staring at a window full of ladies' lingerie. The café clientele, your average blue-collar workers, gazed with eyes a-popping as the new customer in fancy dress came through the door.

Sometime later we were 'fetched' and ushered into a lift that took us to the third floor. As the door opened we were greeted by a lad blowing a bosun's whistle. Jack was invited to inspect the guard of honour of sea cadets lined up in front of the buffet table by a warrant officer who was a dead ringer for Santa with his flowing white beard.

We were seated at the top table for the speeches and toasts, and then I was invited to assist a very young, red-faced Naval reservist warmly dressed in a Navy blue woolly-pully to cut the ceremonial cake. This was followed by dancing. 'If you were the only girl in the world . . .' my partner hummed nostalgically, clutching me close to his shiny buttons as we waltzed sedately round the floor. I closed my eyes and dreamt of . . .

Then there was the monthly cultural tour organised by the senior wives of the South African Defence Forces that, as an Attaché wife, I was expected to attend. We trailed obediently round museums, heritage sites and even a hospital; my husband called them 'hearts-and-minds tours' but I called a lot of them boring. Lisa and I awarded each other Brownie points for good behaviour. One memorable visit, however, made up for all the rest—the day we spent at the De Wildt Cheetah Research Centre.

The farm was situated near Hartebeestespoor Dam, surrounded by the spectacular Magaliesbergs. After a short 'cheetah chat' from a charming young man called Eugene Maurais, we climbed on to the backs of open Land Rovers and circled the farm, taking with us yellow sacks filled with the carcasses of day-old chickens and lumps of beef to hurl over the fences at feeding time. There were many cheetahs to see, including a rare King cheetah—a cheetah with stripes down his back and a magnificent product of mutation. Only three were known in the world.

We saw four 'teenagers' and a dozen or more 'pensioner' cheetahs, and some feeding mothers in the maternity unit. Other endangered species were present, such as fluffy-headed brown hyenas and Cape wild dog and caracal. The highlight of the expedition was being allowed into a pen with three hand-reared cheetahs that were perfectly content to be stroked and petted just like big, purring pussy cats.

In September it was time for the deCandoles to return to England. It was sad to see them go; Lisa and I had had so many laughs together. Fortunately, David and Anne Hanson were good replacements.

In May 1984 our own tour was due to end. The Ambassador told Jack that he had been informed that his relief was to be a Group Captain Grindley, whose wife was called Zandra. The round of farewell parties and receptions lasted several weeks. Unlike the proverbial rolling stone, we gathered moss to add to our heavy baggage. There were shields and wall-hangings and a handbag made from elephant skin. The ladies of the tennis club presented me with 'coffee-table' book of glossy photographs of Pretoria, duly signed. The largest gift was handed to me while I was standing in line to greet our guests at our farewell reception. The package was so heavy I nearly dropped it. Inside was a soapstone carving of a gentleman in a loincloth doing something vaguely vulgar with his right hand. I deposited him in the cloakroom, where for all I know he still resides. A most treasured farewell memento we brought home was a certificate that recorded that we had soared across the veldt in a hot-air balloon early one perfect April morning.

So the last wreath had been laid and the last hand shaken; it was time to pack my hats away in their box and hand over the keys of the house to our successors. Our great South African adventure came to an end as the aircraft lifted off the runway, and I looked down on the vast expanse of veldt for the last time, realising how lucky we had been to have had the opportunity to live in, and explore, such a staggeringly beautiful country in such style.

Living under the apartheid regime had not been comfortable, though I do have to say that we never worried about our security as we travelled around the country, nor did we live behind electronic gates as so many seem to do nowadays. The only time I recollect encountering a policeman was when one threatened me with jail for crossing a white barrier line when driving down to Durban! I was let off with a warning.

Our journey took us home via Egypt, where we spent seven action-packed days of tourism until, exhausted, we climbed aboard our British Airways aircraft for the last part of our journey home. On the platform at Haslemere railway station, I used up the last photograph in my camera and took a picture of Jack pushing our luggage piled up on a trolley. There was not a porter in sight to help.

Once more, we were back in the real world.

— 22 —
Hindhead

So it was home to Hindhead—back to our cottage with the eyebrow windows. The day when Jack would retire from the Royal Navy was fast approaching. Soon he would start a new career. After many years in the Silent Service he would move on to a secret life in the Foreign Office and I would be able to volunteer my services as secretary of the local tennis club, knowing that I would not have to quit the job at the drop of my hat. The only travelling we would do from now on was the holiday kind.

It was time to unpack the crates and put down some roots, a prospect I viewed with a mixture of sadness and pleasure. As for my hatbox—it still resides beneath my bed. Occasionally I dust off the straw and velour brims and wonder if I should wear one, but somehow I never do.

I just don't know why I keep them. Sentimental—that's me.

. . . a mixture of sadness and pleasure.